THE ELECTRICAL UNIONS AND THE COLD WAR

THE ELECTRICAL UNIONS AND THE COLD WAR

Generation of Resistance

BY JOHN BENNETT SEARS

With a foreword by
NORMAN MARKOWITZ

INTERNATIONAL PUBLISHERS, New York

Original edition titled *Generation of Resistance* by Infinity Publishing Co., 2014
This Edition, 2019 by International Publishers Co., Inc. / New York
With Foreword by Norman Markowitz, *© 2019*

Printed in the United States of America

Library of Congress Cataloging-in-Publication Data

Names: Sears, John Bennet, author.
Title: The electrical unions and the Cold War : generation of resistance / by John Bennet Sears ; with a foreword by Norman Markowitz.
Description: New York : International Publishers, 2020. | Includes bibliographical references and index. | Summary: "Electrical workers and their unions were at the vortex of the arguments that shook the labor movement and the country during the Cold War. This book recounts and interprets that experience"—Provided by publisher.
Identifiers: LCCN 2020026913 (print) | LCCN 2020026914 (ebook) | ISBN 9780717807703 (paperback) | ISBN 9780717808243 (mobi) | ISBN 9780717808250 (epub)
Subjects: LCSH: Electric industry workers—Labor unions—United States—History—20th century. | Working class—Political activity—United States. | Electric industry workers—Labor unions. | United States—Foreign relations. | Cold War.
Classification: LCC HD6515.E32 S43 2020 (print) | LCC HD6515.E32 (ebook) | DDC 331.88/12131097309045—dc23
LC record available at https://lccn.loc.gov/2020026913
LC ebook record available at https://lccn.loc.gov/2020026914

ISBN-10: 0-7178-0770-3 ISBN-13: 978-0-7178-0770-3
Typeset by Amnet Systems, Chennai, India

Contents

List of Illustrations

Tables

Foreword

In the first half of the 20th century, there were two major schools of labor history. The established, anti-socialist one represented by John R. Commons, Selig Perlman and Philip Taft dealt with the institutional political history of the trade union movement, relating in a fairly narrow fashion that history to the larger pattern of U.S. history. The class conscious, socialist-oriented school, nurtured by the Communist Party and represented most by Philip Foner, also dealt with the political and institutional history of the trade union movement, but in a much broader context. This school of thought related that history to class struggle and a larger social development. The Cold War in the universities saw the purge of this socialist-oriented labor history just as labor history itself was struggling to get off the ground and left a vacuum in labor scholarship as it left a vacuum in the larger labor movement.

When a new progressive labor history took shape in the 1960s, it too, in the work of David Montgomery, Herbert Gutman and many others, was clearly Marxist and socialist influenced, but it looked to labor's social history – to the experiences of workers and communities, away from trade union political history and to a lesser extent the larger political history. While much of this was very positive, in both exploring workers experiences and making questions of ethnicity and gender central to understanding American labor history, the significance of traditional institutional labor history was put on a back burner. Perhaps because to confront the Commons school on those questions was too dangerous at a time when the defenders of ideological and institutional redbaiting remained very powerful both in labor scholarship and the labor movement. Since 2008 there have been very positive changes in the study of U.S.

labor history as historians like Rosemary Feuer, Jacob Zumoff, and others have from various perspectives followed the earlier pioneering work of Roger Keeran on the UAW to study the largely positive contributions of the CPUSA and its activists to the building of unions, the formation of trade union community coalitions and the mounting of successful strikes. However, most of this history is centered on the great upsurge of the 1930s.

Now John Bennett (Ben) Sears has written a remarkable book which uses the institutional political history methodologies of the Commons-Perlman Taft school and their many imitators over the generations but stands these interpretations on their collective heads. Using both primary and secondary sources, supplemented by interviews with participants, he has traced the history of the electrical workers unions in a remarkably even-handed manner. In his study of the United Electrical Workers (UE) at the height of the cold war, Sears' book remains a model of what scholarship should be.

Sears has written a history of which the late Philip Foner would have been proud and one that trade union leaders would respect. It is the sort of careful narrative of events which will aid both students of the specific history of the UE and those of the larger postwar labor movement. Today, this history is more important than ever, as American labor confronts a Trump administration that has attacked it relentlessly on all fronts. Sears shows that even under the worst conditions, short of open dictatorship, left trade unionists can mount a serious resistance to employers, factional rivals, and government if they continue to work with and for the workers they represent. Given both the Trump administration and the state of the judiciary today, this remains a very important lesson for all trade unionists. Sears is also even handed in developing his carefully reasoned complex political narrative, avoiding polemical attacks on the right within the union in order to connect the history of this remarkable left union with the larger history of the U.S. In the process, Sears makes clear both the achievements and the setbacks that the union faced until the cold war consensus in labor finally collapsed in the late 1960s. His conclusion, that the left and center-left labor politics remained an important factor in the UE (and he suggests the larger CIO) through this period, is perhaps his most important analytical contribution. It helps break down simplistic distinctions between the "old" and the "new" left in our understanding of labor history. Historians dealing with the postwar civil rights movement are also finding similar developments, that is, pre-Cold War left and Communist activists continuing under very different circumstances to play an important role in developing civil rights struggles.

The UE is a large industrial union whose leadership cadre was drawn from CPUSA activists and non-Communist class-conscious industrial unionists in the 1930s and 1940s. This leadership prevailed over an internal opposition, which routinely used red baiting against it, by developing and implementing policies which membership could understand, accept, and benefit from. With the development of the cold war, however, employers, elements of the CIO leadership, the right opposition within the union, and the U.S. government attempted to portray progressive unionists, the UE leadership included, as "enemies within". This posed special problems for both the industrial labor movement generally and for the UE in particular. Even today, although the AFL-CIO leadership is no longer actively collaborating with the global cold warriors and internal red baiters the policies of the cold war decades, starting with the Taft-Hartley law, have reduced trade union membership to nearly pre-New Deal levels and have greatly undermined labor and social welfare protections.

Sears follows this larger political history as it was developed through struggles in the UE locals and national leadership. What he finds differs from the traditional Cold War stereotypes, which in more subdued forms, continue to influence both scholarship and journalism on labor history today. The left leadership of the UE for example was, in most instances, flexible, seeking alliances to defend traditional industrial union positions, and appealed to both the immediate economic interests and to the broader class and social consciousness of its members. The right opposition, on the other hand, represented most consistently through the period by James B. Carey, used anti-Communist ideology as a justification for its own shifting policies and, having little trust in its own members, relied instead on direct alliances with government and indirect ones with employers to gain power.

In the case of the UE the cold war ideology of the time accused progressive unionists of working in a "rule or ruin" way, shifting policies, promoting anti-democratic internal union politics and establishing dual organizations but this is exactly how the anti-left forces within the UE often acted, even to the point of establishing a dual union, the IUE after they failed to gain control of the UE. Although they failed to destroy the UE the anti-left forces did successfully undermine the labor unity that would have been necessary to address major questions facing the workforce like automation and the export of capital and to reverse the general post war attack on labor rights.

Some locals merged with the IUE but, as Sears documents, on favorable terms. The thinking of some of the UE leadership at this time is captured by Sears' who quotes Pat Barile, long time Communist activist and then president of UE local 428, who said: "Practically every day of my life, we would have to be—the local leadership—giving out leaflets, explaining what was going on in the world; the Cold War, red-baiting, what it was; lies about the UE, what the split was....negotiate a contract, there would be another raid...and not only in my shop...we were consuming money and we were consuming workers' rights in the struggle and it had to end....". I have known Pat Barile for many years and have had the pleasure to work with him in many people's struggles. In 1969, while working on my doctoral dissertation, I interviewed James B. Carey, then head of the American Association for the United Nations, a position his cold war friends had gotten for him. Carey had been the leader of the right faction of the UE. It was in his name the raids Pat Barile fought against were organized. After the interview Carey took me to a bar. He was a sad, lonely man, reminiscing about some of his old union comrades, including those he had fought against and tried to purge.

Carey is long gone. In terms of playing any positive role in the workers movement, he was gone decades before he passed away. but he will live in infamy for a statement attributed to him at the end of World War II: "In this war we fought with the Communists against the Fascists. In the next war we will fight with the Fascists against the Communists." That war of course was the cold war and Carey, while he was perhaps just venting his anger at the left leadership which had defeated him, would be a soldier in it fighting against the interests of the workers and trade unionists. Pat Barile on the other hand is still in the struggle and, as long as I've known him, has never been sad, lonely, or isolated. While his eyesight is not what it was, his vision remains as strong as it ever was.

For both students of U.S. labor history and activists of all kinds, John Bennett Sears', *The Electrical Unions and the Cold War* is an enormously valuable work in relating larger issues to the day to day detailed struggles of the labor movement in the U.S. This new edition deserves a wide readership. It also should serve as a model for narrative histories of the post WWII trade union movement who came to make up the AFL-CIO

Norman Markowitz, New Brunswick

Preface

In the summer of 2005, the American labor movement got more media attention than it had since Ronald Reagan fired the air traffic controllers a quarter of a century earlier. The bulk of it focused on the impending split in the AFL-CIO brought on by disagreement among top leaders over organizing and political strategies. However, the organization faced crucial issues in another area as well. At its national convention in July, following months of internal discussion among its member unions, the labor body passed a strong resolution calling for "rapid withdrawal" of U.S. troops from Iraq. Most trade unions have, since World War II, not taken such forthright positions critical of United States foreign policy, but organized labor has changed since the Cold War years. During those years, the AFL-CIO's top leaders gained a reputation as consistent supporters of the government's foreign policy. How had this situation come about? This issue caught my interest in a personal way three decades ago.

As a young teacher in 1972–73, I experienced trade union activity in real life for the first time. The public school employees of Philadelphia conducted a three-month strike that left us all changed people when it finally ended. The strike actually had two parts: three weeks in September and then two more months in January and February. On the first day we went back out in January, my mother drove by our picket line to see how we were doing in the 17-degree chill. She could have shared with us some of her knowledge about workers and unions then, but she must have decided to let her oldest son learn by experience.[1]

1. Only many years later did she let slip that union organizer/activists Powers and Mary Hapgood had been frequent visitors at the family's house near Wilkes-Barre, Pennsylvania, during the late 1920s.

One thing we all learned was to value support from other workers. I struck up an acquaintance with a worker during that strike that led over to a long, winding path to this project. James B. (Jack) Hart, field organizer for the United Electrical Workers District 1, made an impression for a couple of reasons. His years as a worker in the industry and as an organizer for the union, which he finally began to talk about, had given him a deep understanding of the principles of organized labor. In addition, his physical appearance impressed people. They usually remembered the large dark-skinned African American man with nearly white hair and the gruff voice.

At the time, I did not realize how unusual Jack Hart was or how riveting was the story that his labor activity represented, although a few curious and tantalizing facts had begun to surface. The Vietnam War had generated such widespread opposition by that winter that the Nixon Administration had to agree to withdraw the troops. I knew that some unions, such as Jack Hart's, had given support to the anti-war movement, but I also knew that the leaders of the AFL-CIO had supported the government's war policy in Southeast Asia. How could this be? How had this situation developed? Finding answers to that question has taken longer and led to more people and places than I could ever have imagined. As I began to read and inquire, the big picture that emerged seemed clear enough.

For the three decades following the AFL-CIO merger of 1955, the dominant leaders of organized labor in the United States earned their reputation as a bulwark of support for the Cold War, and especially for the foreign policies of our nation's government. While AFL-CIO national conventions passed resolutions, that body's International Affairs Department acted, under a succession of Republican and Democratic administrations, almost as an arm of the State Department.

Did this strong support for Cold War policies accurately reflect the sentiments of union members and, if so, to what extent? That part of the picture is not so clear; authors and scholars have disagreed. On the one hand, it has been suggested that the tradition of labor support for conservative foreign policy exemplified by George Meany, and earlier by Samuel Gompers, has resulted from widespread support for such activity among workers.

Carl Gershman wrote after the Vietnam War, for instance, that "the fact that the tradition of Gompers and Meany has persisted over the years suggests that it is rooted in more than the proclivities of one or two personalities. Rather these leaders themselves were products of the American labor movement."[2] This judgment had a long life as the conventional wisdom and all that needed to be said on the matter.

On the other hand, others have argued that the foreign activity and policy of these labor leaders were not the result of the desires of workers, but of forces outside the labor movement. According to Ronald Radosh, "Since the days of the revolutionary Industrial Workers of the World, there has been no independent union movement controlled by its own rank-and-file and not tied to the machinery of the state." Radosh goes on to suggest, however, that workers have accepted this situation when he predicted that, "When... a new movement is fashioned, American workers will begin a long overdue assessment of the assumptions behind adoption of a backward and reactionary foreign policy."[3]

The uncertainty regarding the attitudes of working people on international matters is understandable in view of the way in which decisions on foreign policy-related issues have been reached. Of all the areas of activity of the AFL-CIO, foreign affairs traditionally involved the least membership participation. In the AFL, and later the AFL-CIO, foreign affairs have been the property of high level committees such as the AFL Free Trade Union

2. Carl Gershman, The Foreign Policy of American Labor (Beverly Hills: Sage Publications, 1975), p. 74.

3. Ronald Radosh, American Labor and United States Foreign Policy (New York: Random House, 1969), p. 29.

Committee or the AFL-CIO International Affairs Department, over which the membership has exercised little or no control.[4] These bodies generally reached foreign policy decisions with a minimum of membership input, and their international activities were carried out in an atmosphere of secrecy.

Under these circumstances, American labor's international posture and its domestic implications stimulated little scholarly interest.[5] Diplomatic historians generally wrote off the labor movement as an insignificant factor. Labor historians, on the other hand, until recently, confined themselves largely to work on domestic issues. Those who addressed international matters did so primarily in order to emphasize the extent of organized labor's cooperation with official United States foreign policy. With some notable exceptions, historians assumed that, since workers in the United States primarily concern themselves with day-to-day problems of survival, they have little interest in matters of international scope.[6] Even the debate between the "old" and the "new" labor history, while breaking significant new ground, has generally avoided connecting the subject to international issues.[7]

This situation requires attention in light of the concept of Marx and others that the concerns of labor are

---

4. See Roy Godson, American Labor and European Politics (New York: Crane Russak, 1976) pp. 49-50 for the AFL Free Trade Union Committee; George Morris, CIA and American Labor: The Subversion of the AFL-CIO's Foreign Policy (New York: International Publishers, 1967); and Gus Hall, "Foreign Policy Crisis at the Top," People's Daily World, February 26, 1987, p. 4-A for the AFL-CIO.

5. This situation may be changing. See Victor Silverman, Imagining Internationalism in American and British Labor 1939-49 (Chicago: University of Illinois Press, 2000). On the Vietnam War specifically see Edmund F. Wehrle, Between a River and a Mountain; The AFL-CIO and the Vietnam War (Ann Arbor: University of Michigan Press, 2005).

6. Among the exceptions are Morris in CIA and American Labor and Philip Foner, American Labor and the Indo-China War (New York: International Publishers, 1970).

7. See Daniel J. Leab, Ed., The Labor History Reader (Urbana, Ill.: University of Illinois Press, 1985).

inherently international. The turbulent history of the twentieth century, with its intense international and class conflict, suggests that the two fields, labor and diplomatic history may be able to illuminate each other. In our own country, scrutiny of the labor movement during the three decades following World War II reveals a story more complex than that suggested by the familiar image of labor as the Cold War monolith. It includes principled men and women confronting intractable issues and others who attempted to build careers on one primary issue: opposition to "Communism" and Communists. In fact, in the United States, the major issues that divided the labor movement were seldom unrelated to international or foreign policy matters. The following pages will, I hope, prove helpful in provoking discussion and encouraging inquiry into these questions.

I've had a hard time deciding whether to change or update the discussion or the conclusions at the end of this book. I have decided to leave them as they were written a decade ago. The enormous challenges confronting working people in our country and around the planet have only intensified since that time, and so have the efforts of workers and their organizations to meet those challenges.

Acknowledgments

This book has been an adventure for the author. The project originated as a doctoral dissertation completed in 1988 at Temple University and has undergone substantial revision since the summer of 2004, when my retirement from teaching once again made it possible for me to devote time to the project. During that span of more than two decades, I have received the help, support, and advice of many people. During my numerous visits to the two primary repositories of electrical workers' records, I was fortunate to encounter archivists who had both the expertise and the patience to make sure that my time was productive. The support first offered by Mark McCulloch more than twenty years ago was continued more recently by David Rosenberg and Wendy Pflug at the UE Archives at the University of Pittsburgh. When I first visited the James Carey IUE collection at Rutgers University, Bill Miller was in the early stages of organizing that union's records. Upon my return nearly two decades later, the help of Tim Corlis and Bob Golon enabled me virtually to pick up the story almost as if I had never left it.

The research could not have been undertaken without the help of many other people. I would like especially to thank the staff at the Walter Reuther Library of Labor and Urban Affairs, Wayne State University; and the staff at the Seeley G. Mudd Manuscript Library, Princeton University; who provided such valuable assistance twenty years ago. More recently, I have benefitted from the efforts of the staff at the Tamiment Library and Robert F. Wagner Labor Archives at New York University and from James Quigel of the Historical Collections and Labor Archives at Pennsylvania State University.

Over three decades ago at Temple University, I was fortunate to have the help of faculty members who were rigorous and thorough in their criticism, but supportive and constructive in their approach. I must thank especially Kenneth Kusmer for his initial guidance and suggestions, his sustained interest, and his persistent attention to detail as well as style and content; Waldo Heinrichs for his encouragement, his probing questions, and his careful reading of so many drafts; Herbert Ershkowitz for his challenging comments and his willingness to share his knowledge of the labor movement. All deserve much credit for their guidance in thinking through complex issues.

Others who supplied valuable suggestions were David Jacobs, Roger Keeran, Jim Lerner, Miriam Crawford, Peter Whelpton, Bob Brown of UE District 1 at the time, and Joe O'Brien of IUE District 1. Thanks must also go to all those people who so readily agreed to be interviewed and to share their experiences. Edward Boehner made available his personal papers as well as his memories. All the activists and workers I have met in and around the labor movement over the years have helped to shape my worldview and guide my thinking. The hospitality of Edie and George Fishman, Maxine Matz, Sue Webb and Sam Webb made it possible for me to travel and stay as long as I needed to in places far from home.

Of course, many thanks must go to my family. My wife Margaret Sears, my parents Ellen and John Sears who both lived to see the dissertation finished but not the book, and the three sons and one daughter who have grown up along with this project—all deserve recognition for their support and their persistent interest in my work.

Finally, the conclusions reached and any mistakes found here are my responsibility alone.

Chapter 1

Labor in Post-war America

The Background

THE youthful, combative secretary-treasurer of the CIO was given to making off-the-cuff remarks. Precisely what he said to his influential listeners on that January day in 1950 is lost to history. He may have read from his prepared text, but in that case, we have no way of knowing which version he had in front of him as he spoke. He may have departed from the text and blurted out an ad-lib. According to the one New York paper that quoted him, he predicted, "In the last war, we joined with the Communists to fight the Fascists. In another war we will join with the Fascists to fight the Communists."[1]

This brief comment seems to have passed with little notice among those in his conservative audience gathered at New York's Waldorf Astoria Hotel, but its appearance in the press caused a stir in the labor community. The occasion, the "All American Conference to combat Communism," was sponsored by the American Legion and drew two hundred participants representing a range of organizations, but apparently only two from labor. The speaker, James Carey, and his organization, the Congress of Industrial Organizations, found themselves issuing numerous explanations and clarifications

---

1. New York Herald Tribune, January 29, 1950, p.16. The New York Times reported that Carey spoke but discreetly ignored any mention he might have made about joining with the fascists.

in the following days and weeks.[2] Did the secretary-treasurer speak for his two and a half million members and was that body calling for war? How could he make such a suggestion less than five years after the defeat of fascism in the most destructive war in history? Why had he appeared on the same platform as noted anti-labor speakers? Explanations were forthcoming, but never a denial.

The secretary-treasurer's remarks reflected the dilemma faced by organized labor's leaders in the United States at the time. Under intensifying pressure from business, media, Church, and government sources to prove their "loyalty" in a global contest with "Communists," U.S. labor leaders faced daunting challenges and difficult choices. How could they move their trade union and social agenda forward in such an atmosphere? How could the labor movement maintain its newly established strength? The new unions in the CIO found these questions especially urgent. CIO leaders had, in the fall of 1945 at the close of World War II, played a central role in establishing the World Federation of Trade Unions as a new force in international labor which, they hoped, would help move the post war world in a peaceful and prosperous direction.

World politics had undergone seismic shifts by 1950, however. The Legion's "All American" conference occurred in a rapidly changing, politically charged atmosphere of looming crisis. The nation's commercial press featured accounts depicting changes around the globe as imminent threats to Americans' security. Most recently, the Soviet Union's successful testing of atomic weapons and the collapse of the Chinese Nationalist government and the birth of the People's Republic of China had jarred the U.S. foreign policy establishment. The

2. IUE Papers, Special Collections, Rutgers University Libraries, Record Group 1, President's Office, Box 1, Speeches, Statements and Addresses of James B. Carey, Folder 11 "American Legion Speech" (hereafter cited as IUE Papers). This would not be the last time Carey's fellow CIO officers would have to clarify or explain his remarks. See chapter IV.

response of corporate America and the commercial media to these events had thrown American labor leaders, and the leaders of the CIO in particular, on the defensive. The 1935–45 decade had seen workers of varying skill levels, varying ethnic and racial backgrounds, and diverse political ideas stream into the house of organized labor by joining the CIO. And the CIO included Communist and other left-oriented activists and organizers.

The invitation to speak at such an affair may have flattered the CIO Secretary-Treasurer, but his appearance there did not solve his problems. Cold War pressures had already reached into his organization and into his union, the United Electrical Workers. The experience of the electrical workers and their unions during the three decades after World War II not only makes a riveting story, but it also suggests lessons for us to ponder more than half a century later.

The deepening Cold War of the late 1940s posed a special problem for organized labor in the United States. American policy makers, with increasing vigor and persistence, identified the Soviet Union as the nation's number-one adversary. They viewed the Soviets not as simply another imperial power, but as a special new and growing danger, one compounded by the fact that the USSR claimed to represent working people.[3] American workers, many having just returned from a war against fascism, were again called upon to prove their "patriotism."

As a result, deciding whether to support official State Department policy became crucial for labor. This was especially true of the Congress of Industrial Organizations (CIO), since the older American Federation of Labor

---

3. Foreign Relations of the United States, 1950, 1: pp. 235-292. National Security Council report NSC-68 March 1950 said in part, "The Soviet Union, unlike previous aspirants to hegemony, is animated by a new fanatic faith, antithetical to our own, and seeks to impose its absolute authority over the rest of the world." While this became the official justification for U.S. Cold War policies, evidence makes it difficult to accept the idea that this was the primary motivation for such policies. See the discussion of the Cold War "consensus" later in this chapter.

(AFL) had since World War I supported United States policy abroad. The CIO constituted a new element in American labor and its international outlook was uncertain.[4] The conservative wing of the CIO, including most of its top leaders, at first reluctant, showed an increasing willingness to support official policy and to accept the Cold War scenario. While some "mainstream" historical writing may still give the impression that they had no options, the record suggests that their decision to support the Cold War was not an easy or foregone conclusion at the time, and not even clearly in line with the majority of their members.

The left, and many others, in labor took the opposite position, arguing that imperialist United States policy was the primary danger. The left in the CIO saw the Cold War as one program that aimed to move aggressively in both the domestic and international arenas in order to move the agenda of American big business interests. Left-wing leaders, activists and their allies saw the American labor movement as a potential counterweight that could—and should—play a central role in presenting an alternative agenda for the country in the post-war world. It is a telling historical irony that the UE was forced to defend itself against charges of its alleged international ties, while it was, in fact, the CIO right-wingers who pursued international contacts and allowed themselves to be drawn into the milieu of the U.S. foreign policy establishment. While U.S. trade unionists spent most of their time dealing with urgent domestic matters, it was the foreign policy related disagreement that would never go away.

4. For the origins of what the AFL and later the AFL-CIO came to call "free trade unionism" see Wehrle, Between a River and a Mountain, pp. 3, 9-10, 12, 15-16. For the CIO see Leroy Lenburg, "The CIO and American Foreign Policy, 1935-1955" (Unpublished Ph.D. Dissertation, Pennsylvania State University, 1973), chapters VI and VIII; and Frank Emspak, "The Breakup of the Congress of Industrial Organizations (CIO) 1945-1950" (Unpublished Ph.D. Dissertation, University of Wisconsin, 1972), chapter VII.

This argument permanently scarred the basic industrial section of the labor movement. One industry particularly affected was that of electrical manufacturing. Here, the major original trade union, the United Electrical, Radio and Machine Workers (UE) won a reputation both for aggressive collective bargaining and organizing and for its opposition to the nation's Cold War foreign policy. So intense was the conflict that erupted in this industry that the UE did not survive in its original form. During much of the period of this study, the UE faced determined opposition not only from employers and from its primary rival in the industry, the International Union of Electrical Workers (IUE), which had split off from the UE, but also from other unions, Congressional committees, and other organs of the U.S. Government.

To be sure, the attack on American industrial unionism took more casualties than the UE. What happened in the electrical and machine industries reflected events in the broader labor movement during the period. But the opposition to official Cold War policy had more strength in the UE than in the other major industrial unions. The refusal of the right-wing forces in the union to accept the union's positions, or to compromise, on this issue was a primary reason for the split. The example of the electrical workers provides insights into the nature of the disagreement after World War II and demonstrates that the argument did not end with the expulsion of the UE from the CIO in the fall of 1949. In fact, the issue has periodically resurfaced with surprising intensity.

The inherent importance of international and foreign policy issues for American workers demands an examination of labor opposition to the Cold War. While other examples exist, this study will focus on the electrical manufacturing industry. As noted above, historians have to some extent studied the official AFL-CIO stance in support of Cold War policies, as well as the activity of the organization's International Affairs Department in numerous countries on behalf of that policy. The other side of the debate has gone almost unnoticed, encouraging the impression that labor gave total support to the Cold War. The other side of the debate has started to get some attention recently; it needs more.

In any case, the right-wingers in the CIO soon decided to support the entire Cold War program, both domestic and international. By the time of James Carey's speech to the American Legion's New York conference in January 1950, they had already showed their hand and were in the process of expelling their "left wing" unions. Opposing the Cold War on either level would require extraordinary courage of American workers.

The experience of the electrical unions suggests that, while it may have been temporarily submerged for a period after 1955, opposition has existed since the early Cold War years when it was considered important enough to be the object of concerted attack by the United States Government and major corporations. But the UE survived, continued to organize, regained respect in the labor movement, and gained membership as well during the 1960s, while it adhered to its positions on foreign policy. The IUE, on the other hand, by the late 1960s became one of the AFL-CIO unions expressing opposition to the Vietnam War. These facts call into question the image of rank-and-file workers as heavily pro-Cold War. Previous research has documented the attack on the UE and on the left in other unions, although the long-term influence of the attack—suppression of debate on foreign policy questions—has not been emphasized. The survival of opposition to Cold War policies in the labor movement is what needs examination.

This study will examine opposition to the Cold War in the electrical and machine industry from the end of World War II until the United States agreement to withdraw from Vietnam in 1973. It will attempt to address the issue of whether and to what extent opposition existed among electrical workers. Because Cold Warriors did not limit their program to foreign affairs, opposition did not always involve overt protest against Washington's foreign policy. Rather, both sides in the debate understood that the foreign policy disagreement was part of a larger controversy over who the primary adversaries of labor really were and what the role of labor in the United States should be. Did the primary threat to the welfare and survival of American workers come from the Soviet Union and Communists, or did it come from the corporations who employed so many of the workers?

The argument surfaced in other areas besides foreign policy. For example, one recurring point of difference involved collective bargaining aims, the most basic "pure and simple" trade union issue. How should unions confront and deal with the powerful corporations who employed their members? In the electrical industry this frequenetly emerged as the "profit sharing" debate. The IUE during the 1950s generally made the achievement of an "equitable profit sharing arrangement with industry" a goal of its collective bargaining efforts with the major electrical manufacturing firms. The UE negotiators rejected the profit sharing approach, preferring to bargain for defined wage and benefit increases, rather than tying workers' income directly to the firms' profitability in any given year. One IUE internal document charged that the "political philosophy of those who controlled the UE was anti-profit sharing" and therefore made employers less likely to deal favorably with that union in negotiations.[5] The differences between the UE and IUE leaders included traditional trade union issues as well as foreign policy disagreements.

To some degree, the foreign policy issue was simply a "smokescreen" used to weaken American labor in the name of national unity. During the Korean War, AFL and CIO leaders served on numerous government boards and hesitated to challenge the government's wage guidelines, despite their dissatisfaction with the

5. Memo by IUE assistant president David Lasser, June 15, 1953, IUE Papers Box 32 Folder 5, "UE Publications, Clippings, Bulletins, Releases 1953."

Truman Administration's domestic policies and with the role assigned to labor in the war mobilization program.

However, the evidence powerfully indicates that the foreign policy question was important in its own right. In the first place, this single issue was considered the test of a person's loyalty. Where dissent on other questions, such as collective bargaining priorities, might be permissible, the concept of "bi-partisan" foreign policy made dissent on this question particularly sensitive in the intensifying Cold War atmosphere of the late 1940s. This especially applied to labor, since the primary enemy identified by the press, Congressional committees, the State Department, and corporate leaders now loomed in the form of the USSR claiming the title of "first workers' state."[6] The central role of labor in their thinking was most bluntly suggested by General Electric president Charles E. Wilson in October 1946, "The problems of the United States can be captiously summed up in two words: Russia abroad, labor at home."[7] Labor was thus called upon to declare itself: "American" or "red," loyal to its country or its class. Labor leaders and workers who refused to accept this as a valid or meaningful choice faced an array of powerful forces.

The foreign policy issue diverted labor leaders from their domestic tasks in another way also. It drew labor leaders into activity abroad. In the world after 1945, U.S. leaders saw a supportive labor movement as an indispensable weapon in the Cold War abroad. The use of labor emissaries, at first in Western Europe and soon in other parts of the world, became an accepted and valued tactic in the execution of American foreign policy, due to labor's ability to gain acceptance where official

---

6. The enormous sensitivity of labor leaders on this question was evident at the 1965 AFL-CIO convention during the discussion on the Vietnam War resolution. For UAW secretary-treasurer Emil Mazey's remarks on this subject, see chapter VIII.

7. Richard O. Boyer and Herbert M. Morais, Labor's Untold Story (New York: United Electrical, Radio and Machine Workers of America, 1955, 1965, 1971), p. 345.

diplomats could not.[8] Labor's agreement to support official Cold War policy therefore carried with it consequences in both domestic and international affairs.

The effort to secure labor support for the Cold War met opposition in basic industries and especially in electrical manufacturing. The UE did not agree with the developing foreign policy of the Truman Administration, which the CIO leadership supported beginning in 1948, or with the direction in which the CIO moved on domestic issues after 1947 when the United Auto Workers became the first CIO union to cooperate with the Taft-Hartley Act. It was clear from the beginning of this period that bringing electrical workers into the Cold War fold would be difficult.[9]

Given the potential for resistance to Cold War policies among electrical workers, on one hand, and the acute desire of forces outside the labor movement to bring them into the Cold War "consensus," on the other, the likelihood of confrontation in the industry becomes apparent. How this conflict developed forms a central theme in our story.

One other circumstance gave the situation in this industry special interest and importance. The UE's first president, James Carey, was especially active, both at home and abroad, in support of Washington's foreign policy. He developed working relationships with leading members of the foreign policy establishment. However,

---

8. See Peter Weiler, "The United States, International Labor, and the Cold War: The Breakup of the World Federation of Trade Unions," Diplomatic History (Winter, 1981)k, pp. 1-22. In the words of Supreme Court Justice William O. Douglas in 1948, "...American labor carries good credentials to western Europe. Doors tightly closed to all others may open at its knock." See Congress of Industrial Organizations, Final Proceedings of the Tenth Constitutional Convention, November 1948, p. 268.

9. The UE was not the only union in which opposition to Cold War policies existed. The CIO expelled ten other unions in 1949 on charges similar to those against the UE, that is, being "Communist dominated" or "loyal to a foreign power." The largest were the International Longshoremen and Warehousemen (ILWU), the Mine, Mill and Smelter Workers ("Mine-Mill") and the Fur and Leather Workers. Opposition to the Cold War was found in other unions as well.

the union's 1941 convention had not re-elected him to the presidency. While Carey continued as Secretary-Treasurer of the CIO, he was without a rank-and-file constituency. The initial prestige and influence of the IUE, chartered by the CIO to replace the UE in 1949, rested in large part on Carey's reputation and connections outside the labor movement, including his ties with the foreign policy establishment. Carey's tenuous position, and his eventual downfall, suggests that the Cold War consensus was never consolidated in the electrical industry, and that many workers, even after leaving the original union, regarded the UE, its leaders, and its program as the true representatives of their interests during the nearly three decades after World War II.

Terms and Definitions

A number of terms appear throughout this work that require definition. Some, while not normally associated with the labor movement, bear directly on the thesis presented. For instance, historians have used the term "foreign policy establishment" to describe the men involved, directly or otherwise, in formulating the nation's foreign policy. One author suggests that the term "establishment" was borrowed from British journalism where it was used to refer to "a group of powerful men who know each other..., who share assumptions so deep that they do not need to be articulated; and who contrive to wield power outside the political or constitutional forms: the power to put a stop to things they disapprove of..., the power, in a word, to preserve the status quo."[10]

Arguing that such a group existed in the United States during the early Cold War period, and that it had particular influence in foreign affairs, Godfrey Hodgson has suggested that its members came from three distinct categories: internationally minded bankers, lawyers and

10. Godfrey Hodgson, American in Our Time (Garden City, New York: Doubleday, 1976), p. 112.

corporate executives; government officials; and academics. Members of this group included Secretaries of State such as Dean Acheson, John Foster Dulles, and Dean Rusk; other high level diplomats, such as Averill Harriman; and close presidential advisors such as McGeorge Bundy, Walt Rostow, and Henry Kissinger. Although some "internationally minded executives" did not always play a direct role in policy making, names such as C.D. Jackson, one time editor of *Fortune* magazine, and General Electric President Charles E. Wilson frequently appear when authors discuss foreign economic policy of the post World War II period.[11]

Members of the foreign policy establishment expressed very definite opinions about the labor movement. Dulles, for example, was described as "anxious that American unions and labor leaders exert their influence among their foreign counterparts so as to give encouragement to anti-Communist elements within the labor movement." The same account continued that "...because they shared this aim...Mr. Dulles and George Meany came to develop a close association."[12] At the same time, Dulles believed in encouraging "anti-Communist elements" in the labor movement in the United States as well. In the spring of 1946, reporting on the first session of the United Nations, he singled out the new international labor center, the World Federation of Trade Unions (WFTU), as a special threat to the post-war order. He wrote:

> The Assembly was split by the same controversy which in many countries divides the ranks of labor into two factions. Member states, whose governments were communistic in tendency or subject to the political pressure

---

11. Ibid., p. 115; see also Blanche Wiesen Cook, The Declassified Eisenhower (Garden City, New York: Doubleday, 1981), p. 298. Some business executives, of course, played more direct policy-making roles, such as Assistant Secretary of State William Clayton in the Truman Administration.

12. John Foster Dulles Papers, Seeley G. Mudd Manuscript Library, Princeton University, Dulles Oral History Project, Interview with James P. Mitchell by Philip A. Crowl, July 22, 1964, p. 4.

> of Communist parties, sought a position of special privilege for the World Federation of Trade Unions, with which the CIO is affiliated but not the AF of L. It seemed that the purpose was to enable that Federation to achieve a position such that, through its influence on many governments, it could dominate the Assembly....[13]

Here, Dulles made assumptions about the nature and aims of the WFTU which its leaders rejected. They argued that the United States delegation at San Francisco in 1945 played a central part in denying the WFTU any meaningful role at the UN.[14] The CIO was a founding member organization of the WFTU, which the AFL had refused to join. In this report, a prominent member of the foreign policy establishment had linked the CIO to the forces that he identified as the main threat to peace and security.

Another important feature of the "establishment," besides its interest in foreign policy and its views on the labor movement, was its bipartisan nature. Despite differences, there were indeed deeply "shared assumptions." Upon reading Dulles's report, then Under Secretary of State Dean Acheson wrote complimenting him for his "searching and excellent analysis."[15] The term "foreign policy establishment" will, then, refer to that loose-knit, but identifiable group of men whose shared assumptions, values, and position made them a powerful force in foreign policy making.

Another term occurring frequently in this work is the "Cold War consensus." This term refers to the broad

---

13. Draft of Dulles speech to the Foreign Policy Association dinner, Philadelphia, March 1, 1946, Dulles Papers, Box 30, file "Re Soviet Union and the Communist Party 1946." Dulles further publicized his ideas in a two-part series in Life magazine in June 1946. See his article, "Thoughts on Soviet Foreign Policy and What to Do About It," Life, 20 (June 3, 1946) pp. 113-126, especially p. 118 for the reference to the WFTU and the CIO.

14. William Z. Foster, Outline History of the World Trade Union Movement (New York: International Publishers, 1956), p. 404.

15. Acheson to Dulles, May 28, 1946; Dulles Papers, Box 30, file "Re Soviet Union and the Communist Party 1946."

agreement among members of the establishment that, during the decade after 1955, was assumed by many to characterize American politics. It was based on a compromise between liberals and conservatives which provided that the New Deal, although scaled down, would not be scrapped entirely, but that the primary goal of the nation's foreign policy was the "containment of Communism." The consensus concept rested on the assumption that America's most urgent problem originated abroad and not at home: the "Communist challenge" or the "Communist threat." Two national commissions, one the President's Commission on National Goals and the other funded by the Rockefeller Foundation, reached conclusions to this effect.[16]

The "consensus" formed a key part of the "deeply shared assumptions" of the foreign policy establishment, but it had less appeal for forces, such as organized labor and working people generally, who did not share the establishment's stake in preserving the status quo. Given the Dulles summary of the UN's first session, it is hardly surprising that members of the foreign policy establishment played active roles in attempting to bring the CIO into the consensus. But those who challenged the consensus concept doubted that it accurately expressed the nature of United States foreign policy after World War II. The UE, for example, called attention to another term, which, in the opinion of its leaders, more adequately described American policy: the "American Century." To UE officers and activists, this was a "big business" term meaning business should "run America... and run the world for its own benefit."[17]

Even members of the establishment occasionally indicated that they, too, doubted that the concept of "containing Communism" and building a consensus to support such a goal accurately expressed the essence

16. Hodgson, America in Our Time, ch. 4, pp. 67-98, especially p. 72. The Eisenhower Administration commissioned Goals for Americans; the Rockefeller Fund issued Prospect for America.

17. United Electrical Workers, General Officers Report, 1946, p. 8.

of the nation's foreign policy. One historian has quoted C.D. Jackson, for instance, to the effect that American businessmen would have to sell American capitalism "to a not particularly receptive world," in order to secure economic world leadership. Another has quoted President Truman's 1947 speech at Baylor University in which he argued that the post-War situation required the United States to export American "freedom of enterprise" to the rest of the world.[18] In other words, Cold Warriors themselves felt that the defensive connotation of the term "containment" did not accurately describe a policy with its own active designs on the rest of the world. In short, the Cold War consensus, although implying agreement, was itself the subject of varying interpretations and, indeed, of controversy.

The terms "left" and "right" appear often in these pages. Labor historians have used these terms to define the contending groups in the labor movement after World War II. We will attempt to use the terms as the participants did. The "right wing" in the United Auto Workers, according to James Prickett, consisted of a coalition of "conservative Catholics and militant socialists... united solely around the limitation of Communist influence in the union."[19] In the UE, members who opposed the leadership and eventually formed the nucleus of the rival IUE regularly referred to themselves as "right wing" and to their group as the "right wing caucus."[20] Therefore, the term will refer here to the trade unionists in the electrical industry who attempted first to limit "Communist influence" in the CIO, and later to remove it completely.

---

18. C.D. Jackson quoted in Cook, The Declassified Eisenhower, p. 298. Truman quoted in D.F. Fleming, The Cold War and Its Origins 1917-1960, volume I (Garden City, New York: Doubleday, 1961), pp. 436-437.

19. Prickett, "Communists and the Communist Issue in the American Labor Movement," pp. 5-6.

20. See UE Local 1102 Review, September 1949, IUE Papers, Box 30, folder 5 "Post Convention 'Right Wing' Material." The press also used the term widely; see clippings in Box 30, folder 8, "Charges against 'Right Wing' leaders."

Since the leading spokesmen for the right in the electrical industry by 1949 tied the effort to remove Communist influence from the American labor movement with the crusade to "contain Communism" on a world scale, it comes as no surprise that they accepted a role in the Cold War consensus. Of course, we should remember that the term "right wing" in the labor movement carried a different meaning than it did in national politics; right-wing politicians were generally not friends of labor. Also, right-wing labor leaders disagreed with members of the foreign policy establishment on many issues. Corporate executives and lawyers generally did not share the views of labor leaders on collective bargaining priorities, for example. But, by making opposition to "Communism" at home and abroad the overriding issue, these labor leaders frequently found themselves aligned with forces with whom they had little or nothing else in common.[21] James Carey's American Legion appearance serves as one example.

The terms "left" and "left wing" are also best explained by the trade unionists who identified themselves as such. One leading organizer in the movement for industrial unionism, for example, later wrote that the CIO "had a strong and well entrenched left-progressive wing (which the AFL had not), leading some 20 percent of the organization as a whole." Reviewing the role of the left, he continued that:

> This progressive force, which had played the most active part in building the CIO during the big organizing drive of 1935–45, was fully in tune with the anti-fascist spirit of

21. Pricket, "Communists and the Communist Issue," p. 6, writes of the non-Communist radicals who joined right-wing union caucuses, "Their willingness to support repressive measures against Communists (which were often used against them later) and to ally with distinctly conservative forces to defeat Communists meant that they played a right-wing role in the labor movement." In n. 2 on the same page, he continues, "Many anti-Communists were sincere, genuinely radical workers who nevertheless played a conservative role. This suggests that anti-Communism has a reactionary dynamic, quite apart from the perceived politics of its adherents."

> World War II, and its influence had resulted in giving the CIO an advanced program in many respects—regarding Negro workers, political action, international organization, etc.[22]

Besides being a leading labor organizer, William Z. Foster, author of this passage, was also a leading member of the Communist Party USA. The role of the party in the industrial union movement was significant and has been the subject of much speculation and debate. It deserves adequate attention at the outset. Most authorities agree that the party was the largest and most influential force on the left in the industrial union movement. We should recall Saul Alinsky's 1949 assessment of the role that Communists played, "Every place where new industrial unions were being formed, young and middle-aged Communists were working tirelessly.... The fact is that the Communist Party made a major contribution in the organization of the unorganized for the CIO."[23] The party was an integral part of the human drama involved in building the CIO. However, simply to equate the "Party" with the "left" may not give an accurate picture.

Roger Keeran has suggested the existence during the 1930s and 1940s of a "Communist milieu," membership in which "was probably as important as membership in the party" itself. Party membership in any case is frequently difficult or impossible for the historian to determine. This milieu included party members, but also many other people who read party-related literature and belonged to mass organizations such as the International Labor Defense, the National Negro Congress, the American League Against War and Fascism, and the American Student Union. Beyond organizational contacts, however, they frequently shared other interests. They listened to the same music: Paul Robeson, Woody

22. Foster, Outline History of the World Trade Union Movement, p. 472.
23. Saul Alinsky, John L. Lewis; An Unauthorized Biography (New York: Putnam, 1949), p. 153.

Guthrie, or the Almanac Singers; they read the books of Howard Fast and Richard Wright, and the poems of Langston Hughes. In short, they "shared a common vocabulary, a common subculture, and many common aims."[24] In addition, many workers who never became part of the subculture apparently felt the Party's influence through contact with individual Communists, reading Party literature or attending public meetings. As another author has suggested, "...Many formerly conservative workers were converted into strong supporters of their left leaders.... The political education they received from social and intellectual contact with Communists had a profound impact on their lives."[25]

The left, then, was larger than the party and included workers who, while perhaps not in agreement with or conversant with every position the party took, basically accepted the party's activity and influence as valuable and positive. For instance, Albert Fitzgerald, the long-time president of the UE, whom we shall meet presently, told an interviewer in 1968 that "they added some vitality to the organization. I don't think you can make any progress in the unions or in the country or any place else, unless you've got a left that's struggling like hell for certain kinds of programs...I never at any time saw them as a threat to the UE or the CIO."[26] Whether the left extended beyond the party and its active supporters is debatable. Other workers, especially during the '35–'45 decade, simply did not make the presence or absence of Communists in their union the determining factor in their own activity. In other words, large numbers of workers did not favor excluding Communists from unions. The exclusion of Communists was precisely the

---

24. Roger Keeran, The Communist Party and the Auto Workers' Unions (Bloomington: Indiana University Press, 1980), pp. 25-26.

25. Gerald Zahavi, "Passionate Commitments; Race, Sex, and Communism at Schenectady General Electric, 1932-1954," in Journal of American History, vol. 83, no. 2, September 1996, p. 521.

26. Fitzgerald, interview by Ronald Filippelli, October 10, 1968; transcript in Pennsylvania State University Archives of Labor History.

point on which right-wing leaders, James Carey, Harry Block and others, based their activity by the late 1940s.

The CIO certainly included many workers who considered themselves neither left nor right wing. The term "center" is useful in describing workers in this large and varied category. The center forces in the CIO frequently determined whether the balance tilted in favor of the left or the right. It has been suggested that the CIO's original success resulted from the strength of the "left-center coalition" in basic industries. This view holds that the willingness of many union members and their leaders, who were not organizationally or philosophically of the left, to work with the left made industrial organization possible and kept right-wingers from vigorously pressing demands for the exclusion of Communists.[27] The Cold War in the labor movement was, therefore, not simply an attack on the left, but an attempt to weaken or disrupt the left-center coalition as well.

The left-center coalition was strong in the electrical union. The split in electrical unionism of the late 1940s is generally discussed in terms of the "left wing" UE and the "right wing" IUE. The record suggests, however, that while the IUE leadership fits our definition of the right, the UE cannot accurately be labeled a "left wing" union. Rather the UE was led by a left-center coalition; its president after 1941, Albert Fitzgerald, has been described as a "center force." Fitzgerald was not identified with the left, and his election to office in 1941 did not result from action initiated by the left.[28]

Therefore, this study will attempt to address the question: To what extent did the left-center coalition, which led the drive for industrial unionism in the electrical industry during the 1930s and 1940s, and which later

---

27. Emspak, "The Breakup of the CIO," pp. 2-6, 17-18, 23.

28. Neither Prickett, "Communists and the Communist Issue,"(pp. 10-12) nor Fillipelli, "The Electrical Workers," (pp. 234-235), found a basis for the contention that the UE was "Communist controlled." The original charge seems to have been based on the assumption that Communist activity or

suffered reeling setbacks, present a serious, legitimate and viable alternative for American labor during the three decades after World War II? Did this viewpoint find significant support among electrical workers or other industrial workers? The issue of foreign policy and international affairs will figure prominently in our discussion because it was the most evident and sensitive point of disagreement, although not the only such issue.

The Issues

The alternative proposed by the left-center coalition can be briefly summarized. It rested on the idea that labor's interests called for labor to play a more independent role in the life of the country than the AFL had yet undertaken, or than the CIO leaders envisioned after approximately 1947.[29] This included, in the first place, a means to express its own political agenda, as the CIO Political Action Committee (PAC) had begun to do, or as it could eventually do through a labor-led political party.

Early in the period covered here, however, the nation witnessed the apparent, and at least temporary, failure of an independent political initiative in the 1948 presidential election. Did this remove the possibility of offering any alternative to the AFL or CIO programs? The UE proceeded on the assumption that the 1948 election results did not foreclose all possibilities of pursuing labor's independent program. The UE was not alone in urging a more independent stance for labor. In the auto workers' union, the right-wing leadership faced internal resistance until well into the 1950s. The UE was,

---

influence amounted to "domination" or "control." For more on Fitzgerald's election and the UE leadership, see chapter II.

29. David Brody, Workers in Industrial America (New York: Oxford University Press, 1980), pp. 234-237. Brody argues that AFL-CIO leaders followed the American labor tradition by choosing to accept a limited and subordinate role in the nation's political life.

however, the largest union whose leadership adhered to its left-center outlook.[30]

The UE differed from the AFL-CIO, and its main rival, the IUE, on important questions that were not overt Cold War issues. One leading authority has argued that the "divergent conceptions of the role of trade unions in the United States" led to sharply different collective bargaining approaches to "shop floor" issues, such as incentive pay and seniority during the decade of the 1950s.[31] Also, during the recession of 1957–1958, while key industrial unions, such as the auto workers, campaigned for a form of guaranteed annual income through Supplemental Unemployment Benefits (SUB), the UE argued that the priority should be to win a reduction in the workweek, a demand that the major employers resisted much more stubbornly. Walter Reuther's decision not to pursue the shorter workweek met resistance in the UAW, and the UE proposal received major press attention. The UE leaders saw the AFL-CIO's refusal to adopt this issue as a major goal as consistent with that organization's past reluctance to chart an independent course for labor.[32]

Similarly, the UE's response to the call for legislation to combat union "corruption" during the late 1950s differed from that of the AFL-CIO. While AFL-CIO leaders initially cooperated with Congress members in attempting to draft the Landrum-Griffin Bill, they felt betrayed

---

30. Prickett, "Communists and the Communist Issue," pp. 295-296, discusses the situation in UAW Ford local 600. This local, the UAW's largest with 60,000 members, continued to elect left-wing leaders until March 1952 when the union's national executive board ended the left's elected representation by removing five alleged Communists from the local's general council. See also March of Labor 3, April 1951, pp. 9-10, "Ford Vote Rocks Reuther," in UE Archives, series D 11, file 113 B, University Library System, University of Pittsburgh.

31. Mark McColloch, "The Shop-Floor Dimension of Union Rivalry" in Steve Rosswurm, ed., The CIO's Left Led Unions, (New Brunswick, Rutgers University Press, 1992) pp. 184 ff.

32. UE News, January 28, 1958, p. 9, "Reuther Acts to Scuttle UAW's Main Demand"; also February 3, 1958, p. 9 for opposition to Reuther's dropping of the shorter workweek proposal offered by Ford Local 600 president Carl Stellato at UAW special convention.

when the final version did not meet their expectations and condemned the law. The UE argued that certain leaders of the larger labor body, including the IUE's Carey, had invited passage of the bill by cooperating with legislators whose aims differed from those of organized labor.[33]

However, the specific areas of disagreement between the UE and the leaders of the AFL-CIO that always seemed to get the most attention related more directly to the Cold War. The UE, for example, argued that support for the Marshall Plan, for the subsequent increased military spending during the early 1950s, and for the Korean War were not in labor's interests. Indeed, by 1951, the union claimed some vindication on these points as AFL and CIO leaders expressed frustration with the results of the European aid program and with the treatment they received by the Truman Administration's war mobilization agencies.[34] After the Korean War, the UE urged opposition to the legislation in Congress aiming to outlaw "Communist controlled" unions, but which, its leaders claimed, threatened the independent activity of all unions. While the AFL and CIO opposed the Brownell-Butler Bill late in the hearings, they did not publicize its significance to their members as did the UE.

To summarize, the UE, while taking many positions in common with the AFL and CIO, had some basic disagreements, but the overriding difference was acceptance or rejection of the U.S. government's Cold War policies. This disagreement had both international and domestic manifestations, but the two were always related. During the late 1960s when the Vietnam War became the critical issue, the relationship between the international

33. See UE News, September 14, 1959, p. 4 for the UE criticism; AFL-CIO, Proceedings, Third Constitutional Convention, San Francisco, September, 1959, pp. 617-618 for the AFL-CIO's position on Landrum-Griffin: "Despite the AFL-CIO's sincere and conscientious efforts, Big Business combined with reactionary and misguided legislators in Congress to thwart labor's honest efforts for a legitimate reform bill. Instead these anti-labor forces entered into an evil alliance with the purpose of crippling all of organized labor."

34. See chapter III.

and domestic sides of the Cold War debate re-emerged, as evidence of opposition to Washington's foreign policy increased, but foreign policy had always been a part—sometimes open, sometimes submerged—of a larger disagreement.

How could organized labor best advance the interests of American workers? The dominant Cold Warriors in the AFL and the CIO may not have shared all the views of internationally minded business executives, but they did believe that expanded United States influence abroad would benefit American workers. Control of foreign markets and raw materials by American firms would mean jobs in the United States.[35] Once they accepted this corporate thinking, they found that their own input was minimal. A corollary of this theory was that consistently high military expenditures, necessary to defend economic interests abroad, also generated employment.[36]

Labor's Cold War leaders did not always state their concerns solely in economic terms. One of their favorite arguments for supporting the Cold War was their desire

35. Lenburg, "CIO and American Foreign Policy," pp. 224-225; Radosh, American Labor and U.S. Foreign Policy, p. 5. AFL leaders referred to their international agenda as "free trade unionism" beginning in the 1940s. The term was intended to give the impression that they were both anti-Communist (which was true) and independent of ties to official government organs (which during much of the period of our study apparently was not). See Wehrle, Between a River and a Mountain, pp. 3, 9-10, 12, 15-16.

36. Labor leaders did not generally state this view for the record, nor did unions often pass resolutions urging increased military spending. However, indications are that some feared the effects of cuts in such spending. See, for instance, Anthony Sampson, The Arms Bazaar (New York: Viking Press, 1977), pp. 213-214 for the comments of Gerry Whipple, UAW regional director in California, on the B-1 bomber, "The B1 is the best deterrent we have, and it's got a helluva lot of plusses: it provides a very necessary job program, and it stimulates the aerospace industry." See also the remarks of Joseph Beirne, president of the Communications Workers in the New Republic, May 16, 1970, p. 8 for a similar point of view.

On the other hand, William Winpisinger's criticism of dependence on military production in April 1985 indicated that Whipple's argument was not universally accepted by labor leaders in the aerospace industry. Then President of the International Association of Machinists (IAM), Winpisinger noted the "boom and bust" cycle of employment in military-related industries. See Economic Notes 54 (February, 1986), p. 4. The same point was made by

for acceptance or for the "respectability" of their movement. Their fear of losing precious and recently won advantages increased dramatically after World War II as the attitudes of government officials and the commercial media towards the Soviet Union became increasingly negative. The search for "respectability" would become an especially divisive issue in the UE by 1947 when the right-wing caucus publicly charged the union's leaders with ignoring the need for it.

The left, or the left-center coalition, had a sharply different view of promoting the basic interests of American workers. The UE argued year after year in its literature and publications that the Cold War and accompanying large annual military budgets damaged the interests of working people because they caused inflation, produced nothing consumable, and diverted resources from the uses most important for workers and their families, such as expanded health care and educational facilities. Military spending benefitted primarily the arms manufacturers and other corporate interests, according to this point of view. The corporations who exploited the people and resources of developing nations were the very ones that attempted to do the same to American workers.[37]

Given the layered but seemingly intractable nature of the internal disagreements, the argument over American labor's international ties comes as no surprise. At the end of World War II, the CIO leaders and the leaders of its largest unions, anxious to establish their organization as a legitimate alternative to the AFL on the international labor scene, responded actively to the initiatives of British, Soviet, and other trade union leaders and played an instrumental role in founding the World Federation of Trade Unions (WFTU). Among these

---

Ernest DeMaio, former president of UE District 11 in a conversation with the author on November 22, 1985, when he observed that the general rule in such industries was "feast or famine."

37. See for example, UE Policy, 1948, p. 30 or UE Policy for any of the years of this study; also see Lenburg, "CIO and Foreign Policy," p. 157.

were UE president Albert Fitzgerald and CIO secretary-treasurer James Carey.

When Phillip Murray and other CIO leaders turned against the left in their own organization, they also broke the CIO's ties to the WFTU. After November 1949, the CIO joined the AFL in promoting a newly organized anti-Communist international labor center, the International Confederation of Free Trade Unions (ICFTU). Although the UE national leadership maintained no formal contact with the WFTU after 1950, the UE News reported on WFTU conferences, and some UE districts sent representatives to meet with WFTU member unions during the early 1950s. Even these contacts soon ceased, however, as Cold War pressures intensified. The near total lack of contact between American trade unionists and the WFTU would remain for decades one of the most enduring results of the Cold War in the labor movement.[38]

The apparent dominance of the AFL-CIO leadership's position should not obscure the more complex underlying situation in American labor. What is obvious is not always the whole truth, or even the most important part of the story. Despite the formal isolation of the UE and the other unions expelled from the CIO (and the eventual disappearance of most of them through merger or otherwise joining with AFL-CIO unions), the record suggests that the Cold War stance of the AFL-CIO leadership never had unanimous support in labor's ranks. After stubbornly surviving for a decade and a half, this sentiment re-emerged with renewed vigor during the mid and late 1960s.[39]

---

38. People's Daily World, March 11, 1987, p. 2-A, reported that the State Department had denied visas to eight Soviet trade unionists who had been invited to attend a health and safety conference, by the IAM, and that the denial was in line with the "official" AFL-CIO position. See also PDW, December 29, 1987, p. 2-A, "McCarran visa curbs eased, but... Ban Remains on Unionists from Lands of Socialism."

39. See The Nation, December 27, 1965, pp. 516-518, "Strong Arm of the Status Quo" on the AFL-CIO convention of that year; and November 27, 1967,

Finally, in addressing the issue of whether or not the left-center leadership in the electrical industry presented a serious alternative for American labor, the size of the UE's membership deserves attention. This union, one of the CIO's largest during the 1940s, suffered heavy losses during the 1950s and then grew again during the 1960s, although it never approached its original size. The UE's opponents cited the losses to buttress claims that the union was a "dying" or "discredited" organization, and that the membership, in disagreement with the policies of its leaders, awaited the first opportunity to leave the union. Historians have used membership figures to demonstrate the decline of the UE's influence during the 1950s.[40] The story of electrical unionism during the Cold War period, however, suggests that the UE membership figures tell only part of the story. In analyzing these figures, several factors require consideration.

In the first place, counting union membership is never easy. Leo Troy and Neil Shefflin have collected data based on the per capita dues payments reported by the unions. This method may yield nominally accurate figures, but understate the influence of unions, since it does not count workers who may have signed union cards in work places where collective bargaining rights have not been won. Especially in the case of the UE, the external difficulties the union faced in collecting dues during much of the period discussed here suggests that this method should be used only with care.[41]

---

pp. 561-563, "Labor Meets for Peace" on the Labor Leadership Assemble for Peace.

40. Joseph Rayback, A History of American Labor, Expanded and Updated (New York: Free Press, 1966), p. 420; Ronald Schatz, The Electrical Workers; A History of Labor at GE and Westinghouse 1923-1960 (Chicago: University of Illinois Press, 1983), p. 232.

41. Leo Troy and Neil Sheflin, The Union Source Book (West Orange, New Jersey: Industrial Relations Data and Information Services, 1985). Dr. Leo Troy told this writer that the UE membership on pp. 6-21 is undercounted in this volume because the union's Canadian membership was subtracted twice, once by the union and once by the authors. The UE was, he said, the only union to subtract its Canadian membership before reporting per capita dues payments. Telephone conversation, June 24, 1987. See tables 1 and 2.

Even if one accepts the lowest estimate at the lowest point during this study, the UE was never in danger of going out of existence and retained considerable and recognized influence in communities where it had significant membership. In addition, the UE's growth during the mid and late 1960s, as indicated by the figures, could have been a factor in changing the attitude of the IUE leaders toward the UE.

Finally, when assessing UE membership figures, we will argue that the union's influence extended well beyond its own officially counted membership. Many workers in shops that left the UE continued to support the UE program throughout this period. In several shops, including the largest plants, UE activity continued long after the shops voted, frequently by narrow margins, to leave the union. In some cases, shops returned to the UE, but even where they did not, there was evidence of continuing support for the UE's program. Finally, developments of the late 1960s, such as the Labor Leadership Assembly for Peace and later the National Co-ordinating Committee for Trade Union Action and Democracy, suggest that the UE positions expressed the sentiments of many workers outside the electrical industry whose leaders supported the Cold War. When assessing the UE's membership and influence during this period, the words of author Bert Cochran, not a friend of the UE, come to mind. He allowed that, given the circumstances of the Cold War, "The wonder is not that they lost heavily, but that they survived at all."[42] The historian is compelled to examine such wonders closely.

The period covered by this work was one of transformative changes in the electrical manufacturing industry as well as in the national and international economy. The two most fundamental changes affecting electrical workers were the increasing pace of automation and

---

See also Albert Blum, "Why Unions Grow," Labor History 9 (Winter 1968), pp. 40-41.

42. Bert Cochran, Labor and Communism: The Conflict that Shaped American Unions (Princeton: Princeton University Press, 1977), p. 293.

the geographical dispersal of production facilities in the industry. Both of these changes occurred in such a way as to cause frequent conflict between labor and employers, and both were key parts of corporate America's increasingly aggressive program.[43]

For example, labor saw the geographical expansion of the major electrical firms as part of a management program to transfer operations out of the northeastern United States to other parts of the country—and later to other countries—where labor costs were lower and the workforce unorganized.[44] The dispersal of factories also meant that workers would be employed in smaller plants rather than the giant facilities in Schenectady, East Pittsburgh, Lynn, Erie, or Lester (South Philadelphia), Pennsylvania. The CIO was aware of this trend as early as 1951 and warned that it was part of a conscious effort to reduce their militancy. The *CIO News* published a report of a meeting of high level industrialists addressed by General Electric's Charles Wilson in December of that year. Here, Wilson had urged that the new plants constructed under the (Korean) war mobilization program and paid for through tax amortization certificates would be smaller and located in small communities to avoid the concentration of a large labor force.[45]

The introduction of new technology in the industry also generated widespread labor-management conflict. David Noble argues that management's primary motivation in introducing tape run machine tools in the way it did was primarily to maintain control of the production process in the hands of managers rather than of

---

43. Schatz, The Electrical Workers, pp. 232-238. On the introduction of new technology at General Electric during the post-World War II period, see David Noble, Forces of Production: A Social History of Industrial Automation (New York: Alfred A. Knopf, 1984).

44. UE Memo, "The Financial Condition of the Westinghouse Electric Corporation," August 16, 1957; United Electrical Workers/Labor Collections, Archives Service Center, University of Pittsburgh (hereafter UE Archives), Westinghouse Conference Board Series, file 435.

45. CIO News, December 31, 1951; article was reviewed in the UE News, January 21, 1952, p. 3.

skilled workers. Noble suggests that the stated goal of increased efficiency was, in fact, a secondary issue and that management's desire for control determined how the new technology entered the industry.[46]

The UE took the position that these changes—automation and the dispersal and relocation of facilities—and Cold War policies were part of the same program. This was not the position of the AFL-CIO leadership. While these leaders recognized technological change in the hands of management as a threat, they refused to relate this to United States foreign policy or the Cold War. Disagreements with corporate employers stopped at the boundaries of the United States. If there was occasional disagreement, it was when AFL-CIO officials attacked corporations or the foreign policy establishment from the right, charging them with being "soft on Communism." In terms of the real life, everyday problems of workers, the record suggests that the UE program did offer a serious alternative to labor support for the Cold War.

On the matter of technological change, Noble observes that "The cultural fetishization of technology... which focuses attention upon fashion and forecast, on what is forever changing... has allowed Americans to ignore and forget what is not changing—the basic relations of domination that continue to shape society and technology alike."[47] By the late 1960s, after two decades of Cold War, developments indicated that many labor leaders were remembering how much had not changed in the relations between labor and management. Their memory appeared to have been jarred by rank-and-file unrest that brought leadership changes in several major unions by the end of the period addressed here. The IUE was one of these unions. These developments, UE

46. See David Noble, Forces of Production; A Social History of Industrial Automation (New York: Alfred A. Knopf, 1984), especially chapter 11, pp. 265-323.

47. Ibid., p. xii.

leaders felt, justified their longstanding opposition to the Cold War policies of the nation's leaders.

In order to understand the changes in the American labor movement during the three decades after World War II, we must account for the survival of the UE, but, equally important, we must account for the continued support for the UE program that persisted among many workers who, for various reasons, did not stay in that union. This program included positions on foreign policy and international issues as well as domestic trade union questions.

Chapter 2

The UE and the Cold War Debate in the CIO

The Union

The end of World War II saw the UE holding its position as one of the big three unions in the CIO. Along with the auto and steel workers' unions, the UE had given leadership to a movement that had caused one economist to suggest that the country was "shifting from a capitalistic economy to a laboristic one," and the president of the U.S. Chamber of Commerce to observe that, "by any... yardstick, labor is a power in our land."[1] The UE's first president, James Carey, had been elected the CIO's first secretary-treasurer, a post he continued to hold in 1945.

While the three large basic industrial unions shared characteristics, including their size and importance in the economy, each had its own unique origins. The UE, for instance, had grown out of several previously existing entities: local unions, "federal" unions affiliated with the AFL, and company unions whose members had accepted the industrial union concept and voted to affiliate with the national union. There was not, for instance, an "electrical workers' organizing committee" during the mid and late 1930s, as there was a Steel

1. The first quote is from Sumner Schlichter, "Are We Becoming a Laboristic State?" New York Times Magazine, May 16, 1948, p. 11; the second from Eric Johnston, America Unlimited (Garden City, New York: Doubleday, Doran and Co., 1944), p. 176.

Workers' Organizing Committee.[2] In March 1936, fifty delegates from independent and federal AFL unions met in Buffalo and founded the United Electrical and Radio Workers of America. The independent representatives came mostly from large, heavy equipment factories in the General Electric and Westinghouse chains, the federal representatives from radio plants, or from the "light" side of the industry. When a group of industrial machinists withdrew from the International Association of Machinists to join the new union in 1937, the organization's name became the United Electrical, Radio and Machine Workers of America.[3]

The three top officers of the union represented these three constituencies. We should say a word about the union's leaders here, although we will become more thoroughly acquainted with them later. As colorful and arresting a group of individuals as any in literature, they have attracted the attention of some historians. How effectively they performed their duties as trade union leaders was a matter of sharp disagreement during the early Cold War years. The seriousness and intensity of the charges directed at them compel us to look carefully at how they interacted with their members. James Carey, a young Philco worker with a college degree from night school at the University of Pennsylvania, was elected president. Recognized for his role in organizing Philadelphia area radio workers, Carey would soon become Secretary-Treasurer of the CIO, as well as President of his own union.[4]

---

2. This point about the origins of the UE is made by James Prickett in "Communists and the Communist Issue in the American Labor Movement," ch. 6; see also Ronald Fillipelli, "The United Electrical Workers," ch. 1; James Matles and James Higgins, Them and Us, part I, "Organizing"; also Ben Riskin interview, October 9, 1986, tape in author's possession.

3. Matles and Higgins, Them and Us, ch. 3 "Pounding on AFL Doors," pp. 37-50; also Interview with James Matles by Fillipelli, May 6, 1968, pp. 17-26, Pennsylvania State University, Historical Collections and Labor Archives.

4. See Carey's biography by labor archivist Bob Golon online at "IUE Labor Archives Project," Rutgers University, Special Collections and Labor Archives.

Julius Emspak, a young tool and die maker from Schenectady was elected secretary-treasurer. Emspak's family had a tradition of political activism in the city; his father had been active in the campaigns of Charles Steinmetz, socialist candidate for mayor and an employee of the General Electric Company. Emspak had gone to work in the factory at the age of 14, had attended Union College on a GE loan program, had gone on to graduate school at Brown University, and returned to work for GE.[5] The third position, director of organization, went to James Matles, a Brooklyn machinist who had come to New York from his native Romania at the age of 19 in 1929. Unsatisfied with the policies of his AFL union, Matles had led 15,000 industrial machinists into the CIO electrical and radio workers' union. Although a number of the original union activists were older skilled workers in the electrical plants, the top leadership posts were consciously assigned to younger men.[6] Given this feature of its history, it is accurate to say that the union was organized from the bottom up. The locals and districts enjoyed a considerable degree of independence from the national leadership in terms of choosing officers and administering finances.[7]

A look beyond the top leadership reveals an organization that represented a membership of varied backgrounds and skills and exhibited a decentralized and free-wheeling character, which veterans and observers

5. Material about Emspak is from the interview with James Matles by Ronald Filippelli, dated October 5, 1968, Pennsylvania State University, Labor History Archives; clippings of Emspak's obituaries in several newspapers dated April 27, 1962, UE Archives, Record Group 1, Box "Emspak Correspondence 1936-62" ff "Emspak, Julius-correspondence-death"; Emspak's testimony before the HUAC, December 6, 1949, U.S. House of Representatives, Subcommittee of the Committee on Un-American Activities, Hearings Involving Communist Infiltration of Labor Unions Part II (81) H1293, p. 834; and from the summary of Emspak's interview in the Columbia University Oral History Collection in Schatz, The Electrical Workers, pp. 92-95. The UE News serialized a brief biography of Matles during the winter of 1955-56 as told to editor Tom Wright.

6. Matles and Higgins, Them and Us, pp. 53, 137.

7. Frank Emspak, "The Breakup of the CIO," pp. 24-25.

still mentioned years later. A word about the democracy that the UE claimed to practice is necessary here in view of the charges later leveled at the union's leaders during the late 1940s and the 1950s. One veteran organizer and district president recalled, for example:

> Because we were a very democratic union, in a sense, the membership kept our feet to the fire. Not that we objected to it. It was a two way street; we defended the rights of the members; the membership defended us and the policies that we were pursuing because building any union is not following simply what the members want. Yes, you defend and advance their interests, but if you are leaders, you lift their sights a little bit. So that you're not only fighting for immediate needs, but also for the long range interests of the workers.[8]

As the union organized and grew, it faced issues that required it to keep the "two way street" open in both directions. The relatively large percentage of women workers in the electrical manufacturing industry, for instance, and the entrenched management practices discriminating against women workers, forced the union to address the issue of winning equal pay for women, or eliminating "women's jobs" or women's rates. The union's claims to have addressed this issue aggressively and to have made progress under complex circumstances find support in the record.[9]

Similarly, while the number of African-American workers in the industry was small, they tended to be concentrated in certain shops and locations, a situation that raised the issues of equal opportunity and of Black

---

8. Interview with Ernest DeMaio, former president of UE District 11, October 2, 1986, tape in author's possession.

9. See Ruth Milkman, Gender at Work: The Dynamics of Job Segregation by Sex During World War II (Urbana: University of Illinois Press, 1987.) Also see Schatz, The Electrical Workers, p. 30 and especially his layered discussion on pp. 119 ff.; and UE News, January 7, 1952, p. 8 for discussion of a Labor Department report on women in the industry.

representation and leadership. While the union's efforts to expand opportunities for Black workers in the large plants met resistance from the companies and often from white workers, the policy continued. African American officers and stewards were elected, and the union urged locals to maintain functioning fair practices committees. The UE's national Fair Practices Committee was led by Ernest Thompson of District 4 in the New York-Northern New Jersey area, and by the 1950s, Black district leaders included Sterling Neal, president of District 7 (Ohio and Kentucky) and William Burch, vice president of District 11 (Illinois, Wisconsin, and Minnesota).[10]

In terms of workers of European ancestry, the electrical manufacturing industry included members of widely diverse ethnic groups. However, employer policies ensured that ethnic divisions in the workforce "coincided with the occupational hierarchy" during the 1930s. Thus, workers of northern European descent were likely to perform the most highly skilled operations while those of southern or eastern European ancestry worked on refrigerator assembly lines or in the foundry.[11] The union, therefore, faced a management tradition of stratifying workers according to ethnic background, a point to which we shall return.

Two clauses in the union's constitution, which were regarded as protections of internal democracy, were debated but never changed. One was the clause prohibiting the national officers from receiving salaries higher than the average pay of the highest paid workers in the

---

10. James B. Hart, former chairman of the Fair Practices Committee in UE Westinghouse Local 107, told in a July 26, 1986 interview how he, an African-American, had overcome resistance and been elected chief steward of an integrated department at the plant in the late 1940s. After being re-elected several times, Hart was hired by the union as a field organizer during the 1960s and continued in that post for nearly two decades.

According to Matles, one of the factors that caused him to lead members out of the International Association of Machinists and into the UE was the IAM's "secret ritual" barring anyone but "Caucasians" from membership. See Matles interview by Fillipelli, pp. 23-25.

11. See Schatz, The Electrical Workers, p. 29 for the ethnic makeup of the electrical manufacturing workforce in 1930.

union. When, at the 1946 convention, a delegate allowed that the officers should receive a raise to bring their salaries closer to those of other labor leaders, the officers entered the debate to argue that such a move would set a dangerous precedent and alter the democratic nature of the union. The constructive and basically good-natured character of the debate on this issue contrasts sharply with the heated and bitter exchanges that erupted when political and foreign policy related issues took center stage as the Cold War deepened.[12]

The other clause generating debate, frequently not good natured, referred to politics. The preamble to the UE constitution stated the intention to organize all workers in the industry "regardless of craft, age, sex, nationality, race, creed, or political beliefs." The issue of limiting members' rights because of their political beliefs first came before the union in 1941 when a small local in Pittsburgh attempted to insert a clause in its constitution denying "Nazis, Fascists, and Communists" the right to run for local office. The union's national executive board overruled the local, stating that a local did not have the power to limit members' rights to run for office or to choose their officers.[13] The issue was not disruptive at that time, but the events of 1941 deserve mention because later accounts and interpretations of what happened differed sharply.

At the 1941 September convention, the young President Carey lost his bid for re-election. Although Carey's defeat changed the political makeup of the leadership, the movement to oust him did not stem primarily from political differences. The challenge to Carey originated with members of General Electric locals who charged that

12. UE 1946 Convention Proceedings, pp. 193-196.

13. Matles and Higgins, Them and Us, pp. 130-131. On the issue of membership rights see Prickett, "The Communist Issue in the American Labor Movement," chapters 2, 6 and conclusion, p. 422. Prickett argues that members of the right-wing opposition in the UE had more rights than did the left in unions controlled by the right. The International Ladies Garment Workers (ILGWU), for instance, resorted to mass expulsions of left-wingers during the 1920s.

he spent more time at his job as CIO secretary-treasurer than he did at his post as UE president. They nominated the thirty-four-year-old president of the UE's New England district (District 2) and treasurer of the Massachusetts CIO Council, Albert Fitzgerald. The left joined the forces supporting Fitzgerald, but the effort extended to "a number of anti-Communists who resented [Carey's] cavalier handling of people and his lack of attention to his union job."[14]

Carey's defeat did not end his activity in labor leadership as he retained his post as CIO secretary-treasurer. Carey was CIO president Philip Murray's choice,[15] and the UE officers agreed to support him in the interest of maintaining unity and avoiding a left-right split in the CIO at the time.[16] In fact, he initially appeared to accept the new arrangement that would allow him to devote full time to his CIO position. Fitzgerald was not identified with the left, and he had, in common with Carey, Irish ancestry and a Catholic background. However, his public statements soon indicated that he would not base his leadership on appeals to anti-Communism, as Carey had begun to do, and that he agreed with the interpretation of the union's constitution adopted by the executive board earlier in the year.[17]

On the other hand, the other two officers, both re-elected in 1941, were identified with the left and probably were, or had been, familiar with the "Communist milieu" of the 1930s. Matles, trained as a machinist in his native Rumania, had been active in the Trade Union Unity League during the early part of the decade.

---

14. Herbert R. Northrup, Boulwarism (Ann Arbor: University of Michigan, 1964), pp. 42-43. For a comprehensive account of this election see Ronald Fillipelli and Mark McColloch, Cold War in the Working Class (Albany, SUNY Press, 1995), pp.58-63

15. Harry Block interview, March 17, 1987.

16. This agreement was a "major mistake" according to UE organizer Ben Riskin, because it gave Carey, after World War II, exposure and influence which did not derive from his standing in his own union, and which was instrumental in splitting the CIO. Riskin interview, October 9, 1986.

17. Prickett, "Communists and the Communist Issue," pp. 329 ff.

Emspak, raised in a family of electrical workers in Schenectady, came from a Catholic household characterized, nonetheless, by left politics and anti-clerical ideas.[18]

Therefore, after Fitzgerald's election, the UE leadership had to function as a left-center coalition, the officers agreeing on basic union policy, but not always on political issues. The union's critics would later charge that Fitzgerald was simply the titular head of an organization that was actually controlled by Communists. While recent researchers have debunked this charge,[19] the sharp difference of opinion about the nature of the union's leadership remains unsettled and reveals much about the politics of the labor movement at this time.

During the war years, the UE's new president carved out his role as a team player among CIO leaders, serving as a member of the organization's political action committee and joining the labor effort to elect FDR to a fourth term. By the late 1940s, however, as Cold War tensions rose inside and outside the CIO, Fitzgerald's refusal to attack the left in the UE and his activity in the broader political arena generated considerable media scrutiny. As the 1948 presidential season entered the fall stretch, for instance, one columnist pondered the active participation of "Big Fitz" in the Progressive Party campaign.

> How a portly, ruddy-faced Boston Irishman gets mixed up in all this funny business takes considerable explaining.... [He] considers the top triumvirate of the CIO [Carey, Philip Murray and David McDonald] mere tools of the church and not true servants of the labor movement... he looks upon himself as a middle-of-the-roader whose function is to make the radical and conservative wings

18. The UE News serialized a short biography of Matles during the winter of 1955-56 as told to editor Tom Wright. See ch. 6 below. The background of Emspak was gleaned from Fillipelli's interview with Matles, p. 28, and from Emspak's interview in the Columbia Oral History Collection.

19. See Fillipelli, "The United Electrical Workers," pp. 234-235; and Prickett, "The Communist Issue," pp. 353, 370, 422-428.

> of [the] labor movement work together.... He is just an extemporaneous talker, utterly unsophisticated. He has a number of other pet hates, in addition to Murray, Carey, McDonald and company. He hates Truman. He hates the press. He thinks all newspaper men are a bunch of liars who merely obey the orders of union hating bosses. [He] likes Henry Wallace and is a complete follower of his line. He thinks Wallace is right in his stand on foreign affairs, civil rights, opposition to the peacetime draft, price control, housing—the whole works.[20]

On the other hand, another observer wrote years later that the union "had fallen under complete Communist control in 1941, the largest union ever to succumb."[21] The author of this statement, Arthur Goldberg, would be remembered both for his association with the industrial union movement and with the foreign policy establishment. Harry Block, an original organizer of Philco UE Local 101 and later a founder of the IUE, was more graphic in a 1987 interview, labeling Fitzgerald "a weak sister, entirely" who refused to side with the right-wing opposition in the UE during the late 1940s.[22]

In response to this estimate of the UE leadership, Donald Tormey, a former leader in Fitzgerald's home local at the Lynn, Massachusetts General Electric plant, offered a different assessment:

> Fitzgerald was nobody's stooge or patsy. He was highly popular in the UE among the membership.... The Harry Blocks of this world were very disappointed with Fitz. He wouldn't red-bait and he fought against their red-baiting. He never tried to be a big shot and he wouldn't let others

---

20. New York World Telegram, September 2, 1948, p. 18, "UEW Chief Fitzgerald is One of Labor Movements's Enigmas," by Peter Edson; clipping in UE Archives, RG 1, Box 1, File Folder "Fitzgerald Personal Correspondence 1947-54."

21. Arthur Goldberg, AFL-CIO; Labor United (New York: McGraw-Hill, 1956), p. 180.

22. Harry Block interview, March 17, 1987.

> make him out to be one. There was Murray's union and Reuther's union and Dubinsky's union and even Hillman's union, but there was no Fitzgerald union. It was the UE and everybody knew the rank-and-file ran it. They held conventions every year to keep it that way. The "weak sisters" in the UE ran away in 1949 to join the red-baiting, Cold War McCarthyism that is in many ways still with us. Harry Block helped lead the runaway. Fitz helped lead the resistance.[23]

The persistent tension between the opposing views of the UE appeared at least once in the words of the same person. Father Charles Owen Rice of Pittsburgh, one of the UE's most active critics during the post-World War II decade, had partially changed his mind by 1966. In calling for a reunification of the electrical industry, Rice modified the charge of "Communist control," but stopped short of reversing himself and labeling the charge false:

> The UE was raided by everyone and its strength fragmented. The unions which succeeded it were neither so efficient nor so democratic. Yes, the UE was democratic. It had been set up that way. I do not know whether or not it changed its constitution so as to be less democratic but its successor unions certainly adjusted theirs.[24]

Rice failed to mention that one of the "adjustments" made by the "successor unions" had been the barring from office, or expulsion, of Communists or alleged Communists who had helped "set up" the union and whom he himself had targeted during the early Cold War. In fact, he again labeled them as "blindly obedient Stalinists" in the same 1966 article quoted above.

The fact that the UE had grown out of previously existing entities did not mean that it neglected to organize

23. Letter from Donald Tormey to the author, April 11, 1987.

24. Monsignor Charles Owen Rice, "Ecumenism in Labor," The Pittsburgh Catholic, June 9, 1966; this clipping was in the personal files of Edward Boehner, former secretary of UE local 107.

new members. In fact, the union played its part in the successful CIO organizing drives of the 1936–1946 decade. By 1945, the UE had grown from its 1936 membership of 23,000 to over 450,000.[25] Indeed, one group of activists that attracted the intense interest of Congressional investigators during the decade and a half after World War II was the union's staff of hired organizers. The Congressmen suspected that since the leaders controlled the paid staff, here was the mechanism through which they exercised political influence over the members. Ironically, however, although the UE leaders were never responsive to questions about their politics, they willingly gave detailed explanations to Congressional Committees and put on the public record how many organizers they had, how they were hired, and what duties they performed.[26]

In any case, the union represented workers of varying ethnic backgrounds and skills in large and small shops in virtually every northeastern state, in the mid-west and on the west coast. Its reputation in the CIO was recognized by President Philip Murray at the UE's 1946 convention when he told the delegates that "your decisions oft times influence the judgments of the national body because of the tremendous interest you manifest in the progress of the movement to which you are affiliated." Murray went on to thank the delegates for "the splendid support that has been given me... by your organization and its officers. They have done so royally, sustained and maintained and fought for all national

25. See table 1.

26. United States House of Representatives, Subcommittee of the Committee on Un-American Activities, Hearings Involving Communist Infiltration of Labor Unions, Part II, 81st congress, 1949, pp. 834-835. Emspak told the subcommittee that the union had 120 field organizers who reported to the 20 international representatives. The staff was supervised by the General Executive Board made up of the district presidents and another representative from each district plus the three national officers. He also explained the hiring process. For more on UE staffers, see Michael J. Bonislawski, "Field Organizers and the United Electrical Workers: A Labor of Love, Struggle and Commitment 1935-1960," unpublished PhD dissertation, Boston College, 2002.

policies and supported the President of this organization in the furtherance of those policies...."[27]

The diversity of the UE's membership has been cited both as a strength and as a weakness. A leading authority on the origins of electrical unionism has suggested that, "It is not true to say...that outside forces were solely responsible for factional conflict in the union movement. On the contrary, union political struggles expressed profound social divisions among workers." He demonstrates, for instance, that, during the late 1940s, groups of younger workers challenged older union leaders in two large electrical plants in western Pennsylvania. He argues that, in both cases, the younger insurgent groups represented a new view of unionism that emphasized "demands for higher wages" as opposed to the older depression era leaders who were mainly concerned with "demands for job security."[28]

Hard fought union elections, I would agree, may reflect serious differences among workers, but factional conflict does not always result in the establishment of two rival unions. We will attempt here to determine if a factor or group of factors was decisive in causing the split in the electrical workers' union, a split which occurred in 1949 and which, despite being partially healed in 1969 and later, continued for decades to haunt the labor movement. This question relates to our primary concern: the role of the left-center coalition in post-war electrical unionism. If, for example, it could be demonstrated that workers left the UE because they were dissatisfied with the leaders' performance in collective bargaining, or because they believed their leaders were corrupt or incompetent, or because of some other action on the part of the leadership, this would indicate that the union did not represent a legitimate trade union alternative to the policies of the AFL-CIO during the period in question. If, on the other hand, outside pressures caused

---

27. UE 1946 Convention Proceedings, p. 57.

28. Schatz, The Electrical Workers, ch. 8, especially pp. 216-217.

workers to leave a union whose leaders and program they supported, then a case can be made for the opposite point of view.

Even if one accepts the contention that outside pressures were not solely responsible for factional internal disagreements, the question posed here remains unanswered. Factions and disagreements do not uniformly lead to irreparable divisions in labor. They certainly did not always do so in the UE. In the western Pennsylvania cases, for instance, the results differed. In Erie Local 506, the challenge to the leadership succeeded, but the local remained in the UE. In East Pittsburgh Local 601, two labor board elections, heavily influenced by numerous outside forces, were necessary in order to remove a majority of the local, although not the entire local from the UE. The union's organizers and activists appear to have considered its diversity a challenge, but more a strength than a weakness.[29]

At the end of World War II UE members had reason for optimism, although widespread concern and uncertainty existed regarding the transition to a peacetime economy. While the union and the CIO did win victories during the early post-war years, the late 1940s brought stagnation and setbacks for the industrial union movement. This young movement, which had generated such broad support among industrial workers, faced powerful and determined adversaries. External forces, including the needs and designs of the American foreign policy establishment, would impact heavily upon it.

The Union and the Gathering Cold War

The year 1949 marks a qualitative change in the fortunes of the industrial union movement in the United States. The split in the CIO drastically changed that organization. In 1945, it had presented a unified front, proud of

29. This point comes through in many of the interviews with activists done by this author and others.

its independence and its newly recognized influence in the nation and on the international scene. By 1949, it was bitterly divided, truncated and on the defensive. The story of the CIO's transformation from one condition to the other has been told.[30] What has yet to be emphasized is the role of the right-wing in electrical unionism in the events of the late 1940s. This was significant, despite the failure of its leading spokesperson, James Carey, to gather widespread support within his own union.

The CIO undertook two notable initiatives during the first year after World War II, one in the United States, the other internationally. At home, surging wartime inflation, which had occurred while the unions observed a wage freeze and a no-strike pledge, produced a surge of militant activity in basic industries. This resulted in the massive 1945–1946 winter strikes in steel, auto, and electrical manufacturing that, at one point in early 1946, shut down much of the basic industrial capacity of the nation. The UE played a key role in the strikes since it represented not only General Electric and Westinghouse workers, but also those in the electrical division of General Motors.[31]

This imposing display of labor's power at home was matched by a bold initiative abroad. The CIO leaders, eager to establish their organization as an alternative to the AFL in the international arena, responded to the overtures of British and Soviet trade unions and participated in the formation of a new international labor center. Two meetings were held during 1945 which succeeded in founding the World Federation of Trade Unions (WFTU) in Paris in October.

30. See Emspak, "The Breakup of the CIO"; Fillipelli, "The United Electrical Workers" chapters 4 and 5; also Richard O. Boyer and Herbert M. Morais, Labor's Untold Story, pp. 340-370; and for a view favorable to the right, see Max Kampleman, The Communist Party vs. the CIO: A Study in Power Politics (New York: Frederick A. Praeger, 1957).

31. On the 1946 strikes see Matles and Higgins, Them and Us, pp. 6-7, 140-148; Noble, Forces of Production, pp. 155-157; Northrup, Boulwarism, pp. 20-23; Fillipelli, "The United Electrical Workers," pp. 132-137; Schatz, The Electrical Workers, pp. 142-146.

A few words about the founding of the WFTU are in order in view of the role played by the CIO right-wingers in splitting the organization four years later. At the February meeting in London, with the war not yet over, the CIO's Carey chaired the Peace Settlement committee and thus played a significant role. His report was enthusiastic.

> Indians and Chinese from the Far East, Arabs and Jews from Palestine, Negroes from Africa and the Caribbean, Catholics, Protestants, Mohammedans[sic] and Hindus—all were represented.... Soviet delegates sat side by side with the leaders of the Christian trade unions of Europe...a true parliament of world labor.[32]

He gave the impression that the conference had essentially succeeded in laying the basis for a new global labor federation. The U.S. representatives, under the leadership of Carey and Sidney Hillman along with those from the Soviet Union had overcome the resistance of the more conservative British delegation and set the stage for the formal inauguration of the WFTU at the second meeting planned for September. The one cloud on the horizon was the blast from AFL president William Green, who had declined to attend, charging that the London conference threatened a "dual, rival movement" to the established European dominated International Federation of Trade Unions (IFTU).[33]

Both Carey and Fitzgerald attended the founding conference in Paris in the fall. The UE was an early and consistent supporter of the WFTU, and both were active among the founding delegates who developed the organization's structure.[34] Following the Paris conference,

---

32. UE Archives, RG 4 Box 6 FF "World Federation of Trade Unions Conference 1943-45."

33. Ibid. FF "WFTU 1945."

34. For more on the founding of the WFTU, see John P. Windmuller, American Labor and the International Labor Movement 1940-1953 (Ithaca, N.Y.: The Institute of Industrial and Labor Relations), 1954, pp. 116-118;

an eleven-member CIO delegation, led by Carey and including Fitzgerald, made a nine-day visit to the Soviet Union. The CIO publicized the delegation's journey in a pamphlet that included pictures of the CIO leaders in the USSR and the text of Carey's report to CIO president Murray. The Americans visited factories and workers' clubs and attended cultural events; they were shown war-damaged industrial plants in Moscow and Leningrad and heard from factory managers and workers about the Soviet Union's urgent need to rebuild and raise living standards. When the delegates met with Soviet Foreign Minister Molotov, he frankly stated his conviction that the nation's primary task was rapidly to raise the living standards of its people in peacetime. At a press conference at the offices of TRUD, the publication of the central council of Soviet trade unions, Carey expressed support for U.S.-Soviet cooperation, saying,

> ...any other Americans who could see what we have seen would be moved by the same feeling of deep human sympathy which we have felt and by the same desire to assist and co-operate in the great tasks in which the Soviet people are now engaged. We believe that America can assist greatly by supplying many of the machines and other products which the Soviet Union so sorely needs, and that in doing so we shall be promoting our own prosperity....

Fitzgerald likewise told a meeting of factory workers at the Kirov machine plant in Leningrad that, as a result of the Americans' visit,

> You have gained friends who are going to insist that our government do everything in its power to aid you. We've seen the price you have paid to establish freedom for all

---

also Ginger and Christiano, The Cold War Against Labor, vol. One, pp. 187-199, essay 23, "The CIO Joins the International Labor Movement," by Len De Caux. For Fitzgerald's role, see UE 1946 General Officer's Report, p. 32, and Kampleman, The Communist Party v. the CIO, p. 325.

peoples of the world. We in America are determined that no force within or without is ever going to turn us against your people again.

Both men would soon have reason to wonder about the wisdom of their statements: Carey because he seems to have changed his mind, Fitzgerald because his prediction did not come true.

While this trip soon disappeared from the radar screen and the memory of the CIO, it was seen as significant at the time. In his introduction to the pamphlet, Murray emphasized the importance of "knowing the truth about the Soviet trade union movement and [of] promoting friendship and understanding between the peoples of our two countries." Perhaps referring to AFL criticism, he continued "unfortunately, there are those who seek to sow the seeds of distrust and suspicion... and who seek to divide rather than unite the world."[35] Thus, by the spring of 1946, the CIO had demonstrated its influence and willingness to act on both the foreign and domestic fronts.

However, the CIO would soon face powerful opposition to its new success. The display of nationwide strike solidarity had the effect of intensifying a corporate offensive that was already underway and that built into a conservative employer assault during the following year. The election of a Republican majority in Congress in the 1946 mid-term elections and the passage of the Taft-Hartley Labor Management Relations Act in June 1947 signaled the direction of the political winds at the time.[36]

---

35. CIO pamphlet in UE Archives, Report of the CIO Delegation to the Soviet Union, submitted by James B. Carey, Chairman. For an account of the thinking of CIO leaders on international matters, see Victor Silverman, Imagining Internationalism, ch. 9, especially pp. 144-155.

36. The role of anti-labor industrialists and publishers in financing Republican senatorial candidates in 1946 is suggested in David Oshinsky's account of the Wisconsin primary and general elections of that year. See his Senator Joseph McCarthy and the American Labor Movement (Columbia: University of Missouri Press), 1976, pp. 9-10, 52-54.

The response of labor to the Taft-Hartley Act did not immediately show obvious or insurmountable division. The restrictions on trade union activities were widely denounced, and most CIO union leaders indicated that they would refuse to cooperate with the Labor Relations Board (NLRB) under the new law. While the *UE News*, with its regular reference to Taft-Hartley as a "slave law," was perhaps more vigorous than some other union publications, organized labor generally shared that assessment. A crucial part of the new law, section 9h, required union leaders, but not corporate executives or managers, to sign affidavits stating that they were not "Communists" or "pro-Communists." While this requirement would soon come to highlight the schism in the industrial union movement, it did not immediately cause irreparable harm. In August, when Walther Reuther persuaded a bare majority of the auto workers' executive board to vote for compliance, other labor leaders continued to refuse.[37]

At this point, we should consider the possibility that the division in the CIO actually originated with the disagreements between Walter Reuther, then head of the union's GM department, and the UE leaders during the 1946 strikes. The UE represented some 27,000 workers in the electrical division of General Motors, centered in the Dayton, Ohio Frigidaire locals. In early February, with the UAW still on strike, Reuther complained bitterly that the electrical union had settled on their own and had undercut his efforts at winning a superior settlement with GM. He told a conference of UAW leaders that because of UE's "secret negotiations" with General Motors, he intended to mount a campaign "to take over the UE workers in GM." While this episode undoubtedly contributed to the later animosity between the auto

37. For the UAW executive board meeting, see Emspak, "The Breakup of the CIO," pp. 172-173. Although the board voted to comply with the Taft-Hartley Act in August, Reuther did not officially notify the Labor Board of the union's decision until November, after the CIO convention had indicated the growing rift over the Marshall Plan

and electrical leaders, it was not clear at the time that Reuther would prevail in any power struggle inside the CIO. Fitzgerald sent UAW president R.J.Thomas a terse response, not released to the press, arguing that Reuther had turned down all UE proposals for joint action in dealing with the company. Other CIO leaders agreed that the "publicity crazy" Reuther had caused the problem by operating on his own before and during the strike.[38] So relations between Reuther and the UE were not warm after 1946, but the CIO was still a unified body.

The developments that turned disagreement into division in the CIO and disrupted the left-center coalition were directly related to foreign policy. During 1947 the foreign policy establishment and the Truman Administration initiated policies that for the first time overtly and officially demonstrated their intention to abandon the wartime cooperation with the Soviet Union. During that year, the Administration requested funds from Congress for foreign initiatives that confirmed its support for the "containment of Communism" or, alternatively, the "American Century."

On March 12, for instance, when President Truman went before Congress to request aid for the embattled Greek monarchy, he based his appeal on the need to meet the threat to Europe posed by "armed men led by Communists."[39] On the other hand, six days earlier, in a speech at Baylor University that received more press in Europe than in the United States, the President had spoken of the urgent and pressing need to export American "freedom of enterprise" to the rest of the world.[40]

On June 5, the day after passage of the Taft-Hartley Act, Secretary of State George Marshall presented the

---

38. Fitzgerald to Thomas, February 22, 1946, UE Archives, RG 1.2, Matles, James 1937-75 Box 1, FF "Correspondence–General Motors 1946-50"; Time, February 25, 1946, p. 20, clipping in same file folder.

39. For an analysis of Truman's speech, see Richard Freeland, The Truman Doctrine and the Origins of McCarthyism: Foreign Policy, Domestic Politics, and Internal Security 1946-1948 (New York: Alfred Knopf, 1972), pp. 97-101.

40. Denna Fleming, The Cold War and Its Origins 1917-1960, vol. 1 (Garden City, New York: Doubleday, 1961), pp. 436-437.

Administration's proposal for a multibillion-dollar aid program for Europe. Although the Marshall Plan is popularly remembered as the model of a successful foreign policy, it generated intense debate both in the United States and in Europe, caused much controversy and confusion regarding the motives and goals of American foreign policy, and became an especially sensitive issue in the CIO.[41] The debate over the Marshall Plan reveals much about the split in the CIO and deserves major attention here.

The CIO and the right-wing leaders of its major unions actively supported the Marshall Plan (formally the European Recovery Program or ERP). Their spokesman testified in support of the plan before Congressional Committees. The UE leadership vigorously opposed the plan and issued detailed literature explaining the union's position. The argument was not limited to abstract foreign policy ideas, as the two sides based their views on their perceptions of the needs of American workers. Most importantly, the Marshall Plan debate in the CIO had significance beyond the immediate issue. It was on this question that the CIO leadership altered its previous practice of allowing member unions to take independent stands on political matters, as it had on the Taft-Hartley Act, for example.[42] Finally, securing CIO support for the Marshall Plan became a personal project of CIO secretary-treasurer Carey. But, why did the CIO leaders take such an uncompromising stand on this particular issue? Their decision did not come easily, and strong reasons existed for taking a less rigid position.

The origins of the ERP lay in the perceptions of members of the American business community of the needs

41. For the popular press image, see Stanley Karnow, "Marshall Had a Message for Today." Phildelphia Inquirer O-Ed page, June 5, 1987. For a detailed discussion of the controversy and confusion, see Freeland, The Truman Doctrine, pp. 151 ff.

42. Foster in his Outline History of the World Trade Union Movement, pp. 473-474, writes, "Never before had the CIO or AFL attempted to assume the right to decide the course of their affiliated unions in such matters."

of the nation's economy at the end of World War II. The world that emerged from the war presented what leading American businessmen saw both as expanded opportunities and daunting new problems. On the one hand, the possibility of expanding American capital's influence into areas of the world previously dominated by European empires created unprecedented possibilities. Unlike every other major industrial nation, the United States, having escaped the ravages of modern warfare, found itself in a decidedly strengthened position. United States corporations had benefitted handsomely from government orders and support during the war, and corporate leaders appeared eager to accept the challenge of spreading "freedom and enterprise" to other parts of the globe.[43]

However, American business and political leaders had cause for anxiety as well as optimism, as they viewed the new world situation. The fear of post-war depression appears to have haunted them even as they contemplated their advantageous new situation. The immediate prospect of large scale demobilization and the return to the civilian workforce of millions of servicemen, as government orders evaporated, provided a grim counterpoint to the long-range unlimited investment possibilities.[44]

In addition, the foreign policy equation now included a new and unsettling factor. The Soviet Union's increased prestige and influence after World War II presented the United States with a situation previously unknown, and the USSR was viewed as a new and different foreign policy problem for Washington. However, policy makers were unsure and divided over what to expect from the Soviets. Some hoped that Moscow would cooperate with Washington's program for the post-war world, including Europe, east and west. When this hope proved false, the

---

43. Fleming, The Cold War and Its Origins, pp. 436-437.

44. See Freeland, The Truman Doctrine, p. 15 for the apprehensions of American policy makers. For their optimism, see Blanche Wiesen Cook, The Declassified Eisenhower: A Divided Legacy (Garden City, New York: Doubleday, 1981), pp. xv-xvi.

foreign policy establishment confronted the task of pursuing post-war economic policy without the cooperation of American's largest wartime ally. Thus, the European Recovery Program developed as a plan aiming to consolidate the United States economic position in Western Europe and isolate the Soviet Union.[45]

This suggests that American policy makers did not view the USSR as an imminent, or even a potential, threat to the security of the United States, but rather as an obstacle to their global post-war policy plans, in short, an obstacle to the fulfillment of the "American Century." At the same time, they viewed with acute apprehension the post-war strength of the left in Europe and especially the influence of Communists in the labor movements of Western Europe. Indeed, American diplomats and others expressed frustration at the "soft" attitude of Western Europeans on the "issue of communism."[46]

It appears, then, that members of the foreign policy establishment did not all believe the most extreme characterizations of the Soviet Union or its intentions, characterizations which eventually provided the justification for expanded peacetime military budgets,

---

45. See Robert Messer, The End of an Alliance; James F. Byrnes, Roosevelt, Truman, and the Origins of the Cold War (Chapel Hill, University of North Carolina Press, 1982), p. 182, p. 264, n. 2 for the varied points of view in the State Department; Hugh DeSantis, The Diplomacy of Silence: The American Foreign Service, the Soviet Union and the Cold War 1933-1947 (Chicago, University of Chicago Press, 1980) for the false hopes of State Department officials; Freeland, The Truman Doctrine for the development of the Marshall Plan.

46. Gabriel and Joyce Kolko in The Limits of Power, p. 379, suggest that "Washington did not really believe the Soviets were the major problem. The ERP policy would have been the same had the USSR not existed. The basic problem was to reconstruct a capitalist Europe... which was a direct response to the imperatives of the American economic system." At the same time, the Kolkos do allow that policy makers considered "the USSR's very existence... a reminder of the profound weakening of European capitalism and the traditional order after World War I, and potentially a catalyst for undermining capitalism in the future," p. 4.

For an example of the frustration American leaders felt with the lack of enthusiasm for the Cold War among Western Europeans see the American Federationist, January, 1952, p. 4, "George Meany Finds Europe Soft on Communism."

permanent war preparedness, and the entire Cold War program.[47] Some observers may still argue that the ERP was necessary to prevent Soviet domination of Western Europe, but it seems at least as plausible to argue the reverse: The image of an imminent Soviet "threat" to Western Europe was used to justify a European recovery plan that might otherwise founder in Congressional committees.[48] In any case, the ascendance of hard line Cold Warriors in the State Department by 1947 meant that the CIO leaders would feel increasing pressure to support the Marshall Plan.[49] The eventual acceptance by Murray, Carey, and other right-wing CIO leaders of the most extreme anti-Soviet positions forced the labor left and what remained of the left-center coalition to uphold positions that they believed deserved the support of all labor.

For their part, American business and government leaders, perceiving both problems and opportunities in the post-war world, turned their attention to international matters. The nations of Western Europe, the largest trading partners of the United States, appeared to face imminent economic crisis, and to lack the means to purchase American products. This condition led to the development of plans for large-scale American aid to Europe.

Clearly, however, widespread suspicion regarding the nature and intent of the proposed aid plan existed on both sides of the Atlantic. Weak and uncertain support for the Administration's proposal for European recovery surrounded the debate in the CIO. Both the left and the

---

47. Although the most extreme characterization was only stated in its final form much later, in NSC-68 in March 1950 (see chapter 1, n. 10), rudimentary expressions of the thesis appeared earlier. See the John Foster Dulles article in Life, June 3, 1946, pp. 113 ff., "Thoughts on Soviet Foreign Policy and What To Do About It."

48. See Freeland, The Truman Doctrine, pp. 66-69, 100-101, 277-283 for his argument that the Truman Administration found it necessary to create "emergencies" to secure passage of aid to Britain and Western Europe on more than one occasion.

49. Silverman, Imagining Internationalism, pp. 169-173.

right in the CIO saw a danger in the probability that the aid program would be administered primarily by corporate and business leaders. CIO president Murray made public, in the form of a letter to President Truman's Non-partisan Committee on Foreign Aid, a list of ten CIO criteria that the aid plan should meet.[50] The first was that the aid should be applied in amounts adequate to enable European nations to develop or rebuild an industrial base, and without strings attached in the form of American control over European political or economic affairs.

The CIO's second major concern related to the effects of the recovery plan on working people in the United States. The CIO president's letter expressed the fear that the European relief plan would cause shortages in the United States and stressed the need for corporate leaders to agree to increase the nation's industrial capacity and for the nation, in the event of shortages at home, to distribute available goods equitably "without regard to income." Thus, the CIO leadership indicated its reservations and uncertainty regarding the aid plan's intent and execution.

By the fall of 1947, the issue of European relief loomed large. When the CIO convention met in Boston in early October, Murray had not yet released the CIO conditions for support of any aid plan. The labor body had not publicly rendered a judgment on the results of the Nonpartisan Committee's work as measured by the CIO criteria, and Murray's actions and positions reflected the unsettled situation. While speakers emphasized the importance of helping Europe rebuild, no substantive discussion or analysis of the actual ERP proposals occurred. The UE delegates and other Marshall Plan opponents, reasoning that no specific plan was on the floor for discussion and hoping to preserve unity in the

50. Emspak, "The Breakup of the CIO," pp. 214-215.

CIO, did not push the issue.[51] The convention approved a compromise foreign policy resolution that mentioned aid to foreign nations but not the Marshall Plan by name. The convention never did go on record in support of the ERP. However, Marshall was a featured speaker; in his remarks, he stressed the importance of labor support for the ERP and appealed for such support in order to save "the characteristics of Western Civilization on which our government and manner of living depend."

After Marshall's speech, greeted with "thunderous applause," the foreign policy debate turned bitter as right-wing speakers attacked the Soviet Union, savaged Americans who did not join the attack, and stated their support for the Marshall Plan. UAW President Reuther and Textile Workers' president George Baldanzi both expressed these views, and Murray himself indicated that he interpreted the foreign policy resolution as including support of the European Recovery Program.[52] Although the CIO did not formally declare its support of the ERP until the January 1948 meeting of the executive council in Washington, the <u>CIO News</u> carried articles supporting it earlier. Following the executive council vote, secretary-treasurer Carey testified in favor of the bill at Senate hearings, and the *CIO News* carried a two-page feature including questions and answers about the aid plan.[53]

In March, the CIO issued a statement applying its ten-point criteria to the Senate ERP bill. The statement indicated the leadership's awareness that the

---

51. UE Washington Representative Russ Nixon to Giuseppe DiVittorio, Italian Confederazione Generale de Lavore, April 14, 1948, UE Archives RG 4 Box 6 FF "WFTU 1947-48." Nixon wrote that the "progressive wing at the CIO convention felt afterwards that they should have fought more definitely on the issue of foreign policy."

52. CIO <u>Convention Proceedings</u>, 1947, p. 260 for the quote from Marshall; for summaries of the convention, see Emspak, "The Breakup of the CIO," pp. 208-213; and Leroy Lenburg, "The CIO and American Foreign Policy," pp. 166-168. Reuther was, at the time, in an internal battle for control of the UAW where resistance to his policies continued into the 1950s.

53. <u>CIO News</u>, January 12, 1948, p. 5; February 9, 1948, pp. 6-7. The executive council vote was 33-11 with the "left led" unions in opposition.

CIO conditions had not all been met. According to the CIO's assessment, the bill would meet the requirements regarding Europe and would not impose conditions on receiving nations. However, the safeguards regarding American workers were less evident. These issues would have to be fought "independently" of the Marshall Plan bill. However, the CIO leaders considered the creation of the Economic Cooperation Administration and a Civilian Advisory Board as positive steps that would insure the ERP's independence of the State Department.[54]

While the CIO leaders backed the proposal for European recovery despite their reservations, the UE took the opposite position. The union had previously noted what it labeled as a shift in the Administration's foreign policy away from the war-time cooperation with the USSR, and the 1946 UE convention had expressed its apprehension. The foreign policy resolution that year called on the President to "return to the foreign policy of FDR," to remove the "big business" representatives from the government, and to call for a meeting of the great powers in order to "call a halt to the... division of the world into conflicting spheres of influence, and to halt the reactionary drive for war."[55]

In March 1947, the *UE News* responded to Truman's policy address on the Greek Civil War with a full-page report of an opposing speech by Henry Wallace. Wallace was a national political figure who had already stated his foreign policy differences with the Administration. His removal from the Democratic ticket and replacement by Truman as Vice Presidential candidate in 1944 had been widely interpreted as a defeat for the liberal and labor elements in the Democratic Party and had contributed to the strained relations between Truman and the CIO after Roosevelt's death. A second episode had occurred in September 1946 when Truman had removed Wallace from his post as Secretary of Commerce after

54. Emspak, "The Breakup of the CIO," pp. 214-215.
55. UE Convention Proceedings, 1946, pp. 229-230.

Wallace had publicly differed with the "get tough with Russia" policy in a speech at Madison Square Garden.

In March 1947, Wallace spoke out again, charging that the Administration policy toward Greece undercut the United Nations because of its unilateral character. This was the speech carried by the *UE News*, which noted that Wallace's remarks had received scant attention in the commercial press.[56] By printing the speech and commenting favorably, the union hoped to enter and expand the national debate on foreign policy.

The union's 1947 convention met in September two weeks before the CIO and presented a sharp contrast. In the UE the right-wing forces continued to find themselves isolated and in opposition to the majority of the nearly 1,000 delegates. The foreign policy question brought sharp and heated debate, but the resolution eventually adopted overwhelmingly by the convention clearly indicated the majority sentiment. Adhering to the union's position of the previous year, the resolution urged that the United States Government be taken "out of the hands of Wall Street" and "redirected to the needs of the people."

The right opposition and its spokesperson, ex-president Carey, took the significant step of presenting a "minority report" on the foreign policy issue. While the report included conciliatory language, its overall content provoked intense debate and exposed the fundamental disagreement between left and right. It called on President Truman to establish a "clear foreign policy" that would enable all people to attain "full economic and political democracy," and urged that the United States "not support Communist dictatorship, re-establishment of Fascism or decadent monarchies."[57] The majority of the delegates interpreted the posing of "political democracy" on the one hand against "Communist dictatorship," on the other as an attempt to justify the rationale for the

56. UE News, March 29, 1947, p. 9.

57. UE Convention Proceedings, 1947, pp. 294-297.

European Recovery Program. They apparently reasoned that, if "Communist dictatorship" constituted the threat to "political democracy" in Europe, and if it could be equated with the "re-establishment of Fascism," then the entire Cold War foreign policy of unilateral emergency aid to Greece and aid to other western European nations, coupled with isolation of the Soviet Union, was justified and necessary. The minority report made no mention of "Wall Street" or its influence on the nation's government.

The 1947 convention demonstrated the seriousness with which the UE leaders viewed the developing situation in the nation and in the labor movement. Organization director Matles, in a major address, blasted Carey and former District 1 President Harry Block by name for organizing the UE Members for Democratic Action (UEMDA), an opposition group that had embarrassed the union by issuing critical statements in the national press.[58] Matles charged that the UEMDA had not made specific criticisms of the UE leadership, but had instead publicly praised General Electric president Charles Wilson while claiming that the UE under its present leadership lacked "respectability." The UE leader suggested that Carey desired a "respectable union" that, "in order to win press approval," would refrain from seeking wage increases.[59]

The foreign policy debate and Matles's remarks underlined the connection that the UE leadership and the convention majority saw between foreign policy and matters at home. They argued that the Administration's foreign policy, exemplified by the European Recovery Program, aimed to benefit major American corporate interests. Support from the labor movement for these interests abroad would lead to submission to the same forces at home. Therefore, Carey's advocacy of what would soon become the CIO position on European

58. Fillipelli, "The United Electrical Workers," p. 143.
59. UE News, October 4, 1947, p. 3.

recovery and his attitude toward GE President Wilson were two sides of the same policy.[60]

In May 1948, the UE issued its own detailed analysis of the ERP bill. It argued that the bill failed to meet the original CIO criteria and aimed to serve the interests of American firms whose profits the bill specifically protected.[61] The union's statement claimed that the plan failed to protect the living standards of American workers or the independence of European nations receiving aid. One particularly curious feature of the proposal appeared, the UE observed, to give the United States control over the export policies of European nations, and at the same time to indicate the Marshall Plan's political nature, despite the State Department's position that the aid was offered to all nations. Receiving nations would be forbidden to export to eastern Europe any commodities that the United States would itself refuse to ship there. Thus, the trade policies proposed for the United States were "liberal" only within distinct limits and were not without strings.

Also, the UE pointed out that certain goods would not be shipped to Western Europe at all. Generally, these included goods that would enable the region to rebuild a heavy industrial base, such as unfinished steel and certain types of machine tools. Finally, the fact that the ERP would be administered unilaterally by an American

---

60. Former UE activists frequently made the connection between foreign and domestic policy in interviews and letters, for instance, Ben Riskin and Ernest DeMaio interviews; also former Local 201 leader Donald Tormey in a letter to the author December 11, 1986.

61. See UE General Officers Report, 1947, pp. 508; this report would have been prepared by the UE's research department under Nathan Spero along with the Washington office under the direction of legislative representative Russ Nixon, who subsequently corresponded with European labor leaders about the ERP. The depth of the research and the restrained passion in Nixon's letters suggest that determined opposition to the plan did not all originate in Europe. See Nixon to Benoit Frachon of the French CGT, March 23, 1948; to Giuseppe diVittorio, Italian CGL, April 14, 1948; Nixon to Louis Saillant, WFTU, November 11, 1948. UE Archives, RG 4 Box 6 FF "WFTU 1947-48." See also Frank Emspak's discussion of the UE statements on the Marshall Plan in "The Breakup of the CIO," pp. 217-220.

agency and would bypass the United Nations indicated Washington's intent to keep it under American control. From the UE's assessment, it was clear that the "UE and the right wing of the CIO were in fundamental disagreement over the question of European relief."[62]

But the question persists: why was this the issue on which the right-wing forces refused to compromise and over which disagreement turned to disunity? The left and the forces opposed to the Marshall Plan in the CIO did not oppose the principal of post-war aid to foreign nations; they argued that administering the plan through the United Nations was the principled course to take. Also, they were willing to let the disagreement stand and to find common ground on other issues such as collective bargaining goals. The UE leaders withdrew from the CIO Political Action Committee only when Philip Murray insisted that member unions support the Democratic ticket in 1948. When they resigned, they stated their intention to work with local CIO-PAC's in congressional elections wherever possible, even as they charged that the CIO-PAC nationally had become "an appendage of the Democratic machine," and that "Democratic candidates could now take labor for granted."[63]

Opinion polls at the time seem to give support to the positions of the ERP's opponents in the CIO. The proposal for unilateral American aid to Europe was, among those aware of the issue, highly controversial in the United States in the fall of 1947. In October, less than half of the people questioned in an American Institute of Public Opinion poll had heard of the Marshall Plan; by November, public awareness had increased somewhat to 61 percent. The October poll indicated that even the idea of lending large amounts of money to western European nations lacked wide support. Among those best informed

62. Emspak, "The Breakup of the CIO," p. 220.
63. UE General Officers Report, 1948, pp. 50-53.

about the plan, less than half (49 percent) favored it; among other groups disapproval was even stronger.[64]

Was the United States simply turning inwards, returning to pre-war "isolationism," and losing interest in the problems of other nations? According to another AIPO poll taken a month earlier, this was not the case. When asked whether they approved of the UN suggestion that "all employed people throughout the world give one day's pay to the UN to help the underfed children of the world" (a proposal closer to the UE position because it utilized the UN), 74 percent of the respondents approved.[65]

Similarly, polls in the fall of 1947 yielded decidedly mixed results concerning the political nature of the plan and the nation's developing Cold War foreign policy. Responses to questions about "Russia" appeared to depend on the phrasing of the questions. For instance, in answer to the question, "Do you think the United States is being too soft or too tough in its policy towards Russia?" 62 percent of the respondents answered "too soft." On the other hand, when asked how important it was to be on friendly terms with Russia, 56 percent of those polled considered it important whether or not the Soviet Union developed an atomic bomb.[66]

We are faced with highly inconclusive results regarding public opinion on the issue of the United States role in European recovery. The urgency with which the CIO leaders supported the ERP was not motivated by the plan's popularity. In addition, the criticisms leveled at the ERP by its opponents in the labor movement were not frivolous ones. It was true, for instance, that American officials did indeed intend to bypass the United Nations. Assistant Secretary of State and former textile executive William Clayton argued, "The U.S. must run this show."[67] The opposition of dominant sections of European labor was so adamant that simply to dismiss

64. Public Opinion Quarterly, XI (Winter 1947-48), p. 675.
65. Ibid.
66. Ibid. pp. 653-654.
67. Freeland, The Truman Doctrine, p. 169.

it as proof of Soviet manipulation appeared curious, especially for the CIO, which had sent a high level delegation to the USSR slightly more than two years earlier.[68] The apprehension among European workers regarding the plan's consequences actually received support from State Department officials, who predicted that workers in Europe would be required to make "sacrifices in their standard of living" and "accept temporary unemployment."[69]

Why, then, when their own analysis showed acute awareness of its shortcomings, did the CIO leaders agree to support so vigorously a unilateral, unpopular big business plan for European relief? They appear to have had two basic reasons for their decision. First, they believed that, precisely because the plan had corporate backing, no other plan would stand a chance of winning Congressional approval. Second, in accord with their philosophy of fundamental convergence of interests of labor and management, as mentioned in chapter 1, the CIO had, by 1947, already developed a working relationship with the Washington foreign policy apparatus. This relationship, although not smooth and not without stresses, nevertheless trumped other factors in determining the CIO's stance. CIO Secretary-Treasurer

---

68. The plan's opponents in the CIO apparently felt that the views of European workers deserved consideration. DeMaio, in his October 2, 1986 interview for instance, contended that the plan was widely regarded in Europe as an American big business "shakedown." He may have had a point; according to a poll released by the French Institute of Public Opinion in September 1947, 47 percent of the respondents believed "Mr. Marshall's proposal" was dictated by the "need to find external markets to avoid economic crisis in the U.S.," while 18 percent believed it had been dictated by a "sincere desire to aid Europe's recovery." POQ, Winter 1947-48, p. 675.

Freeland, in The Truman Doctrine, p. 168, writes that Truman's March 1947 speech "was a direct attack upon the largest political organizations in France and Italy" and that it "foreboded a division of Europe into American and Soviet spheres of influence, which offended nearly everyone else."

69. Peter Weiler, "The United States, International Labor and the Cold War; The Breakup of the World Federation of Trade Unions," Diplomatic History, vol. V, no. 1 (winter 1981), p. 13.

Carey played a central role in building and maintaining the relationship.

As early as 1945, Carey had testified before a House Committee on behalf of the "Clayton Plan," the Assistant Secretary of State's proposal for increasing United States investment in, and exports to, Latin America. This plan met opposition from the left-led Confederation of Latin American Workers (CTAL), which viewed it as an attempt to retard the industrialization of Latin America and perpetuate the economic dominance of the United States. The CIO, on the other hand, supported the plan despite the fact that the two labor centers had cooperated before and during World War II. Carey, presenting the CIO testimony, stated that "several of our basic industries are dependent upon exports to sustain their high levels of production.... There seems to be a direct correlation between domestic prosperity and foreign trade."[70]

Carey's personal involvement with foreign policy grew in part because his post as secretary-treasurer frequently placed him in the position of representing the CIO at conferences or on committees. This process did not go forward easily, and Carey attempted to resist State Department pressure to conform to the policy line into 1948; but the direction was clear, and by the fall of that year, "little...separated the CIO from the AFL."[71] The most significant example of Carey's activity was his work on the President's Nonpartisan Committee on Foreign Aid, established in June 1947 following Marshall's speech. Because the AFL delegate did not attend regularly, Carey found himself the only labor representative.

---

70. Ronald Radosh, in American Labor and United States Foreign Policy, pp. 355-359, successfully makes his point that CIO leaders sided with U.S. business leaders and the State Department against the CTAL. He incorrectly identifies Carey, however, as the "United Electrical Workers chief," which, as we have seen, had not been true since 1941. Thus, in what was for long the leading study of the subject, the impression is wrongly given that Carey represented a rank-and-file constituency.

71. Silverman, Imagining Internationalism, pp. 175-178, provides a more nuanced account of this process than Radosh, but they agree on the end result.

In fact, it was from Carey's report on the Committee's work that Murray drew the ten-point CIO criteria by which the CIO proposed to assess the Marshall Plan. This nineteen-page document reveals much about Carey's view of the Committee and the proposed plan.

Carey found the committee and its eight subcommittees dominated by businessmen and bankers, and felt that its recommendations reflected this composition. He wrote:

> Although the CIO representative has no objection to sitting on committees where labor is outvoted five or six to one, it becomes difficult to be one of eighteen or nineteen. This whole question of labor participation, derived not alone from this experience, but as you know, many others, deserves attention on our part. While on many of these committees it is deemed proper to have representatives from various segments of industry, it seems to be considered sufficient to have only the national labor organizations represented. This not only places labor in a numerical inferiority, but requires the labor representatives to be experts in fields covering the whole of our economy if they are to properly represent their organizations.[72]

The secretary-treasurer particularly noted the "extremely cautious attitude" of the "business banking group" who "constantly had in mind what the business community might think of them...." His estimate of the Nonpartisan Committee, therefore, did not differ fundamentally from that presented by the UE and the Marshall Plan's critics in the CIO.

His response to the conditions he encountered on the Committee, however, led him to a different estimate

---

72. "Report on the President's Committee on Foreign Aid," by James B. Carey, Secretary-Treasurer, CIO, p. 1, Wayne State University, Walter Reuther Library of Labor and Urban Affairs, CIO: Office of the Secretary-Treasurer, Papers 1935-1960 (Hereafter CIOST), Box 126, file "Statements of J. Carey on ECA and ERP 1947."

of the European recovery plan itself. He wrote that, although a few members on the Committee had urged him to sign a minority report, he rejected this alternative and undertook "to get all he could, and if no fundamental principles were violated, to agree to a compromise." In choosing this course, Carey demonstrated a quality that would remain part of his makeup for the rest of his career: his confidence in his ability individually to influence people outside the labor movement, especially businessmen. By the time the Committee's work was finished, Carey felt that he had succeeded in gaining sufficient "compromises" to make the plan worthy of support and, indeed, had committed himself and his organization to providing that support.

He described, for example, his attempts, successful in his opinion, to defeat a proposal that "would have almost had the United States manage Europe's industries, making a field for private investment and securing a profit on the projects."[73] On the matter of the effects of the plan in the United States, Carey, likewise, felt that he made progress in arguing for the necessity of "controls to prevent speculation, further inflation or rising prices." While the committee's final recommendations fell short of calling for controls, Carey felt that it showed an understanding of the viewpoint that "the sacrifices called for must be spread equally among the people." He summarized this section of his report as follows:

> Certainly progress has been made in this field, and while I feel that the majority of the committee is lagging behind the country in its thinking, we have the admission that the resumption of controls is required, and that it cannot be expected that the low income groups will bear the main burden.[74]

73. Ibid., p. 12.
74. Ibid., p. 13.

The CIO representative's general conclusions on the Harriman Committee's work contained a similarly mixed assessment. Although he felt that his personal efforts had yielded results and influenced the outcome somewhat, he understood that his influence had been limited.

> I am under no illusions that the CIO point of view was generally successful in the final draft. It does, however, represent a vast improvement on what would have been secured in the absence of our point of view. In the light of the composition of the committee it is probably as good as could have been obtained....

Carey argued that the importance of presenting a solid front in the legislative effort for the bill demanded unanimous support for the Committee's final draft, although he understood that further work by the CIO would be required to influence the specifics of the plan and its implementation.

> ... in view of the overall character of the report and the difficult fight it will meet in Congress, it was better to have a unanimous report, rather than weaken the whole effort by a minority report.... Insofar as this Committee is concerned, a direct refutation was given to the charges that the Marshall Plan is designed for imperialist purposes or to control the economic or political destinies of other nations.[75]

Carey's position reveals much about the thinking behind the CIO leadership's decisions regarding the European Recovery Program. Clearly, he saw the obstacles to attaining the CIO goals on the Harriman Committee. Also, his experience on the Harriman Committee along with his attempts to cooperate with the State Department since World War II had given him reason to believe that the CIO would meet obstacles in

---

75. Ibid., pp.17-19, for Carey's conclusions.

influencing the actual administration of the aid plan. Yet, he endorsed the final draft without protest, thus playing a very different role than he played in his own union, where he presented a minority report and went public with an organized opposition. He urged the CIO to adopt an all-out campaign, "a public information program," in support of the European recovery proposal. Murray appears to have followed Carey's advice totally on this matter.

Thus, the CIO leadership chose to enter the national debate on European recovery in the camp of the "internationally minded corporate lawyers and business executives" who believed that the Marshall Plan was a vital part of their post-war program, and also that the plan needed all the help they could muster in a skeptical nation. The possibility of an alternative plan, such as that proposed by the UE, appears never to have been seriously considered either by the foreign policy establishment or by the right-wing leadership of the CIO. Leading members of the foreign policy establishment would remember the role that the CIO secretary-treasurer played in providing crucial support.

The CIO right wing, and Carey in particular, did benefit in the short term from their association with the foreign policy establishment. As part of the European recovery effort, AFL and CIO members and officials were assigned as labor attachés to United States embassies in European countries. Although CIO leaders did not make final appointments to these desirable and sought-after posts, they could, and sometimes did, make recommendations. In one notable instance a western Pennsylvania judge, Michael Musmanno, received Carey's support in seeking an appointment as Mission Chief of the Economic Cooperation Administration (ECA) in Italy. Although Carey's attempts to influence ECA Special Representative Averell Harriman did not succeed, Musmanno appreciated the effort. He wrote to Carey, "You know how grateful I am for your spontaneous and enthusiastic interest in the ECA situation... you know that you have in me an eternal friend."[76] Within a year Musmanno returned the favor during the contest between the UE and the IUE at the East Pittsburgh Westinghouse plant about which more will be said in chapter III. In addition to such tangible favors, the CIO leadership also gained "respectability" or at least the appearance of respectability, the lack of which had caused them such concern. In Carey's case especially, the relationships that he developed with members of the foreign policy establishment and Democratic Party leaders would figure prominently in his career. More will be said about Carey's situation in chapter IV.

And yet, in view of their own assessment of the Marshall Plan's results within the next three years, the CIO leadership's confidence in their ability to influence the ERP's administration seems seriously misplaced and ill founded. Their criticisms of the Plan's execution and results in 1950 paralleled the warnings of the UE in 1947 and 1948. In supporting the Marshall Plan, the CIO leaders probably took the first step down the path that would lead, by the 1970s, to labor's being viewed by many as a special "interest group" rather than an advocate for the general welfare of poor and working people.[77]

In any case, the issue precipitated the split in the CIO. It was largely responsible for the failure of the CIO unions to agree on political activity in the 1948 election. This election's unexpected result, in turn, emboldened the CIO right-wing leaders to intensify attacks on and raiding of those unions under "left wing" leadership.

---

76. Musmanno to Carey, August 29, 1949, CIOST, Box 126, file "ECA Labor Division Personnel File Correspondence 1948-1949."

77. David Brody, Workers in Industrial America, p. 239, argues that "In the years since the Great Society, organized labor has been pressed inexorably into the mold of an interest group." At least one source tried to warn Murray of this eventuality at the time. John Williamson, National Labor Secretary of the Communist Party, USA wrote to him in September 1949 detailing the issues on which the CIO had changed its position since 1945 and offering to work "in alliance with you... on the basis of a minimum program representing the economic and political interests of labor and that would allow democracy and autonomy in the affairs of the CIO." IUE Papers, Box 28 FF 5. See appendix for Williamson's entire seven-page letter.

By the fall of 1949, the CIO's situation looked drastically different than it had four years earlier. The Cold War pressures it faced had brought sharply different responses from the left and from the right. This had momentous consequences in electrical unionism. When, on the day before the opening of the CIO's 1949 convention, a nine-member UE delegation met privately with CIO president Murray, the UE members did not receive good news. After Murray refused to guarantee them that he would oppose raids on their union by other CIO unions, the UE leaders decided, in accordance with resolutions of the UE's last convention and of the union's general executive board, not to enter CIO convention.[78]

In the absence of the UE delegates, the CIO convention formally expelled the union and the next day, with delegates from the UE's right-wing opposition (the self-named "committee of ten") in attendance, chartered a new CIO union in the industry, the International Union of Electrical, Radio and Machine Workers (IUE). Although the new union had no formal structure, Murray publicly presented the IUE's charter to CIO secretary-treasurer Carey. Thus, Carey took on the primary responsibility and the formidable task of organizing the new electrical union. The IUE's first convention took place in Philadelphia in November 1949 with Carey serving as chairman. Disagreement surfaced immediately, however, and no permanent leader emerged until the following year when Carey was finally elected president.[79]

The UE decision to boycott the CIO convention got a mixed response from UE supporters because it allowed the union's opponents to blame UE for the split, especially since the other left unions had remained on the scene. One observer wrote that the UE delegation "jumped the gun [by] leaving before the act of their expulsion" and "made it easier for the Red-baiters to split their union."

---

78. Report by UE District 4 president James McLeish to District Council meeting, November 9, 1949, UE Archives D/4-19.

79. IUE-CIO News, December 14, 1950, p. 2.

Another argued that "they should have attended that session and taken advantage of a last opportunity to tell off the clique now running the CIO.... The left unions that stayed in the Convention showed that such a floor fight is effective."[80] These arguments give pause as the breach in the CIO, and the loss of its "strong, well-entrenched left-progressive wing" proved to have such long-lasting effects.

On the other hand, the UE leaders, and the union's convention delegation, did make numerous attempts to find a basis for compromise with the CIO leadership. At the meeting with Philip Murray before the convention opened, they showed him copies of no-raiding agreements they offered to sign with other unions, and, even as the Convention progressed, the attempts at compromise continued—as one executive board member reported shortly after the CIO convention:

> The UE-GEB was in continuous session from Sunday until Tuesday. After repeated attempts to have our convention resolution dealt with seriously and honestly, after being completely convinced that the CIO was set on a policy of expelling and wrecking this union...and after finding that Carey's committee of ten had been seated at the convention as regular delegates, the GEB voted to withhold per capita from the CIO, in accordance with our convention decision....[81]

In addition, observers on the left and in the commercial press agreed that the CIO leadership had decided to expel the left unions as early as the spring of 1949. One on the left wrote that the call for the IUE convention was "ready for mailing before the CIO convention even

---

80. John Swift, "The Left Led Unions and Labor Unity," Political Affairs, XXXII (August 1953), p. 41; George Morris, "The UE Hanging Was Planned Last Spring," Daily Worker, November 7, 1949.

81. McLeish report to District 4 Council meeting, November 9, 1949, UE Archives, D/4-19.

convened... the die was really cast by Murray as far back as last spring."[82]

The breakup of the CIO was part of the global program of the Washington foreign policy establishment. While the CIO was being divided and truncated, a parallel development occurred on the international labor front, when the CIO, along with the British Trade Union Congress withdrew from the WFTU. In January 1949, the British and American delegates, led by James Carey, walked out in the middle of a WFTU executive council meeting.[83] They took this final step despite the compromise that the WFTU executive council had thrashed out, and which Carey had defended, in May of 1948 in Rome. That agreement had allowed each national trade union center to take an independent position on the Marshall Plan, an arrangement which seemed reasonable enough, since it simply recognized that the WFTU could not dictate policy for its member federations. This did not satisfy the CIO's critics, especially the AFL leaders who claimed the CIO was being used "by the Kremlin and its puppet unions."[84] The founding conference of the new anti-Communist International Confederation of Free Trade Unions (ICFTU) took place in London in November 1949, the same month as the founding of the IUE.

The beginning of 1950 found electrical workers facing an uncertain future, given the attacks on their organizations at home and abroad. The argument over the Cold War in American labor did not end as quickly as many

82. George Morris, "UE Hanging Was Planned Last Spring," Daily Worker, November 2, 1949; see also Victor Riesel in the New York Daily Mirror, October 26, 1949: the new "skeleton union is ready to begin operating on ten minutes notice...." And Louis Stark, "CIO Chiefs Tell Showdown Plans," by Louis Stark, New York Times, October 30, 1949. These clippings are in IUE Papers; RG-1, Box 30, Folder 10.

83. Windmuller, American Labor and the International Labor Movement 1940-1953, p. 148.

84. Weiler, "The United States, International Labor and the Cold War," p. 19. See Silverman, Imagining Internationalism, pp. 172-173 for an account of Carey's 1948 trip to Rome with a different emphasis.

observers and participants anticipated, however. The results of the attempts to bring electrical workers into the Cold War consensus in the early 1950s would surprise many Cold Warriors inside and outside the labor movement.

Chapter 3

Weathering the Storm, 1950–1953

The labor movement's fortunes in the early 1950s until recently remained shrouded in mystery. The period has not received the same vivid detailed scrutiny as the years of labor's great offensive of the same length from 1936 through 1939, for example, but a time of such contradictory developments in the nation and the labor movement deserves a close look. While the period saw the peak of Cold War rhetoric and hysteria, it also showed that the most strident Cold War forces would not entirely succeed in undoing the legislative and political gains of the previous two decades.[1]

During this period, the UE faced attacks on so many fronts that its survival required sustained, varied, and high level activity. That the union succeeded in essentially holding its ground during these years contradicts the notion that its leaders were isolated from, out of touch with, or insensitive to the membership. The original charges—that the UE leaders served a foreign and hostile power rather than the interests of the UE members—seem ludicrous today, but they did not die easily. Even among those who allowed that perhaps they were not "foreign agents," the notion persisted that, because the union's leaders refused to abandon their program during the early and mid-1950s, they failed to

1. Hodgson, America In Our Time, p. 72; also James Gilbert, Another Chance; Postwar America 1945-1985 (Chicago, The Dorsey Press, 1986), pp. 126-133.

represent their members. This is a more complex question than the original charge and deserves attention.

After the UE's break with the CIO, did the leaders attempt to serve the interests of their members? Did they have the support of a significant portion of the union's membership in the course they chose? While sharp disagreement grew within the UE over the future of the union by the mid-1950s, these differences were tactical. They involved how the union should respond to its situation, and how best to advance its program, rather than basic differences over what the program should be. The notable feature of the early 1950s in the electrical industry is that the UE, after the 1950 split, survived the Korean War period and, in fact, at times appeared ready to regain shops it had lost. The evidence indicates that a substantial base of opposition to the Government's Cold War policies existed among electrical workers. (See table 1.)

This was a time of extraordinary activity for the UE. We can identify five areas in which the union acted: "bread and butter trade unionism" or negotiating contracts and attempting to win gains for its members; organizing and defending its existing locals against "raids" by other unions; political action that mainly took the form of sending delegations to pressure legislators; opposing discrimination in the workplace; and defending itself or individual members in court or before Congressional committees. The first three of these might fall within the normal range of trade union activity; the union would have to break new ground in the last two: discrimination and political defense.

For example, when we consider the effort to combat discrimination and break down workplace barriers workers beyond the traditional limits of white male dominance, we see a picture more complex than simply that of an isolated union under attack. UE activists and historical researchers have argued that the adverse conditions of the early 1950s forced the union to find new creative methods of struggle. Indeed, former local

Table 1
Membership of Selected CIO Unions, 1945–1954

Union	1945	1946	1947	1948	1949	1950	1951	1952	1953	1954
Auto UAW	892,000	673,000	856,000	893,000	919,000	908,000	1,045,000	1,171,000	1,417,000	1,240,000
Steel USW	736,000	733,000	858,000	881,000	810,000	867,000	1,003,000	929,000	1,101,000	987,000
Electrical										
*UE	467,000	366,000	472,000	500,000	428,000	223,000	222,000	215,000	203,000	182,000
IUE	--	--	--	--	--	74,000	203,000	231,000	266,000	282,000
Clothing	222,000	244,000	275,000	280,000	283,000	275,000	295,000	275,000	288,000	274,000
Textile	248,000	301,000	342,000	332,000	302,000	322,000	301,000	244,000	242,000	200,000
Transport										
TWU	32,000	32,000	53,000	53,000	69,000	69,000	69,000	59,000	59,000	59,000
Newspaper										
Guild	15,000	17,000	21,000	22,000	22,000	22,000	23,000	24,000	25,000	27,000

* Independent after 1949
Source: Leo Troy, Trade Union Membership 1897-1962. National Bureau of Economic Research, Occasional paper 92; 1965, pages A-20 through A-27, A-37.

301 activist and leader, Helen Quirini felt that the split with the IUE had its positive side, at least in the short term, because it enabled the UE to "get rid of the cancer" and freed UE members to intensify the fight inside the union for stronger positions against racial and gender discrimination. Quirini and others played leading roles in this effort, which culminated in the UE national women's conference in 1953. This conference was apparently a first of its kind for a major union and energized UE women around the country to assert their influence.[2]

UE members also gave leadership in the developing Civil Rights movement. Ernest Thompson, leader in northern New Jersey's Hudson County CIO Council and former business agent of two UE locals I the area, served from 1951 until 1956 as secretary of the union's National Fair Practices Committee. In this position, he played a major part in building the National Negro Labor Council that, during this period, organized the first mass job campaigns against employment discrimination. The major employers targeted by the Council included both the Ford and General Electric Companies in Louisville, Kentucky, a city which saw intense competition between the UE and the IUE. Under Thompson's leadership, the Fair Practices Committee built a coalition of Black and women workers to promote their advancement to leadership positions, both in the union and in the workplace.[3]

Of course, the union's work in each sphere of activity was extra difficult because it could not count on help from major sections of the labor movement. During a strike, for example, the UE had constantly to deal with the possibility of other unions raiding striking UE locals instead of offering financial or other support.[4] On the

---

2. See Lisa Kannenberg, "The Impact of the Cold War on Women's Trade Union Activism; The UE Experience," Labor History, 34: nos. 2-3 (Spring Summer 1993), 309-323, especially 315-319.

3. The Ernest Thompson Papers are Manuscript Collection 1180, Special Collections and University Archives, Rutgers University Libraries; his biography can be found on line at www.libraries.rutgers.edu.

4. "Raiding," normally considered a serious matter in the labor movement, became an epidemic in the early 1950s. Under NLRB rules, a raid could be

other hand, the union was never totally isolated during this period. It maintained relations with other unions expelled from the CIO, notably the Mine, Mill and Smelter Workers ("Mine-Mill") and the west coast longshoremen (ILWU). UE members and local leaders frequently continued contacts with their counterparts in other unions,[5] and in the plants that narrowly went IUE, the former UE members remained active union members.

The UE also did not hesitate to publicize the occasional recognition by outside sources of its efforts to continue pushing for progress on social issues. For example, the *UE News* in September 1952 summarized a report by the New York State School of Industrial and Labor Relations that cited the "unusual" degree of rank-and-file participation and attention given to the "practice of discussing grievances and local policy and action to be taken" found in the UE local at the GE plant in Elmira, New York. Similarly, the union took not of evidence supporting its claims of leadership in the field of civil rights. Articles in the African-American press in the early 1950s expressed concern at the general trend in the labor movement. The CIO, the articles charged, was abandoning its commitment to ending segregation and was engaged in organizing "Jim Crow" locals in the South. An article in the *Washington Afro-American* gave credit to the "so-called leftist unions" as the only ones opposing the CIO trend of "conformity with America's traditional policy of segregation and Jim Crowism."[6]

---

initiated by having 30 percent of the workers in a shop sign cards stating their desire to transfer to a new union. A representation election must then be held. The UE's adversaries did not always adhere to this regulation, however, as GE noted before a Congressional Committee. See n. 9 below. The UE believed that the GE example was not the only one. See note 54 below for the Westinghouse Lester results, for instance, where the vote against the UE was less than 25 percent of the total vote.

5. Interview with Pat Barile, former president of UE local 428, August 14, 2001; transcript in Tamiment Oral History collection, Communist Party collection.

6. For the School of Industrial Relations study, see the UE News, September 1, 1952, p. 5. For unions and civil rights, see the Amsterdam News, March

On the issue of the rights of women workers, the UE likewise cited evidence to support its claim. In January 1952, the union's paper devoted an entire page to a United States Labor Department report that charged employers with exploiting women by reserving certain low paying, but frequently crucial, jobs for them. The report specifically noted that in the electrical manufacturing industry often "it is the women who do the production work and make the money for the company" and that the UE had pioneered in the fight for equal pay for equal work during World War II and had succeeded in writing equal pay clauses into 150 contracts as opposed to 50 for the United Auto Workers by 1943.[7]

These efforts to roll back workplace inequality might have encountered more stubborn resistance inside the union had the split with the IUE not happened, and such efforts were not pursued with the same resolve by the IUE after the split. Still, the one issue responsible for the union's breakup and the founding of the IUE was the UE's refusal to support the Cold War foreign policy of the Truman Administration. To survive the coming years, the union would need all the membership participation it could muster. Developments of the first six months of 1950 demonstrated that the price of rejecting official Cold War policy would be great.

In late January, there occurred the well-attended two-day "All American Conference" in New York, which drew 160 representatives from prominent conservative organizations to the Waldorf Astoria. That this conference to "combat communism" included delegates from the Chamber of Commerce, the National Association of Manufacturers, the American Medical Association, and the American Legion may not have surprised UE members, but the presence of representatives from the AFL and CIO indicated that labor leaders had joined the

---

4, 1950 and the Washington Afro-American, February 19, 1950, reprints in the IUE Papers, series A2.05, File Folder "UE 1950."

7. UE News, January 7, 1952, p. 8.

crusade. While initial reports named CIO official Harry Read as chair of the group's continuations committee, the participation of labor representatives at this gathering brought forth a surprised response from enough observers that the CIO soon announced that it had "informally" withdrawn. But the presence at this conference of the leading right-wing trade union activist in the electrical manufacturing industry and his reported assertion that "we will join with the fascists" in another war demonstrated both the distance that the CIO leadership had moved during the previous three years and the breadth of the coming attacks on the UE.[8]

The rush of events in early 1950 left little doubt about the dominant political currents of the time in domestic or foreign affairs. Two days after the New York "All American" Conference, President Truman, under pressure from Congress, ordered the start of production of the hydrogen bomb in what one observer called "the advent of a new phase of the atomic age and a surge ahead of Russia in the race to retain military ascendancy."[9]

The impact that these developments would have on electrical workers soon became evident. The UE represented most of the employees at the two largest electrical manufacturing chains in the nation, General Electric and Westinghouse, as well as Sylvania, Philco, RCA, and others. James Carey, Senator Joseph McCarthy, and others repeatedly trumpeted the charge that because these companies, especially GE and Westinghouse, received sensitive government military contracts, the UE's presence in their plants constituted an intolerable threat to the nation's security.[10] Therefore, the IUE's challenge to the UE presented an opportunity to remove

8. New York Times (NYT), January 29, 1950, p. 19, and January 30, 1950, p. 5. The Times reported that the conference drew 160 representatives from 57 organizations with a combined membership of 50 million. Also, see clippings of the Daily Compass article, February 1, 1950, by I.F. Stone and the Daily Worker article, April 2, 1950, by George Morris.

9. NYT, February 1, 1950, p. 1.

10. UE News, October 2, 1950, p. 2.

this danger. The UE, ridiculing the allegations, always maintained that the IUE's viability depended on crucial support from outside the labor movement, including the Federal Government and the companies themselves.

The National Labor Relations Board scheduled elections in the major electrical chains for April and May of 1950. Since much has been made of the fact that many workers vote against the UE in this "first round" of representation elections, it is imperative to analyze the manner and the atmosphere in which the elections were conducted.[11] In the first place, the fact that NLRB scheduled the elections on a chainwide basis was itself unusual. To do so, the Board had to waive the normal procedure that called for a union to present membership cards signed by 30 percent of the workers in each plant or "unit" in order to appear on the ballot. General Electric later admitted that it took advantage of another Labor Board policy allowing a company to file its own petition for an election if a question arose as to which union represented its employees. GE filed an election petition covering over fifty plants and 100,000 workers as a single unit.

The company's action enabled the fledgling IUE to appear on the ballot in all GE plants, although it had filed no membership cards in many of them. As the had of the Company's labor law department told a Congressional subcommittee, GE had therefore relieved Carey and the IUE of "the need to spend either the time or the thousands of dollars they otherwise would have had to spend in order to sign up sufficient membership cards to get an NLRB election on the strength of his own

11. See Joseph Rayback, A History of American Labor: Expanded and Updated (New York: The Free Press, 1966). Rayback says the IUE "recovered half the original membership in the first three years" but does not mention the circumstances under which the elections were held. Ellen Schrecker, in her essay "McCarthyism and the Labor Movement; the Role of the State," in Rosswurm, The CIO's Left Led Unions does evoke the atmosphere of the 1950s as do Fillipelli and McColloch in Cold War in the Working Class, ch. 6.

petition."[12] The fact that the NLRB also scheduled Westinghouse elections on a chain-wide basis suggests that the same process transpired there.

On the other hand, another development kept the UE from effectively protesting the election procedures. Early in the year, both companies had announced that the nationwide contracts with the UE "would not be in effect" after they expired at the beginning of April, pending the outcome of the Labor Board elections. The companies based their action on an NLRB ruling that an employer could not negotiate a contract with one union "in the face of representation proceedings involving another competing union."[13]

This company action constituted the other half of the pincer m movement in which the employers attempted to squeeze the UE. On the one hand, they filed petitions for elections in their plants, thus initiating "representation proceedings." On the other hand, they argued that they could not now negotiate with the union until these proceedings involving "competing unions" were completed.

The day after Westinghouse announced the termination of its UE contract, the pressure on the union increased yet again. The rival IUE secured a federal injunction preventing General Electric from turning over membership dues to the UE. This was no small problem for the union. As the press noted, the injunction removed a "major source of revenue from the UE" in its efforts to service its locals and fight legal battles. To grasp the

---

12. See U.S. Senate, Subcommittee of the Committee on Labor and Public Welfare, Communist Domination of Unions and National Security, 82nd Congress, 2nd Session, 1952, pp. 432-467, for the complete testimony of GE Labor Relations Counsel William J. Barron.

13. NYT, January 28, 1950, p. 8. See also letter from Westinghouse Vice President W.O. Lippmann to UE International Representative Edward Matthews, January 25, 1950, notifying UE of contract termination and Matthews's reply charging that Westinghouse "bailed out the Company union IUE" by filing petitions in all of the company's UE plants and then citing the "representation proceedings" as an "excuse" for terminating the contract with the UE, January 27, 1950, in the record of the 1949-50 negotiations, pp. 17-18, University of Pittsburgh, UE Archives, Westinghouse Conference Board Series File Folder 404.

full impact of the injunction, one need only recall that the CIO had, years earlier, considered the winning of the "dues checkoff" as one of its major achievements, since it relieved the unions of the constant need to worry about raising funds. Subsequently, union contracts generally required employers to deduct dues from each member's paycheck and transfer the funds to the union. The IUE's injunction, therefore, required General Electric to break its national contract with the UE even before it had expired. The company's Vice President Lemuel Boulware commented that it was "refreshing to see unions apply to the courts for the hated injunction," as this implied "an admission that the injunction is an honorable and useful instrument."[14] Thus, the actions of the IUE appeared to meet the approval of the nation's largest electrical manufacturer.

Under these adverse circumstances, the UE leadership, after an initial period of demoralization following their expulsion from the CIO, displayed remarkable confidence. When Fitzgerald addressed the UE District 1 Council meeting in January, he did not minimize the difficulties, saying that the union had been "hit by government, industry, churches, and people inside the labor movement. In November they marshaled all their forces against us...not a single GE local received a checkoff...." He went to argue, however, that despite the obstacles, the union had received over a quarter of a million dues payments in November and expected to maintain at least that level of membership. In closing, he told the delegates "... the only thing we are going to get rid of... is that messy part of this organization that should have been kicked out in 1941. Today, they have more allies than they had then and the job is more difficult...."[15] While the UE would face problems and choices that not

14. NYT, January 29, 1950, p. 32.

15. Minutes of UE District 1 Council meeting, January 5, 1950, UE Archives, D/1 File 13.

even Fitzgerald could imagine, his statement indicated the confidence of the leadership at the time.

The UE president had accurately identified the union's adversaries. In addition to the opposition of employers and a rival union, the UE also had to face the active participation of the national CIO, clergymen, and at least two branches of the federal government. At the Westinghouse Company's home plant, the generator works in East Pittsburgh, the outcome of the UE-IUE contest required two elections and was largely determined by the intervention of outside forces with power bases in the Pittsburgh area. These included not only CIO president Philip Murray and the leader of the Association of Catholic Trade Unionists, Father Charles Owen Rice, but also former Republican Congressman and HUAC member John McDowell and Judge Michael Musmanno, whom James Carey had supported for an ECA post the previous year. The outside financial and organizational support provided by the CIO and the ACTU meant that the new union could mount a viable campaign.[16]

Events at the other major plants followed a similar pattern, although with local variations and similar results. The forces opposing the UE hammered at the "Communist issue" and "national security." In Lynn, Massachusetts, site of GE's second largest plant, Secretary of Labor Maurice Tobin and CIO President Murray shared the podium at an IUE rally held in the city hall on the Sunday before the election. The content of the remarks of these two prominent figures demonstrates the single-issue nature of the campaign. Tobin told the 1,500 workers present that the election was not a local issue, "but a question of whether a vital industry will be in the hands of Soviet Russia." Murray, again demonstrating how far the CIO leadership had moved since the end of World War II, joined in, stating, "I swear on this platform that this small group of leaders of the

16. For more detail on the East Pittsburgh election, see Schatz's provocative analysis in Electrical Workers, pp. 188-204.

old United Electrical Workers Union have one master—Stalin in Russia."[17]

The elections in both major chains resulted in splitting the electrical workers virtually down the middle. At Westinghouse, the IUE won bargaining rights in 19 plants while the UE won in 18; the IUE won 27,000 votes to the UE's 22,000. At the East Pittsburgh plant, the company's largest, a second vote finally established the IUE as the winner by less than 200 votes out of a total of over 11,000 votes cast. Even with the external pressures in this election, the result may have been different had not the NLRB separated the 400 workers at the Nuttall Gear factory out of the election. The Nuttall workers belonged to the same local union as the East Pittsburgh workers but remained in the UE until the gear factory closed in 1960.[18] The second largest Westinghouse facility, the steam turbine division in Lester near Philadelphia, had not experienced the same level of outside activity. There, the UE won 80 percent of the vote. The IUE captured the large plants in Sharon, Pennsylvania, and Mansfield, Ohio, while the UE won the Westinghouse electric meter division in Newark, New Jersey.[19]

The General Electric vote less than one month later produced a similarly inconclusive result. The IUE claimed victory in 49 plants; the UE, in 40. While the overall vote favored the IUE 53,000 to 36,000, the results in the largest plants were different. Of the three largest GE facilities, the UE won two: the home plant in Schenectady with 19,000 workers and the third largest in Erie with 13,000. At the company's number-two plant in Lynn, UE supporters challenged the narrow IUE victory by placing an ad in a local newspaper signed by 1,200

---

17. NYT, May 22, 1950, p. 8.

18. UE Archives, CB/W-1097.

19. See NYT, April 28, 1950, p. 2 for the overall Westinghouse results; Schatz, Electrical Workers, p. 203, for the East Pittsburgh results and pp. 225-226 for more on the overall results; Philadelphia Inquirer, April 28, 1950, p. 1 for the Lester results.

Lynn workers protesting the appearance of the Secretary of Labor on behalf of the IUE.[20]

The results of this first round of NLRB elections demonstrated that workers in the electrical manufacturing industry had been divided. In an industry where previously one large union had represented workers of diverse backgrounds and skills, unity had given way to division. There were various reasons, certainly, why many workers voted for the IUE, as shall be seen below. Some desired to remain in the CIO; some feared that their shop would lose government contracts if the UE represented them. But the single issue on which the IUE and its backers had based their appeal had been the "Communist issue." This explosive question had transformed a diverse but unified labor organization into two bitter rivals.

On the other hand, the events of the first half of 1950 also indicated that the allegedly "red dominated" UE maintained considerable support among large numbers of workers in the industry. While James Carey claimed 220,000 members for the IUE and headlines proclaimed the end of "leftist rule" in the industry, the UE's Matles told the press his union had withstood the "CIO raids" and remained the dominant electrical union representing over 450,000 workers.[21] Both sides apparently inflated the figures, but the UE clearly remained entrenched and influential in basic industry and could reasonably argue that attempts to dislodge it had not succeeded. While the results appeared to legitimize the IUE, they also suggested the dangers of basing a campaign on the "Communist issue" alone. The IUE received votes in plants where it had no organizational nucleus and claimed no members. This would present major difficulties for the new union in the future. This situation which saw the UE reduced in size, but still large and holding its position, would continue for almost the next

---

20. NYT, May 22, 1950, p. 2; May 27, 1950, p. 1.
21. Ibid., May 27, 1950, p. 1.

four years.[22] During that time the union maintained a significant base of support even in plants where it had lost elections such as at East Pittsburgh and Lynn.

The most notable UE success occurred at the largest electrical manufacturing facility in the nation: the GE turbine and generator works at Schenectady. By the summer of 1951, the IUE filed for a second election at the plant, whose 19,000 workers were represented by UE local 301. Although the UE margin had been substantial the first time, the IUE leaders believed the 7,761 to 5,847 count was close enough that they might have a chance at a future victory. In addition, they understood that their union would have to control the Schenectady local in order to assert genuine dominance and the end of serious "leftist" influence in the industry. Therefore, the local had been, and would continue to be, a focal point of the conflict in electrical labor.[23]

In these conditions, the 1951 campaign started badly for the IUE. Eager to have the issue decided before the opening of national contract negotiations with the company and confident of victory, the UE pressed for an early election. The scheduling of the election on September 14, the day before the start of contract talks, threw the IUE on the defensive from the beginning. The local's influential business agent Leo Jandreau, president William Kelly, and most of its 605 shop stewards were thought to be strong UE supporters.

This election typified contests in the industry during the period in that it attracted considerable attention not only inside the plant, but also in the press and the surrounding community as well. Besides conducting campaign activity inside the shop, the two sides distributed leaflets at plant gates, hired sound trucks, aired radio—and even TV spots—and placed ads in local papers. The UE campaign focused on two main points.

22. See table 1. The UE figures must be considered rough estimates given the difficulties the union faced collecting dues during the early 1950s. In any case, the evidence indicates that the UE's influence exceeded its numbers.

23. See chapter V.

First, the union charged that the opposition was backed by outside forces interfering in the affairs of the local. One UE newspaper ad included the text of a wire that Kelly and Jandreau sent to Congressman John Wood, Chairman of the House Un-American Activities Committee (HUAC). After citing a number of examples of HUAC hearings or subpoenas which had coincided with UE elections, the authors urged the Committee not to interfere this time, saying, "Your Committee will undoubtedly be asked, if it has not already been, to meddle in this election on behalf, as it has done in so many elections in the past. We believe that you should refuse."[24]

Second, the UE emphasized the gains that GE workers had made in "bread and butter" terms during the years since the union had won bargaining rights at Schenectady. One leaflet entitled "What We Have Won" emphasized wage increases, seniority rights, paid holidays, and vacation time. At the bottom, under the heading "What We Are Fighting For," the leaflet mentioned "removal of discrimination against women's rates and elimination of geographical differentials which allow the company to open up plants and move jobs to low pay areas."

While the UE campaign focused on economic "bread and butter" issues, the IUE emphasized national security, "Communist domination" of the UE, and "Communist Russia's campaign to conquer the world." According to the IUE literature, the nation was "engaged in a deadly struggle with Communist Russia" which required the Government to bar any union whose leaders were not loyal to the United States from performing "secret war work." One leaflet correctly pointed out that the Atomic Energy Commission had barred the UE from the atomic energy industry in 1948 and then argued that the union would soon be excluded from all war work. This leaflet

24. Material on the 1951 Schenectady election is in a UE pamphlet, "The Schenectady Story," IUE Papers, Box 31 FF 5.

ended with the exhortation to "Vote American; Vote IUE-CIO."[25]

During the days before the election, IUE supporters paraded outside the plant, carrying signs which read "A Vote for UE is a Vote for Communism" and "No Iron Curtain—Vote IUE," while across the street, behind a cordon of police, UE backers carried signs reading "CIO Goons Scram" and "IUE-CIO Offers One Hot Dog for Each Vote." The UE's decisive victory in the election attracted national attention. The press response indicated how widely perceived was the connection between electrical trade unionism and international affairs. The Pittsburgh Press termed the IUE's 11,542-4,851 defeat "stunning" and noted that the UE had actually gained strength since the previous election. It editorialized that, while most UE members were undoubtedly loyal, there was "considerable question about which side some of their leaders might take in case of a war with a Communist nation."[26]

The conservative *Brooklyn Eagle* used stronger language. Its article expressing grave concern for the nation's safety ran under the headline "Victory for Red-Controlled Union at G.E. Plant Defies Analysis." The article's words typified the most vigorous attacks on the UE:

> Talk to the average G.E. worker in and around Schenectady and he will rattle off the Commie line to you in perfect parrot fashion....
>
> A grass-roots anti-Communist campaign has been going on for the past six years in the electrical industries. Yet 11,500 workers, the vast majority by far non-Communist, by secret ballot have refused to loosen the grip of the Commie leadership upon their economic lives.

---

25. Ibid., p. 29. For the UE and the Atomic Energy Commission, see chapter V below.

26. Pittsburgh Press, September 16 and 20, 1951, reprints in Ibid., pp. SA and S38.

> The fact that the Communists are strewing the mountain passes and the plains of Korea with wounded and dead GIs, fellow American citizens, has had not the slightest effect upon the thinking of these workers in the up-State city.[27]

In other words, the rank-and-file support for the local and national leaders of the union contradicted the expectations of the UE's adversaries. The large vote for the UE led some opponents to another conclusion, however. If Schenectady workers supported the UE, then the fault must lie with the leadership of the rival IUE. The question arose whether James Carey was equal to the task of winning workers away from the older union. Father Rice called for stepped-up government intervention, arguing that "the Communist unions will have to be busted no matter whom it may hurt."[28] The fact of widespread support for the UE clearly proved difficult or impossible for its most determined opponents to accept.

The local 301 election was not the only evidence of such continuing support. In fact, this period saw numerous examples. Schenectady represented one pattern or type of example, where the leadership and a majority of the members expressed a common desire to remain in the UE. We find two other patterns: one in which the UE actually lost the election but retained the allegiance of a significant minority; the other in which the leadership, or some of the leaders, favored leaving the UE but were then overruled by a majority of their members.

At both the East Pittsburgh Westinghouse and Lynn General Electric plants events followed the second pattern. In both of these cases, the UE continued to wield considerable influence even after having lost representation elections. Developments at the Lynn plant during 1953 illustrate the point. During the early months of the

27. Brooklyn Eagle, September 23, 1951, p. 22, reprint in Ibid., p. s37. For actual quotes from local 301 members, see the discussion of the Saturday Evening Post article of October 18, 1952, in chapter V below.

28. Pittsburgh Catholic, September 20, 1951, reprint in Ibid., p. s40.

year, both unions were again in the process of negotiating new national contracts with General Electric. The UE, attempting to establish a basis for jointly facing the company, formally appealed to the IUE on February 7 and again on April 9 to agree on a common bargaining program. Receiving no response to either overture, the UE contacted the IUE locals directly "through leaflets, ads and other contacts."[29]

At the same time, the UE activists in the Lynn plant conducted an active campaign to regain representation rights there, and their efforts met with some success. Based on the widespread perception that union strength at Lynn had ebbed since the UE's defeat in 1950, the UE aimed to collect enough signed cards to present more than the 30 percent necessary for an NLRB election.[30] While the IUE leadership did not respond to the UE appeal for joint bargaining, they did issue a statement calling "agreement with all non-Communist unions in GE for concerted action," a formulation clearly intended to exclude the UE, despite the fact that the two unions together represented the bulk of GE's organized workforce.

At this point, Carey, apparently bidding to maintain control in Lynn, the IUE's largest local, called a mass meeting to review the progress of negotiations with the company. UE supporters in the plant prepared for Carey's visit by distributing leaflets and urging a large turnout. Over 5,000 members of IUE local 201 attended the outdoor gathering at Lynn's Fraser Field despite the wet weather conditions. Here, IUE President Carey, the

---

29. UE News, April 13, 1953, p. 1. This was not the first time the UE leaders had attempted to find a basis for united action and been rejected by Carey. See NYT, March 4, 1952, p. 10.

30. For comments on dissatisfaction at GE's Lynn plant under the IUE leadership, see copies of the "rank-and-file" paper Spotlight written by two workers claiming allegiance to neither union, especially November 24, 1951, p. 2 and January 19, 1952, p. 1., UE Archives, D/2-164. For the UE plans to file for an NLRB election, see UE local 201 paper Score, February 4, 1953, UE Archives D/2-165. For the progress of the UE in collecting signed cards, see reports Charles Newell to Matles D/2-160.

meeting's opening speaker, came into open conflict with the overwhelming majority of the members present. According to a UE report, when a local member moved to strike the words "non-Communist" from the proposal for joint action, Carey responded combatively. He "launched into a most vicious red-baiting attack against the UE and the makers of the amendment, at which point he was booed to such an extent that he had to give up the platform and could not regain it." The local leaders who supported Carey's position were similarly booed. The chairman was compelled to put the amendment which was carried almost unanimously.[31] Thus, the members of local 201 specifically rejected their national and local leaders' appeal to anti-Communism.

The Lynn meeting demonstrated a situation that existed elsewhere in the industry at this time. Although the IUE had succeeded in narrowly winning the labor board election, with outside support such as the Secretary of Labor's visit in 1950, many of the most active members in the plant were UE supporters. While the Lynn local would never return to the UE, it continued to show the influence of the activists who had been UE supporters. The IUE had won the 1950 election by a vote of 6,093 to 5,314, after which all the workers in the plant were eligible to join the newer union. But, the size and sentiment of the Fraser Field gathering so closely paralleled the UE's vote that the results of the meeting indicated that the IUE president could not count on IUE voters for active support.[32]

The desire of these members to unite with their old union to increase their bargaining strength did not succeed in changing Carey's position. By June, the IUE had rejected another UE approach and had accepted the wage

---

31. Matles to UE shop stewards, April 16, 1953, IUE Papers Box 32/FF4 "UE Research Files, UE Publications, Clippings 1953."

32. For the Lynn results in 1950, see NYT, May 27, 1950, p. 1. In December 1953, immediately following a visit by the McCarthy Subcommittee to the city, the IUE won again 5,546–4,806, NYT, December 12, 1953, p. 23.

settlement offered by the company.[33] The UE General Executive Board subsequently recommended the same settlement to its own members, charging that the IUE's refusal to cooperate had prevented a more successful contract settlement and had especially blocked progress for "women and lower rated workers."[34] Although the decision of the meeting in Lynn had not prevailed, it had indicated the substantial sentiment that existed, rejecting Cold War politics and in favor of finding a basis for reuniting the workers in the electrical manufacturing industry. The IUE continued to base its refusal on the Cold War issue.

During this period, the UE's District 1 (Eastern Pennsylvania and Maryland) also faced challenges to the union's continued existence. In the district's two largest locals, a number of leaders indicated by their actions that they were losing confidence in the UE's ability to survive the Cold War attacks. Events at Westinghouse local 107 and the amalgamated local 155 indicated that a significant part of the membership did not share this view. The example of these two locals constitutes the third pattern.

The events of 1949–1950 had an especially stark meaning for District 1. Two of the most prominent original opposition leaders who spearheaded the founding of the IUE came from Philadelphia. James Carey and Harry Block had both worked at the large Philco plant in the 1930s and had figured prominently in organizing the federated AFL local that eventually became the first UE local, Philco 101. Consistently uncomfortable with the course the union had taken after Carey's defeat in 1041, Carey and Block had organized the UE Members for Democratic Action (UEMDA) during the late 1940s and in 1950 had succeeded in bringing the Philco local and the Camden RCA local 103 into the IUE.[35]

---

33. NYT, June 17, 1953, p. 38.

34. UE News, June 29, 1953, p. 1.

35. See Ronald Fillipelli, "The United Electrical Workers," pp. 143 ff for an account of the origins of the UEMDA.

The UE retained strength in the area, however, and the continued existence of the two large UE locals in the IUE president's hometown was especially troubling for the new union. Local 155 was an "amalgamated" local that represented workers at approximately fifty-five small- and medium-sized machine, tool-and-die, and electrical shops. As such, it differed from the locals in the major electrical chains in that it bargained with many different employers in varying situations. Despite the local's widely distributed membership, it included a core of members who took pride in its eighteen-year history in organizing the bulk of the tool-and-die industry in Philadelphia, its production record during World War II, and its attention to issues such as hiring of African-American workers, women's rates, and international questions.[36] From a wartime peak of 7,000, the local's membership had fallen to 4,000 in 1952, the decline resulting in part from the closing of small shops after the war and in part from losses to other unions.[37]

The storm that broke over local 155 in the spring of 1952 demonstrates the pervasive influence that outside Cold War pressures were having on the union. The UE's opponents had apparently started to regroup after the IUE's defeat in Schenectady the previous September. Secretary of Labor Tobin had attended the IUE convention following that election and expressed his disappointment with the results. The ACTU's Father Rice had gone further and suggested that perhaps the IUE needed new leadership in order to bring electrical workers into the Cold War fold. Then, in December, Senator Hubert Humphrey announced his intention to convene his Labor Subcommittee of the Senate Committee on Education and Labor in order to investigate Communist control of unions the following year. We will say more

36. This estimate is based on a reading of The Square Dealer, publication of local from January 1944, in the possession of former local business agent Max Helfand.

37. According to the Philadelphia Evening Bulletin, May 21, 1952, p. 1, the local still represented the bulk of the tool-and-die shops in the city.

about the Humphrey hearings below, but the Senator's announcement was already a part of the larger picture surrounding the events in local 155. When, in addition, Senator Pat McCarran announced that his committee would visit Philadelphia, serious division in local 155 resulted.

In mid-May, a split in the local's leadership surfaced which pitted five of the fifteen executive board members against experienced business agent David Davis. The five charged Davis with damaging the interests of the local's members and demanded that he stand trial before the membership. Although a majority of the executive board voted against holding such a trial, the dissident leaders proceeded to organize a trial meeting that was attended by several hundred people, but boycotted by Davis and his supporters. At the meeting, which received prominent press coverage, two opposition leaders, Thomas Delaney and Samuel DiMaria, presented a long list of charges which reflected those being leveled at the union elsewhere.[38]

Davis had, they charged, brought "scorn and condemnation on the Local" by openly affirming "that he is a member of the Communist Party," had "forced over 2,000 members to leave local 155," and "attacked our Government policies." His politics were "contrary to the aims and aspirations of an American Trade Union."[39] While the executive board members who brought the charges claimed their purpose was to keep the local together by removing Davis, the meeting had the opposite result.

38. The Evening Bulletin, May 25, 1952, p. 3; May 26, p. 2; May 28, p. 5. Also, see Matles letter to UE International Representatives and Field Organizers, May 29, 1952, UE Archives D/1-794.

39. The full list of twelve charges was attached to the Matles letter of May 29 for the information of UE staff members. Matles claimed that the movement to oust Davis had been instigated by Delaney because he had lost the support of the workers at the H. H. Eby Company, one of the larger shops for which he was responsible. Max Helfand, 155 organizer and later business agent, supported this claim in an interview on March 23, 1987, charging that the "issue of Communism" was "phony." It was, nevertheless, the issue on which Davis's opponents based their public appeal.

One faction led by Augustine Gisondi, shop chairman at the Ocean City Manufacturing Company, called for secession from the UE. Delaney and DeMaria found themselves having to stem the secession tide. The meeting broke up without agreement, but Gisondi later told the press that he would urge members in his shop to join the IUE. The majority at the meeting, however, voted to call for new elections for business agent and all executive board posts.[40]

While the events of May 1953 did result in the withdrawal of a number of shops from the UE and the establishment of IUE local 123, a majority of the shops and members remained in local 155. The local did hold an election, and Davis voluntarily resigned his post, but his supporters won and continued in leadership. A closer look at the record indicates that the publicized opposition to Davis and his leadership represented only one section of opinion in the local. Although Gisondi claimed that twenty shops would move to the IUE, a UE organizer's report two weeks later alleged that thirteen shops had actually voted to secede. Charles Fluhrer, who had been president of the local and a supporter of Davis, became acting business agent.[41] Davis continued as a local organizer, an elected position, until he was arrested on Smith Act charges the following summer.[42]

While the local 155 story demonstrated the powerful effect of outside pressures, it also showed that considerable resistance to those pressures existed. While Davis did not personally survive in his original position, the leadership of the local continued on the hands of his supporters and associates. His support in the local was, according to several sources, impressive, and his public membership in the Communist Party did not dissuade

40. Evening Bulletin, May 28, 1952, p. 5.

41. See UE organizer Gene Derrickson's report to Matles, June 12, 1952, for the 13 shops, UE Archives D/1-749. Letter from Fluhrer to Matles October 21, 1952, signed "President and Acting Business Representative," D/1-751.

42. Local 155 Press Release, August 5, 1953, protesting Davis's arrest, UE Archives D/1-805.

many local members from voting for him. In the words of one former local officer, "Most of the membership in the 155 didn't hold that against him because he represented the interests of the people, and he delivered some of the best contracts and conditions for the people in 155."[43] Another former 155 added, "He always based it on what the people were going to want, what they needed, what they stood for... and that's why the workers had real confidence in him."[44]

Even Davis's opponents felt compelled to qualify their accusations. DeMaria, one of the dissident executive board members, told the press that Davis had "done a lot for this local through the years. Nobody can take away from that record. But I am in favor of the motion [to bring Davis to trial]."[45] Thomas Delaney, the other dissident leader, supported this conclusion when he identified one major source of the pressure:

> The ax is about to fall. The infamous McCarran Committee is coming here and that means only one thing—an investigation of UE and local 155 in particular. We knew there would be scare headlines and that shops would be scurrying for cover to get out from under the pressure. We had to act now.[46]

In short, the movement to oust Davis, a leading left-wing unionist, was largely a result of the outside Cold War pressures on the organization. Another press account implied that this was the case after the trial meeting held in Davis's absence, allowing that "The meeting of insurgents in the left-wing Local 155... established one thing

43. Max Helfand Interview.

44. Interview with Louise Koszalka, former H. H. Eby employee and 155 shop steward, February 18, 1987.

45. Evening Bulletin, May 21, 1952, p. 10.

46. Ibid.

if nothing else: There is no organized anti-Communist movement within the union."[47]

UE local 155 survived as a force in electrical trade unionism in the area. The local leadership remained skeptical of the motives of the five board members who had called for Davis's trial. Differences of opinion had existed previously between Davis and Delaney, but disagreement is not disunity. The pressures on the local from outside had transformed disagreement into disunity.

In the UE's other large local in the district, Westinghouse 107, a different situation developed the next summer. Local 107 represented the 7,000 workers at the steam turbine plant in Lester, a community in the industrial belt hugging the Delaware River south of (or down river from) Philadelphia. Here, the local business agent himself called for a change. In July 1953, a month after the execution of the Rosenbergs in New York, and approximately two weeks before the arrest of David Davis and eight other Philadelphians on charges of violating the Smith Act, 107's Francis Bradley issued a statement to the members calling for secession from the UE and affiliation with the IUE-CIO. At a local membership meeting the following night, previously called to vote on the Westinghouse contract offer and now also a forum for debate on the future of the local, it quickly became clear that Bradley's proposal would meet serious resistance. Local president John Monaghan, whose name had appeared on the original leaflet with Bradley's, repudiated the secession move and the "wave of hysteria" that had spawned it, and urged the members to stick with the UE. Bradley resigned his post and stated his intention to continue working for disaffiliation from the UE.[48] The presence of a third union in the

---

47. Philadelphia Daily News, "Local 155 Anti-Reds Lack Organization" by Edward J. Hussie, May 28 or 29, 1952, Clipping in UE Archives D/1-806.

48. Evening Bulletin, July 22, 1953, p. 11; July 23, 1953, p. 35; UE News, August 5, 1953, p. 1.

contest, the International Association of Machinists, complicated the situation, although affiliation with the IAM was never a serious possibility. The IAM's representative in the area, Philip Van Gelder, had previously been a UE organizer, and he told the press that the IAM was 107's "way out" of the dilemma.[49]

Unlike the episode in local 155, the uncertainty in 107 dragged on for months. The IUE used Bradley's defection to repeat the charges of "Communist domination" of the UE, although not local 107 directly. A leaflet carrying Bradley's name and picture entitled "Why I Quit UE" stated that "the issue of Communist control of UE is neither a small issue nor a fake issue...because more than anything else it has been responsible for UE's collapse in membership and in collective bargaining strength." The statement continued, "Thousands upon thousands of local 107 members had become...disgusted with the continuing willingness of UE's national leaders to let UE be used as a tool of the Communist Party and International Communism."[50]

As elsewhere, the campaign to wrest local 107 from the UE included broader forces than merely the IUE. The Westinghouse plant's Aviation Gas Turbine Division (AGT) produced jet engine parts for the Navy Department and employed 2,500 of the 7,000 members of the local. The company had announced that it was considering transferring the AGT work to Kansas City, and this possibility became a key issue in the campaign. In a half-page ad in Philadelphia newspapers, the IUE claimed that the jobs were threatened because the UE was the bargaining agent at the plant "no responsible government official can continue to allow secret defense work in plants where UE has access to it."[51]

Emphasizing this issue, the IUE enlisted the support of local officials including Mayor Joseph Clark and

49. Evening Bulletin, July 22, 1953, p. 11.

50. IUE leaflet in IUE Papers, Box 32 FF 24 "IUE Materials on UE 1955."

51. UE Organizer's Bulletin "107" Campaign," January 20, 1954, IUE Papers Box 32 FF 14.

Congressman William Green, Sr. to lobby in Washington to save the AGT jobs and, as an IUE victory would presumably have that result, to give implicit support to the CIO union. A well-publicized delegation including Clark, Green, Carey, and the IUE's Harry Block traveled to Washington for hearings on the location of the Westinghouse Company's Navy Department work. In addition to using the press, television and radio, the UE claimed, their opponents produced "literally an avalanche of printed literature, on many days three and four different pieces during the course of one day."[52]

The UE later charged that the cooperation between the public officials and the IUE was organized by a Carey aide, IUE assistant president David Lasser, "a leading Social Democrat and an ADA'er. It is he who cooked up the details of this deal through ADA." Also, in addition to local figures, the Westinghouse Lester election attracted the attention of national politicians. On January 7, 1954, a week before the scheduled Labor Board election, Oregon's Senator Wayne Morse suggested on the floor of Congress that the transfer of the AGT work was "dictated by security considerations stemming from the suspect nature" of the UE. He noted that the election the following week would involve three unions, "The UE and two devotedly anti-Communist unions—the IUE-CIO and the IAM. I hope the Defense Department will clarify this matter as a result of congressional inquiries and conferences with Mayor Clark and others."[53]

The challenge to the UE's representation rights generated a surge of rank-and-file membership activity in the plant. Grievance committees were reactivated and new members recruited; a members' group known as the

52. Ibid., p. 4. For the publicity, see the half-page ad in the Evening Bulletin, January 11, 1953, p. 24, placed by the IUE, claiming that the delegation had secured a delay in the AGT transfer. The following day Carey, Clark, and Green were on WIP radio together discussing the AGT situation, Evening Bulletin, January 13, p. 9.

53. Congressional Record, January 7, 1954, p. 56, quoted in UE bulletin "107 Campaign," p. 3.

"Minutemen" which has previously functioned during strike situations re-formed to aid the UE campaign. While the majority of the 32-member executive board supported the UE, new leaders emerged to replace Bradley and Monaghan in the two top positions. Carl Gray was elected President, and Edward Savitsky became business agent, while Nick Onafaro was co-coordinator of the campaign steering committee.[54]

Choosing to concentrate their campaign inside the shop rather than directly counter the IUE media campaign, the local leaders based their effort on the record of the UE and the local in winning gains for the members. The UE's campaign program stated in part:

> ... we stand to maintain our democratic fighting union run by the rank-and-file for the rank-and-file; to preserve the highest wages and best working conditions in the Delaware Valley that we have won in the past 17 years under the banner of UE local 107; to protect our job security through our seniority system which is guaranteed by our Westinghouse contract; to continue our fight to win unity of all Westinghouse workers for joint action in next May's negotiations...; to work for a united American labor movement.[55]

They argued that the local had itself carried on a sustained effort to keep the AGT jobs at the Lester plant and had, in fact, succeeded in having a resolution to that effect passed by the Philadelphia City Council. On the other hand, they contended that the planned expansion of the steam turbine production at the plant offered the best hope for secure employment.

The UE's lopsided victory in the January 14 election not only demonstrated the strength of membership sentiment and gave a much-needed boost to the UE

54. UE News, January 25, 1954, devoted six pages to the election at Westinghouse Lester.

55. "107 campaign," p. 5; IUE Papers, A2.06, ff "1954 II."

nationally. But it also indicated that the goal of the IUE-CIO and its backers—the unification of electrical workers around a Cold War program—was still out of reach. The local press labeled the results "a bitter and embarrassing blow to the IUE and the CIO" which, along with the IAM, had spent a reported 500 thousand dollars on the 107 campaign.[56]

The examples of the two District 1 locals suggest the gross inaccuracy of the allegations of "Communist domination" or "control" of the UE. In the case of local 155, the argument rested on the fact that the business agent was a known Communist. But, the evidence suggests that his position in the local stemmed from the confidence the members had in him rather than from any control he had over them.[57] The challenge to his leadership came only when a group of executive board members decided that, due to the outside pressures, the local's image was suffering and its future threatened. At least one of the dissident board members, Thomas Delaney, had previously aligned himself with the left but had changed his position due to the Cold War pressures.[58]

Westinghouse local 107, on the other hand, was never directly charged with being "Communist controlled." The UE's opponents claimed, in fact, that 107 did not belong in the "red dominated" UE and should choose to leave. The local's persistent refusal to do so puzzled UE adversaries. Activists in and out of local 107 frequently mentioned the influence of members of the International Workers of the World (IWW or the "wobblies") in pioneering industrial unionism at the Lester plant in the 1920s

---

56. Philadelphia Inquirer, January 15, 1954, p. 1, "Red Tinged UE Wins NLRB Poll at Lester Plant." A later edition of the paper changed the headline to read "Independent UE." The results: UE 5,046; IUE 1,048; IAM 488.

57. Koszalka interview; Helfand interview; also interview with Harry Block, former President of IUE District 1, March 17, 1987.

58. Delaney had in 1951 served as secretary of the Trade Union Committee to Defend Labor's Rights. See Delaney to Julius Emspak, November 12, 1951, UE Archives, D/1-749.

and their continuing activity in later decades.[59] In summary, the evidence in District 1 supports the contention that the UE was a coalition of diverse groups with a generally shared concept of trade unionism, rather than an organization dominated by any outside influence. Where the coalition splintered, as it threatened to do in 1953 in District 1, and as it did elsewhere in the labor movement, Cold War pressures were responsible.

At the same time as the union was demonstrating its capacity for survival in such local situations as Schenectady, Lynn, and Philadelphia, it also continued to face serious challenges at the national level. The UE was constantly being investigated. Its national officers, district or local leaders, and some rank-and-file members became targets of investigation. Congressional hearings or news of investigations were frequently timed to have impact on a local representation election, but their influence reached far beyond any particular locality. When two of the union's top officers, Matles and Emspak, were called before a New York City grand jury four days before the 1951 Schenectady election, they were already under federal indictment for "contempt of Congress" for refusing to respond to questions about their politics.[60]

The widest ranging investigations reached beyond the UE and targeted the entire labor movement. While these inquisitions were generally driven by conservative Republicans, one of the most revealing in retrospect was chaired by Democratic Senator Hubert Humphrey. In the summer of 1952, as the Korean War dragged on

---

59. Bradley interview; Block interview; Boehner interview; Gray interview; Matles and Higgins, Them and Us, pp. 181-182. Gray also suggested that the union had succeeded in neutralizing the influence of the local Catholic clergy: "We knew what was going on in Pittsburgh and other areas. We visited the various parishes in the area and told them, 'stay out of it; it's not your province... or we withdraw our dues.' You know what that meant—[we won't] put any more in the collection box."

60. See UE News, October 17, 1955, pp. 6-7 for background of the case stemming from the two officers' refusal to answer questions before the HUAC in 1949. See Schenectady Union Star, September 8, 1951, reprint in The Schenectady Story, p. s20 for the grand jury subpoena.

and a difficult presidential election loomed, Humphrey attempted to pre-empt further Republican attacks and undertook an effort of his own to determine the magnitude of the "national security" problem in the labor movement. His subcommittee heard witnesses from several unions, including the IUE, as well as from scholars and representatives of the General Electric Company. The transcript reveals much about the thinking of the contending forces during the early Cold War years. Although this effort yielded no obvious positive results at the time, it must be said that the less contentious atmosphere stands in marked contrast to many other committee hearings. The UE asked to testify and its representatives, Matles and Russ Nixon, succeeded in getting the union's positions on the record. We will return to this subcommittee in the next chapter, but the UE testimony concerns us here.

Matles and Nixon opened their testimony by entering their prepared statement into the record. It bears repeating in part:

> The traducers of the UE assert as their most basic fabrication that the UE "through Communist domination serves the purposes of Soviet foreign policy." A careful and objective look at the facts thoroughly exposes such slanderous allegations....
>
> The UE is a trade union and, as such, the overwhelming bulk of its activities... have to do with basic trade-union questions and related domestic policies.... Through the year 1947 the UE, as a section of the CIO, participated in the formulation and fully agreed with the foreign policy position taken by the CIO.... In 1947 the split that began between UE and the rest of CIO, insofar as it involved foreign policy, resulted not from a change in UE policy, but in a change of CIO policy. Without deviation, the UE has followed the policy developed by the late Franklin D. Roosevelt....
>
> Sharpest attacks have been thrown at this union because its members have adopted positions on foreign

> policy differing from those of the administration and its supporters....
>
> Had the members of this union declared that war profiteering is fine, we would not be here today....If our members had put their stamp of approval on the tax-price-wage squeeze that is wrecking the country's living standards, we would not be charged with endangering the country's security.... Had we called for atomic war, for $60 billion arms budgets, for distributing America's wealth to corrupt dictators like Franco and Chiang Kai-shek, we would not be under attack here.[61]

In response to questions, they repeated and attempted to expand on the points made in their statement.

Senator Humphrey: You have criticized American foreign policy, have you not?

Mr. Matles: Yes sir, we have.

Senator Humphrey: Have you seen fit to criticize Soviet foreign policy?

Mr. Matles: We would criticize anything we consider to be detrimental to the American people.

Senator Humphrey: Have you ever criticized the American Communist Party?

Mr. Matles: We don't join in that. We are the most red-baited union in America, and you want us to hit ourselves over the head. You want us to join with McCarthy. You want us to join with McCarran. You want us to join with them and hit ourselves over our heads. We would have to be nuts to do that...

You will not find anywhere that we have criticized the "New Leader" with which you may or may not be associated. We have not criticized Norman Thomas. We have not criticized the Socialist Party or anybody else like that. What would you say? That we have endorsed socialism because of that?

---

61. U.S. Senate, Subcommittee of the Committee on Labor and Public Welfare, Hearings, Communist Domination of Unions and National Security, 82nd Congress, 2nd Session, pp. 354-355.

I challenge you to show me a single position that this union has taken in the affirmative to the detriment of the American people.... Show me such a single instance and I will argue with you on that.

Senator Humphrey: Is it your testimony that the UE is not governed directly by or influenced by those persons who are members of the Communist Party?

Mr. Matles: My testimony is that the UE is not directed or controlled by any political party including the Communist Party....

And we have more independence in the locals, districts, and national headquarters of the UE than any of the unions under the CIO.

Senator Humphrey: It is not red-baiting to identify a man who is a Communist as a Communist.

Mr. Matles: There are some men serving jail sentences now because they said they were Communists....

Returning to the pivotal and persistent matter of foreign policy, Matles argued that the UE's problems with the Truman Administration and with the CIO stemmed from its consistency.

> ...The CIO up to 1947 said: we ought to try to live in peace with the world. The CIO resolution in 1947 said that the big powers ought to negotiate a settlement, including Russia. The fact that we say the same thing in 1952 and have continued to say it for five years after the CIO finished saying that does not make them patriots and does not make us Un-American.[62]

The union had, in fact, made this point before and attempted to stress it at every opportunity. The UE argued that the change had been in the CIO and the Administration in Washington. The *UE News* had editorialized

62. Ibid. For Matles's entire testimony, see pp. 486-510, especially pp. 499, 500, 504. The UE News published the excerpts quoted here on July 21, 1952, p. 6.

in February 1950, three months after the UE's expulsion from the CIO, that there had occurred a "great and significant change in the attitude of the politicians who run the government toward the people." The editorial contended that, while the UE "did not always see eye to eye with Franklin Roosevelt, he did not slander the American working people and their unions." Recently, government agencies "from top to bottom" had adopted the "red-baiting" tactics of the Dies Committee.[63] This continued to be the union's position during the next four difficult years.

Another thrust of Matles's testimony deserves mention. While he aired the UE's differences with the CIO and despite attacks being directed at him, he defended the loyalty of the entire labor movement. He closed his testimony by telling the subcommittee that:

> The problem that confronts this country is the repeal of the Taft-Hartley law and the McCarran immigration act, and the repeal of every single piece of repressive legislation that are directed against the people.... You can sleep at ease as far as any section of the labor movement is concerned...from the standpoint of any union or any group of working people being a threat to the security of the United States of America. That does not exist.

This chapter has attempted to argue that, despite its embattled position and the heavy losses during the spring of 1950, the UE essentially held its ground and maintained its membership during the period of the Korean War. A final piece of evidence to support this view comes from a source hardly friendly to the union at the time. An observer from the CIO Editors' Association of Illinois attended the UE national convention in Chicago in September of 1953. He reported being struck by the high morale among the 550 delegates, the "good natured and orderly" proceedings, and the extent of

---

63. UE News, February 6, 1950, p. 2.

delegate participation in convention business. He noted, for example, that he had been invited to attend meetings of women delegates and a Publicity and Education Conference of 250 delegates discussing local leadership problems. He reported that the delegates included 90 to 100 women and 50 African Americans ("Negroes, men and women").

Specifically addressing the international aspect of the UE's program, the report noted that the delegates felt that one advantage they enjoyed in their ongoing contests with other unions was their freedom from "all obligation to justify a foreign aid program which they call giving your money away to help foreign monopolists to prepare for war."

The reporter noted that the "delegates listened with seemingly genuine interest to the main speakers, Fitzgerald and Matles, and to the offerings of their fellow delegates," and concluded that "the fact must be faced that the great majority of UE delegates seem to be friendly, capable, energetic, and sophisticated. In a union fight they should be hard to beat, other things being equal.... One gets the impression that UE in September 1953 is still a confident and formidable organization."[64]

The report also noted one weak spot that troubled many UE delegates. The union's "public rejection and isolation" brought "bitter complaints" from many at the convention and was, in fact, indicated by the total press blackout. The local Chicago dailies and the major wire services had virtually ignored the convention, and no community or religious leaders addressed the gathering. This situation presented a marked contrast to the environment three years earlier when the media had awaited the union's position on the Korean War. Generally, however, this assessment from a CIO press representative belied the allegations of the UE's rivals that the union was dying because the members were

---

64. Confidential Report of the UE's 18th Convention by George F. McCray, trustee of the CIO Editors Association of Illinois, IUE Papers Box 32 FF 14.

deserting their scheming and manipulative leaders. To summarize, the UE during the early 1950s refused to abandon its political or foreign policy positions, continued to seek unity of the workers in its industry, worked on breaking racial and gender barriers facing electrical workers, and demonstrated organizational ability and membership support sufficient to maintain a position of considerable influence in the electrical manufacturing industry.

An examination of the foreign policy differences between the UE and the CIO will show that this remained a central disagreement between the two during and after the Korean War period. The CIO leadership immediately rallied in support of the Administration's decision to intervene in the Korean conflict, while the UE at first offered cautious criticism while expressing support for the troops and later more insistent calls for ending the war.[65] The foreign policy argument stands out because by 1951 the CIO leaders began to voice dissatisfaction with the Truman Administration's lack of progress on its domestic program, as the UE had been doing for years. The next chapter will show that common frustration with domestic developments during the early 1950s was not enough to overcome the disagreement on foreign policy-related issues.

---

65. See CIO News, July 1950, p. 3; July 10, p. 1; July 17, p. 3; July 24, p. 3 for the CIO's support of the Administration's war mobilization program.

Chapter **4**

Pushing Limits: The Electrical Unions and U.S. Foreign Policy, 1950–1955

The Korean War solidified the Cold War in official United States foreign policy. It brought sharply increased annual military budgets, an emergency mobilization program, and further chilled debate on foreign policy. The differing responses of the IUE-CIO and the UE to the Administration's war policy and to changes following the Korean War is the subject of this chapter. How the unions responded to these developments tells us much about the fortunes of organized labor in the United States at the time and since.

In September 1950, when 600 UE delegates gathered in New York for the annual convention, they had the attention of the national commercial press. The shooting war on the Korean peninsula was then barely three months old. By this time, the CIO, now without its "left wing" unions, had already offered the Truman Administration "unqualified endorsement for the prompt steps to end Communist aggression" and called for labor representation in the emergency mobilization program.[1] What, the media wondered, would the UE, largest of the recently expelled "left" unions, say about the Korean situation?

Some of the country's most strident voices, suggesting that events in Korea signaled a new and intensified stage

1. CIO News, July 3, 1950, p. 3; July 17, 1950, p. 5.

in the global struggle with Communism, raised the specter of the "left wing" unions in strategic sectors of the economy, disrupting the war effort through strikes or sabotage. Those unions, some pointed out, represented workers in the western copper mines, in electrical plants involved in military production, and on the west coast docks.[2] The UE delegates, well aware of the circumstances and the pressures on the union, debated the issue at length, both in the resolutions committee and on the convention floor.

President Fitzgerald's opening remarks demonstrated this awareness when he pledged "100 percent support for the American forces" in Korea, but he also asserted that "we have the right and solemn duty to discuss and analyze the causes of war." The president went on to say "if a UE member thinks it was U.S. foreign policy that led us into this mess, it does not necessarily make him a traitor to his country."[3] While Fitzgerald thus attempted to defuse the media speculation, the union still had to adopt a comprehensive foreign policy position.

This was done only after hours of debate. The resolution finally reported out of committee and eventually adopted by the delegates reflected the varying points of view still existing in the union even after the losses of the previous spring's Labor Board elections. As delegate Cliff Cameron observed during the floor debate, the resolution was a "compromise" that represented hours of work by the resolutions committee. The resolution made no specific mention of Korea but, instead, called on the government to:

1. Keep foreign policy out of the hand of big business...;
2. Use our money and resources to support democratic governments and to rebuild economies which will provide trade and jobs...;

---

2. The Pittsburgh Catholic, September 20, 1951, clipping reproduced in The Schenectady Story, p. s40, UE pamphlet in IUE Papers Box 31 FF 5.

3. NYT, September 19, 1950, p. 5.

3. Refuse military or financial support for corrupt or totalitarian regimes anywhere;
4. Participate in a meeting of the great powers, including Russia, to work for peace and non-use of atomic weapons;
5. Make the United Nations the instrument of all peoples throughout the world to win better living standards, peace, and security.[4]

The committee had succeeded in crafting a resolution that satisfied virtually all the delegates, but two hours of floor debate still transpired before they voted approval. George Bobich of local 610 in Western Pennsylvania's Turtle Creek Valley reflected a widely held sentiment when he argued that the nation's foreign policy was an extension of domestic policies which the union opposed. He pointed out that the delegates had "sat here all week criticizing the domestic policy of the leaders of our government and the dirty rotten deal" being perpetrated on the American people, and he continued, "the foreign policy of these leaders is no different from the domestic policy.... They can't be different, it is one program...." Similarly, Francis Bradley, business agent of local 107 favored the resolution because "the bosses who oppress people at home are the same as those who oppress people abroad. The people who wanted to put a dictator in the White House are the ones who have made U.S. foreign policy today."[5]

---

4. UE 15th Convention Proceedings, p. 169.

5. For the convention discussion on the foreign policy resolution, see the UE News, October 2, 1950, pp. 11-12. That the resolution represented a compromise was understood in the union. See James Lustig's report to the District Council 4 meeting, September 28, 1950, p. 3, UE Archives D/4-19. The NYT of September 19, 1950, p. 5, reported that a Cleveland local had submitted a more left-oriented resolution, for instance. Bradley's position is significant in view of his attempted switch to the IUE three years later. Although he desired to change his union affiliation at one point, he apparently never changed his ideas on foreign policy, which he again expressed vigorously to the author in an interview on October 9, 1986.

The UE convention, therefore, adopted a position that may be summarized as "support the troops, but work to end the war, bring them home and work for a comprehensive plan for world peace." Here, the union in fact held to the positions it had taken over the previous three years. By declining to endorse explicitly the Administration's Korea policy, the UE placed itself outside the safe boundaries of what has been called the "in house" debate in foreign policy, not an easy place to be in the early 1950s.

Here, we should pause and consider the significance of the role the UE played by sticking to its foreign policy positions. In the chilling atmosphere of the deepening Cold War, any discussion of foreign policy carried risks and usually took place within the safe boundaries of the "in house" debate. Policy makers might, for example, discuss "how the American empire should be administered, but not whether there should be an American Empire."[6] They might disagree about when to use military force and when to use other forms of influence abroad, but not over the desirability of advancing the interests of the empire. The author who used this term did so in referring to the 1960s and the Vietnam War, but the concept can readily apply to the period of the 1950s as well. Robert Tucker (reluctantly) credits the "radical left" of the Vietnam period with expanding the debate by questioning the basis of the policy—the assumption that America had a right to empire in the first place.

As the history of the CIO shows, and as our discussion here shows, attempts to restrict and narrow any deliberation on foreign policy predated the 1960s. Applying the "in house" concept to the early 1950s, we find different terms in use, but the same situation. The "containment of Communism" was the stated and agreed upon goal of policy, but deciding upon the most effective way to achieve this goal proved elusive and difficult for the

---

6. Robert Tucker, The Radical Left and American Foreign Policy, (Baltimore: Johns Hopkins University Press), 1971, p. 7.

foreign policy establishment. The argument over responsibility for the Korean War, which would erupt during the 1952 election campaign, showed how volatile such a debate could become, but it did not challenge basic Cold War assumptions, in place since the 1940s.[7] The Labor movement, however, thanks to the "left led" unions, was one place where the argument raged well beyond any confining "in house" boundaries. To this unfolding debate, we will now turn.

Developments in electrical unionism during the early 1950s show that strong resistance to Cold War policies existed among electrical workers. On the other hand, forces inside and outside the labor movement considered it crucial to bring electrical workers into the Cold War fold. The creation of a new electrical union did not settle the matter. The UE continued to hold its ground during this period as it also continued to propose alternatives to the policies pursued by "mainstream" diplomatic and political leaders. One of the most energetic crusaders in the effort to bring electrical workers under Cold War leadership was also one of the strongest advocates for labor support for the nation's foreign policy. This was James Carey, past president of the UE-CIO; after 1951 president of the IUE-CIO; and until 1955, secretary-treasurer of the CIO.

Carey did not initially belong to the most aggressive Cold War camp. During the late 1940s, he associated himself with the liberal internationalist wing of the Democratic Party and supported liberal trade policies toward Washington's trading partners in Western Europe.[8] He

7. See NYT, September 23, 1952, p. 1; September 24, 1952, p. 26; September 28, 1952, p. 1; October 3, 1952, p. 1.

8. For Carey's views on United States' trade policy, see Carey to John Kenney, Deputy Director, Mutual Security Agency, August 18, 1952, Walter P. Reuther Library, Archives of Labor History and Urban Affairs, Wayne State University, Congress of Industrial Organizations, Office of the Secretary-Treasurer (hereafter CIOST), Box 129, file folder "MSA Correspondence 1952-1953." Carey's support of economic aid and liberal trade policies toward U.S. allies reflected the CIO position. See CIO News, April 17, 1950, p. 5. Also see Silverman, Imagining Internationalism, pp. 173-178.

served as a member of the Public Advisory Board of the Economic Co-operation Administration which administered the ERP. However, the persistent opposition to the Marshall Plan and the Truman foreign policy in Carey's own industry made the position of this labor "statesman" tenuous and led him to undertake a campaign of vociferous red-baiting in the industry and in the labor movement.

In his attempts to consolidate his position, Carey had no choice but to rely on support from outside his own union and from outside the labor movement. His allies included, in the first place, President Murray of the CIO and Secretary of Labor Maurice Tobin as well as the General Electric Company and the National Labor Relations Board itself. He also found support among liberal members of the foreign policy establishment and, at times, from the most conservative participants in the foreign policy debate. The UE on the other hand came under attack because of its opposition to Administration foreign policy as well as because of its militant collective bargaining positions. The most prominent foreign policy issue after mid-1950, the Korean War, was, in fact, only the clearest example of the broader foreign policy issues confronting the labor movement. On this issue, the Carey-CIO position found more enthusiastic support in the foreign policy establishment than it did among electrical workers, and perhaps workers in other industries as well.

The CIO's quick decision to endorse the Truman Administration's war policy in a sense continued the line it had pursued since the Marshall Plan debates of 1947–1948, and the organization was not alone as politicians of both parties initially supported the Administration. However, while the Korean War may have solidified support for the Cold War, support for the Truman Administration proved short lived, and as the war dragged on, the "in house" debate soon vigorously resurfaced. But, it remained for the UE, as the largest of the unions expelled from the CIO, to show that the disagreements in the nation and the labor movement over foreign policy involved issues more far reaching than simply how to pursue the Cold War.

The UE, preoccupied with defending itself and with its own survival, waited until its national convention in September to comment directly on the war. When it did, its position was not reached quickly, but in the end, it was a logical extension of the union's previous statements. In the spring of 1950, during the first campaign against the IUE in the major electrical chains, the *UE News* had regularly carried articles emphasizing the damage that "red-baiting" threatened to do in national politics. A March 20 *UE News* editorial had condemned McCarthy's attacks on the State Department, arguing that "red-baiting drags everyone down." The June 26 edition of the paper carried an editorial referring to the Stockholm peace pledge entitled "Peace Should Not Be a Dirty Word," and in the same issue, an article appeared on UE locals joining a movement to "outlaw" atomic bombs.[9]

During the summer, the union criticized the Administration's war emergency program and contended that the government aimed to use the war to maintain control over the labor movement. The UE argued, for instance, that, while the Administration had introduced a proposal for a wage freeze and a government agency to enforce it, the House had specifically voted down an "excess profits tax" provision in August.[10]

In September, at its national convention in New York, the union hammered out a more comprehensive position which, as events unfolded, would provide the basis for the union's stance during the next two decades. During the three years of the Korean War, the UE became increasingly outspoken in calling for American initiatives to end it. For example, by early 1951, the union noted the

---

9. UE News, March 20, 1950, p. 2; June 26, 1950, p. 2 and p. 11.

10. Ibid., August 7, 1950, p. 6, "War Mobilization and Red Baiting in Congress," by UE Washington Representative Russ Nixon.

international attempts to halt the shooting in Korea and charged that the Administration had rejected a cease-fire proposal from the Arab nations at the UN which had the tacit support of "practically every important nation in the world including France, Britain, and India." The union's newspaper related Washington's rejection of the proposal to the Administration's goals in domestic policy, suggesting that acceptance of it would have created the wrong political atmosphere in which to gain support for the wage freeze, as well as the tax increase the President had called for to fund the military buildup.[11]

By September 1951, when the UE convened again, the union had reason for some renewed confidence on two fronts: its organizing and its position on the war. Polls showed increasing discontent with the Administration's Korea policy as the war dragged on with no victorious end in sight.[12] Buoyed also by the union's convincing victory in Schenectady a week earlier, the delegates showed more willingness to assert their foreign policy position. The convention this time urged support for Colorado Senator Edwin Johnson's peace resolution of the previous spring and called for the withdrawal "of all non-Korean persons" from the peninsula within four months. The resolution further called for a UN-sponsored "assemblage of the major powers... so that through collective bargaining and negotiations a global formula for peace will be established. And furthermore that there be guaranteed by gradual disarmament the abolition of the use of atomic and other weapons of mass destruction...."[13]

---

11. Ibid., February 26, 1951, p. 2. One authority has recently suggested that key policy makers saw the military budget increase, not as a response to events in Korea, but as a way to get sufficient aid to European countries to enable them to continue to buy U.S. exports and close the "dollar gap" since renewal of the Marshall Plan "was considered virtually impossible in Congress." See Benjamin O. Fordham, Building the Cold War Consensus; The Political Economy of U.S. National Security Policy, 1949-1951 (Ann Arbor: University of Michigan Press, 1998) p. 46.

12. See table 2 and appendix A.

13. UE 16th Convention Proceedings, pp. 277-278. The UE News printed the text of Johnson's resolution on May 29, 1951, p. 2.

This continued to be the UE position until the cease-fire in the summer of 1953. By the fall of 1952, however, the union, while declining to endorse a presidential candidate, called attention to the growing peace sentiment in the country. In an editorial on the election results, entitled "End the War," the *UE News* argued that "the only ones who stand to gain by continuing the war are the reactionary big business interests who find the war politically useful in destroying the rights and liberties of the people.... Eisenhower was elected because people believe he opposes the war and will end it."[14] Hints of the breadth of the submerged peace sentiment in the country had surfaced during the election campaign, expressed especially by leading Republicans, such as New York's Senator Ives who had stated that an Eisenhower victory was the only alternative to "all-out war." Ohio's Senator Robert Taft had earlier in the year claimed that "Truman's war" in Korea was "useless" and "unnecessary." The *CIO News* had maintained its support of the war and specifically taken issue with Taft's position.[15]

It soon appeared that President Truman had interpreted the election results in a similar way. When he asked publicly for proposals to bring the war to an "honorable" end, the UE's Fitzgerald responded by sending him the union's last convention resolution. In his message to Truman, Fitzgerald noted that, since many UE members had sons in Korea, they had strong feelings on the issue. He stated that the proposals came from 325,000 UE members who believed that their position "represents the overwhelming sentiment of the American people."[16]

By the time of the union's next convention in September 1953, the Korean truce had been signed. The union's officers in their report to the members assessed the effects of three years of war on the United States. Their

---

14. UE News, December 8, 1952, p. 2.

15. NYT, October 15, 1952; CIO News, February 25, 1952, p. 5.

16. UE News, December 22, 1952, p. 3. Gallup Poll results from 1951 lent some support to Fitzgerald's assertion. See table 2 and appendix A.

sobering analysis charged that 25,000 American deaths and 140,000 casualties could have been avoided if the resolution of Colorado's Senator Johnson, which the UE supported, had been followed. The foreign policy resolution that year called for a "great power conference" as suggested by Adlai Stevenson, for UN-supervised elimination of atomic and hydrogen bombs and for the "drastic disarmament" of all nations. The resolution noted that the UE had refused to join in the "clamor and program of the Cold War" with its "crushing military burden."

A separate resolution on "peace and jobs" sounded an optimistic note, despite the perceived threat of depression in a war economy faced with the prospect of peace. This threat "should cement the ranks of labor and create new opportunities for united action against unemployment."[17]

While the union regularly called for a change in the Administration's Korean policy and sometimes presented evidence of anti-war sentiment in its ranks or in the nation, it also consistently related the national "emergency" to domestic issues. It was in opposition to Administration policies related to the war mobilization program that the UE succeeded in mobilizing rank-and-file members and in actively calling attention to issues that it saw as crucial for workers. Two particular targets of protest were the Office of Defense Mobilization (ODM) and the Wage Stabilization Board (WSB). President Truman established the ODM in late 1950 and appointed General Electric President Charles E. Wilson as its director. The UE regarded Wilson's appointment and that of General Lucius Clay as his special assistant as proof of the big business-military alliance that aimed to guarantee corporate profits from wartime contracts. The union had already noted the growing influence of leading business executives and corporate lawyers in the Administration's programs and

17. UE Policy 1953, UE Archives, PC 76, resolution on "Peace and Jobs" pp. 32-34; resolution on "Foreign Policy," pp. 34-36.

had criticized the "profiteering on war" as "profits on blood," but Wilson's appointment signaled a new level of influence since he would have "complete charge" of all mobilization activities.[18]

The Wage Stabilization Board, chaired by industrialist Cyrus Ching, presented even more visible evidence of the effects of the war emergency on working people. The WSB made a practice of unilaterally postponing or reducing collectively bargained wage increases. By the winter of 1951-52, the Board's policies generated a "months long" UE protest campaign featuring one-hour sit-downs, half-day walkouts, meetings, and picket lines. On December 13, the UE staged demonstrations against the WSB policies in several different cities which were joined by members of other unions. The following March, a national delegation to the WSB Washington office and a picket line outside "shook up the wage freeze authorities in a very noticeable way."[19]

While the UE rejected the Truman Administration's foreign policy as a corporate dominated operation, the CIO (and the AFL) took a different position. The CIO, in the summer of 1950, immediately and energetically supported the Truman Administration's decision to intervene on the Korean peninsula. By January 1951, the CIO had joined representatives of the AFL on the United Labor Policy Committee and met directly with Secretary of State George Marshall to "renew organized labor's support of our country's struggle against Soviet imperialism." James Carey proved especially energetic in this effort and became the point man for the CIO in advocating support for the policy. In a speech to the Ohio CIO council early in 1951, he labeled the "growing tide of isolationism... Communism's fifth column" in the United States and "branded isolationists virtual traitors... and called on organized labor to educate all

18. UE News, December 12, 1950, p. 7, on Wilson's appointment; October 30, 1950, on "war profiteering"; November 13, 1950, p. 7, on "Wall Street's Men in Washington."

19. Ibid., January 7, 1952, pp. 1, 6, 7; March 17, 1952, p. 7.

Americans on the real way to fight Communism, with arms, with ideas, with economic aid."[20]

Supporting official foreign policy during the Korean War soon presented difficulties for CIO leaders. Before long, they perceived, as did the UE, that not only the mobilization program, but also the foreign policy apparatus and, they charged, the Truman Administration were dominated by representatives of the corporate community. In the spring of 1951, Carey claimed that the Administration had abandoned even the verbal commitment to social legislation and "junked" the "remnants" of the Fair Deal program. In April, he specifically charged that big business dominated the war mobilization effort.[21] The business orientation of the Administration had, by that time, led the labor representatives to take the step of withdrawing from the economic stabilization program, in which the UE said they had no reason to serve from the beginning. In the summer of 1951, however, following the extension of the Defense Production Act, the AFL and CIO leaders agreed to return to the reorganized War Stabilization Board.

The CIO did not confine its criticism to the war mobilization program. Disillusionment with the Marshall Plan surfaced as early as August 1950 when leaders of both bodies returned from Europe charging that the ERP had failed to raise the living standards of European workers and had benefited only employers. They expressed alarm at the dire conditions faced by workers in France, Italy, and West Germany while firms aided by Marshall Plan funds made "huge profits." Teamsters' leader Harold Gibbons alleged that French leaders "manufacture Communism" with their "reactionary attitude," and the group warned that the French people would not be

20. CIO News, January 22, 1951, p. 6; January 29, 1951, p. 6.

21. See Carey's statements in the New York Post, March 8, 1951, on UE leaflet in IUE Papers, Box 31 FF "UE Research Files-UE publications, Bulletins 1951"; also Carey to Truman, January 5, 1951, Ibid. See "Statements of J. Carey on ERP and ECA 1948-1951" for Carey on the mobilization program, CIOST Box 126.

"strong enough to resist totalitarian aggression" if the three basic items of food, clothing, and shelter did not become more available.[22]

Throughout the early 1950s, the CIO leaders persisted in calling for greater labor representation in foreign policy decision making. When the Truman Administration had originally recruited the CIO to support the Marshall Plan, the foreign policy establishment had recognized the value of organized labor in carrying out policy. As early as August 1950, an editorial in the *CIO News* expressed disappointment that the State Department had apparently already forgotten. This statement indicates the rationale for the CIO's persistence in pursuing a course that so often frustrated its leaders during this period.

> There was a time in our history when big international deals were pulled off by foreign servicemen who knew how to dress faultlessly and always used the right fork. But that was before Communism became an international menace.... The State Department [must] face the realities of the current world situation.... There is a big need for shirt-sleeve diplomats who can work with real understanding among the people most likely to swing to communism. And the job can't be done merely by providing the shirt-sleeves with glorified office boy posts.[23]

In short, the importance of giving necessary guidance to a backward-looking foreign policy establishment in the changed international arena was so great, in their view, that CIO leaders would tolerate repeated indignities in the process. Despite its consistent failure to gain influence in crafting the nation's foreign policy, the CIO doggedly adhered to its position of reliable support, while always expressing its dissatisfaction.

The fact was, however, that the electrical manufacturing industry was not consolidated behind the Cold

22. CIO News, August 21, 1950, p. 3.
23. Ibid., August 28, 1950, p. 4.

War policy. While large pockets of resistance to the policy existed in other basic industries, especially in auto, Murray and Reuther could make a credible claim to have brought their unions safely within the limits of the "in-house" debate; Carey could not. His inability to do so put him in a peculiar position. On one hand, his failure to bring the workers in his industry in line behind the Cold War was an embarrassment compared to other CIO leaders. How could he claim to speak for American labor if he lacked the support of workers in his own industry? On the other hand, his anti-Communist crusade boosted his reputation with the foreign policy establishment as a labor leader with the experience and will to combat the "reds" wherever they might be. The response of the IUE leader and his allies to this unsettled situation merits our attention.

The 1951 IUE convention, held under the slogan "Production for Defense," presented a marked contrast to the UE's which took place the same week. The agenda included speeches by several leading personalities in the war mobilization apparatus and the Democratic Party. Secretary of Labor Maurice Tobin, Mutual Security Director Averill Harriman, Economic Stabilization Administrator Eric Johnston, as well as Eleanor Roosevelt, all addressed the gathering. The resolutions adopted on the convention's last day presented an interesting mixture. The union opposed the "unprincipled hysteria-mongering of the Senator McCarthys and McCarrans," but also called for larger appropriations for the Voice of America. One resolution which indicated that the disagreement between the electrical unions went beyond foreign policy issues was the resolution calling for "equitable profit sharing arrangements with industry."[24]

The profit-sharing question suggests the depth of the disagreement between the electrical unions. The UE regularly cited the IUE's position on profit sharing as

24. For a descriptive account of the convention, see the UE News, October 1, 1951, p. 15; for the resolutions, see the NYT, September 22, 1951, p. 6.

a problem in negotiations, preferring to negotiate for defined wage and benefits. An IUE internal document charged that the "political philosophy of those who controlled the UE was anti-profit sharing" and had cost electrical workers money.[25] The foreign policy issue, therefore, was part of a larger disagreement over who were the primary adversaries of electrical workers and what the task of their union should be. The UE program demonstrated its belief that the union existed primarily to protect its members' interests in dealing with their employers and the employers' allies in government. The IUE leadership viewed international communism as a greater threat to its members' interests.

In following this approach to trade unionism, the IUE leaders basically aligned their union with the right-wing Murray-Reuther leadership of the CIO, but Carey at times went beyond the CIO, as we shall see below. The willingness of CIO leaders to tolerate Carey's excesses on the "Communist issue" indicated the importance they attached to their relationship with the foreign policy apparatus. The support and prestige that Carey enjoyed in the foreign policy establishment was more consistent than his support in the trade union movement and was a major factor in his survival in the protracted struggle with the UE.

Carey's relationship with leading foreign policy figures was well established by the time of the IUE's founding in 1949–50. During the early 1950s, this relationship intensified as the president of the IUE (and secretary-treasurer of the CIO), whom they viewed as the "respectable" trade union leader in the industry, continued his well-publicized support for the expanding U.S. role in the Cold War abroad. When the European Recovery Program (ERP) came under control of the Mutual Security Administration in 1951, Averill Harriman became director, and Carey was appointed as a labor member of the

25. Memo by IUE's David Lasser dated January 15, 1953, IUE Papers, Box 32 FF 5.

Public Advisory Board to the MSA. Carey consolidated his reputation as an articulate speaker from the ranks of labor who could be counted on to deliver support for the Mutual Security Program before Congress or the public. Harriman, in a letter to Carey in the spring of 1952, wrote that "your support on the Hill has been very helpful in what I think is the biggest problem that we face—that of getting across to Congress and the public the real issues which this legislation poses."[26]

Carey's ties also extended to forces in the military. For instance, he accepted regular invitations to speak or participate in panel discussions as labor's representative at the Industrial College of the Armed Forces, where Army, Navy, and Air Force officers attended courses on topics such as "Wartime Labor Problems" or "Industrial Relations Problems." Carey felt that the College treated him in the same way that the State Department treated the CIO. By his own account, he attended "cheerfully," yet, as he complained in a letter to Secretary of Defense Louis Johnson, the Board of Advisors of the College included representatives of "many industrial establishments, but not a single labor organization." Many CIO affiliates were therefore "suspicious and in many cases resentful," and labor continued to find itself "in the position of orphans in a charity school."[27] While Carey's complaints elicited only a noncommittal response, he continued to receive letters of thanks for his participation in programs at the College.[28]

The unusual interest that Carey generated among members of the foreign policy establishment during this period is perhaps most strongly suggested by his relationship with such people as Eleanor Roosevelt and

26. Harriman to Carey, April 2, 1952, CIOST, Box 129/"MSA Correspondence 1952-53."

27. Carey to Johnson, April 17, 1950, CIOST, Box 129/"MSA Correspondence 1952-53."

28. See Major General A.W. Vanaman USAF to Carey, February 15, 1950; and Brigadier General J.L. Holman USA to Carey, November 1, 1950, CIOST, Box 38/Ibid.

Secretary of State Dean Acheson. The IUE leader's personal and political friendship with the former first lady originated during the period of the CIO's support for President Roosevelt during World War II and continued during the post-war decade and a half. She considered Carey a reliable source of advice on issues affecting labor during the 1950s.[29]

The Secretary of State also sought Carey's advice and spoke in support of the IUE. Carey's experience in electrical unionism had apparently made him, in Acheson's eyes, something of an expert on Communism in the labor movement. In fact, Carey may have been one of the few labor leaders seriously consulted on matters relating to policy. For example, the Secretary included Carey on a list of sixteen prominent figures invited to a two-day "off the record consultative meeting" in January of 1951. The list of participants included Henry Steele Commager, Reinhold Niebuhr, and Arthur Schlesinger, Jr. as well as the CIO secretary-treasurer. The purpose of the meeting was to discuss the "content of material exposing fallacies of Communist ideology and setting forth some of the aspects of [the] democratic way of life primarily for groups abroad who are subjects of Soviet propaganda." Acheson wired Carey that his "participation would make a real contribution."[30]

Carey's initially ambivalent response prompted a followup letter from the State Department's Director of Public Affairs urging him to attend "as we feel that you have a distinct contribution to make to the discussion."[31] Carey, the only labor leader invited, attended the conference and declined the offer of transportation and housing expenses as his home and office were in Washington. While we do not know what actually transpired

29. See correspondence CIOST, Box 3/"Mrs. Roosevelt 1949," "Mrs. Roosevelt 1951-52," "Mrs. Roosevelt 1953-55."

30. Acheson to Carey, December 15, 1950, CIOST, Box 46/"State Department Correspondence 1950-1951."

31. Francis Russell, Director, Department of State Office of Public Affairs to Carey, December 22, 1950, CIOST, Box 46/Ibid.

at the conference, the background questions supplied to the participants ahead of time included some apparently thought to be in Carey's field of expertise, such as "Can we outbid the communists in points where their appeal is strongest?" and "How?" and "What are the principle audiences abroad to whom anti-Communist arguments should be addressed?"[32]

During this period, the CIO came to Acheson's defense when conservative Senate Republicans charged that he was "soft on Communism" and that the American people had lost confidence in the Secretary of State.[33] Under Truman and Acheson, the State Department considered the CIO a reliable source of support for its developing foreign policy, but that James Carey, as the secretary-treasurer of the organization and as a labor official especially willing to cooperate, was held in special regard.

As we have mentioned, Carey's difficulties in his own union had the curious result of raising his profile with the foreign policy elite. The IUE president, besides supporting official United States policy abroad, was seen as waging a campaign to eradicate a major source of opposition to that policy—the UE. The State Department may have resisted attempts by CIO officials to gain influence in actual policy making, but members of the foreign policy elite willingly came to the support of the IUE leadership in domestic affairs.

During the winter of 1951, for instance, Eleanor Roosevelt sided with the labor leaders in their dispute with the economic stabilization agencies and Defense Mobilization director Charles E. Wilson. She backed Carey on television and in the press. While she generally confined

32. See Department of State, background questions to be used in connection with Conference on "Content of Materials Exposing Fallacies of Communist Ideology and Setting Forth Aspects of Democratic Way of Life" to be held in the State Department, January 10 and 11, 1951, CIOST, Box 46/ Ibid.

33. "Outline of Support of Secretary of State Acheson," January 2, 1951, CIOST, Box 46/"State Department Correspondence 1950-51."

her criticism to Wilson and the Office of Defense Mobilization, she mentioned Carey's campaign against the "communists" in the electrical industry as proof of his reliability and as one reason why he and the other labor leaders deserved more sympathetic treatment from the war emergency apparatus.[34]

The IUE's annual conventions regularly included speeches by leading foreign policy figures as well as other personalities connected with the war mobilization program or the electrical industry. In 1951, Harriman, certainly aware of labor's criticism of the previous year, came to express his appreciation for the IUE's support and to defend the importance and success of the Marshall Plan. The following year, during the Presidential election campaign, Dean Acheson attended and praised the union because it fought communism the "right way" and compared the IUE's program and "fighting spirit" to American foreign policy: "It isn't enough to be anti-communist. You have to lick them with a positive program of your own.... This in a nutshell is the basic idea of our foreign policy."[35]

By 1952, however, it appeared that when such a program failed, other ways to "lick them" could be attempted. Apparently frustrated at his union's inability to oust the UE from the electrical industry, and especially in the GE chain, Carey undertook a campaign of strident attacks on General Electric for its continued recognition of the UE. His conduct in this effort reveals much not only about his tactics as a labor leader, but also about the nature of his support.

Carey had maintained since the founding of the IUE in 1949 that GE discriminated against his union in its contest with UE. He charged that the company, by refusing to distinguish "between a Communist-led union and a democratic American union" demonstrated its lack of

---

34. Washington Daily News, March 7, 1951, clipping in CIOST, Box 3/"Mrs. Roosevelt 1951-52."

35. CIO News, October 13, 1952, p. 12.

patriotic responsibility.[36] In a sense, Carey's charges were the mirror image of the UE allegations that the company had helped the IUE by withholding checkoff dues payments from the UE during 1949–50. The IUE leader charged that the company should immediately have recognized his union as the bargaining agent since it was the CIO affiliate. However, even rudimentary examination suggests that Carey's charges were for public consumption and that he knew they lacked substance. In many GE plants, the IUE was able to produce no evidence of organized membership, and the company had filed its own NLRB petition covering all its plants as a single unit, thus putting the IUE on the ballot throughout the GE chain. The Carey charge, therefore, that the company, by taking an ostensibly neutral stand between an "American union" that at the time existed largely on paper and a "Communist led" union" that was the certified representative in the company's factories, was failing in its patriotic duty, can hardly be taken seriously.

For its part, GE management publicly claimed to take no interest in what it considered the subtle irrelevancies of union politics, even while its actions promoted division. On September 291, 1949, the company took out a full-page newspaper ad entitled "A Plague on Both Your Houses," which argued that the "left-wingers" and the "right-wingers" had "in the end the same objectives." GE Vice President Lemuel Boulware adhered to this public position after the split when he told a meeting of the National Association of Manufacturers the following March that "no union on a national level is any good."[37] Carey's charge amounted to a complaint that the company should do more than it actually did to help an "American" union in its struggle against Communism.

The IUE president escalated his rhetoric following his union's disappointing showing in Schenectady in

36. James Carey, "Summary Report to GE Conference Board," August 16, 1950, p. 3, CIOST, Box 64/"CIO Unions, Office of the President, May-December1950."

37. Carey, "Summary Report," p. 3, CIOST, Box 64/"CIO Unions."

September 1951. In March 1952, Carey publicly rejected the UE's proposal for a joint wage drive in GE and Westinghouse, charging that the UE had "nothing to offer us or the workers of our industry except weakness, moral corruption, and political perversion."[38] Then, in May, the IUE executive board, on Carey's initiative, demanded a Congressional investigation of General Electric, charging that the company, by continuing to recognize the UE, was "undermining American workers' faith in democratic unionism and making them susceptible to appeals of Communist unionism."[39] The IUE president undoubtedly knew that Minnesota Democrat Hubert Humphrey had already announced his intention as Chairman of the Senate Labor Subcommittee to "investigate Communism" in the labor movement.[40]

The Humphrey Subcommittee partially obliged the IUE leadership during its hearings that spring and summer when it called numerous labor and management representatives, including a delegation of executives and lawyers from GE. As we noted previously, these hearings left a more candid record of the thinking of the various parties than some other Congressional headline grabbing efforts. While their end result may not have differed greatly from the others, the Senator seemed genuinely curious to hear what witnesses had to say. This must, at times, have been uncomfortable for him. Carey's testimony here shows a revealing pattern. While he verbally blasted the General Electric Company for what he claimed was its tolerant attitude toward the "Communist controlled UE," the content of his proposals for dealing with the issue closely paralleled management's position and far exceeded the position of the CIO. The IUE president called for a "tripartite committee" of labor, industry, and government procurement agencies to investigate unions "suspected of being Communist dominated" in

38. NYT, March 4, 1952, p. 10.
39. Ibid., May 24, 1952, p. 12.
40. U.S. News and World Report, December 28, 1951, pp. 20-26.

plants holding defense contracts. The committee would have the authority to deny contracts to employers whose workers belonged to a "Communist dominated" union.[41]

Carey's proposal demonstrated his willingness to break ranks with his allies in the labor movement when he saw the need. He had testified as the president of the IUE-CIO. Four days later, when CIO Executive President Allan Haywood presented the official CIO position, differences with Carey emerged. The CIO had consistently maintained that the Taft-Hartley affidavits were an unnecessary intervention in union affairs and that the labor movement could purge itself of "communist" influence. Haywood argued that the CIO had demonstrated success in this effort and that the affidavits had "accomplished nothing worthwhile to date, and probably will not in the future." He admitted that the CIO's effort to win back workers in the expelled unions had been "arduous and expensive" and had taken much of the CIO's energy over the previous two years. Haywood also had to point out that only his statement represented the CIO position and that the organization had made no proposal similar to Carey's.[42]

It appeared, based on Haywood's testimony, that the Murray leadership of the CIO understood the potential anti-labor character of Carey's proposals. In case they did not, the UE's Fitzgerald wrote to Murray to ensure that the CIO president was "fully acquainted with the extremely dangerous proposal for government control of unions" that Carey had put forward. Fitzgerald observed that the "tripartite board" would be stacked against labor, since "the procurement agencies are notorious agents of big business," and were "currently under attack by the Amalgamated Clothing Workers of America-CIO and the

41. U.S. Senate, Subcommittee of the Committee on Labor and Public Welfare, Communist Domination of Unions and National Security, 1952, pp. 239 ff.; see also CIO News, June 23, 1952, p. 12.

42. See U.S. Senate, Communist Domination of Unions and National Security, 1952, pp. 263 ff. for Haywood's testimony.

Textile Workers-CIO for their anti-labor bias in procurement practices."[43]

While Carey's testimony threatened to embarrass the organization of which he was the secretary-treasurer, it would over the next four years help to maintain his own tenuous position in the labor movement. While the Humphrey subcommittee's recommendations, issued in early 1953, did not entirely adopt Carey's proposal, they did show the influence of his testimony. The report denounced employers who attempted to "exploit rivalry" between "Communist" and "non-Communist" unions. In an apparent contradiction, the report denied that it was suggesting that an employer should favor one union over another, but then singled out GE for its "plague on both your houses" attitude and called for a special Justice Department body to deal with reported violations of the Taft-Hartley "non-Communist" requirement.[44]

Despite its criticism of the company, the subcommittee's conclusions also reflected the testimony of GE vice president Lemuel Boulware. He had argued that it was not the private sector's job to weed out Communists in unions and had recommended that Congress create an independent agency to impose penalties on unions designated as "Communist-run." Boulware, responding to the Carey charges of aiding the UE, argued that the CIO was a newcomer to the anti-Communist campaign: "We were making our position clear long before some of those currently most vocal in their anti-Communist professions had ceased to harbor, defend, and associate with those people they now denounce as Communists." While the two had traded barbs, Boulware and Carey had presented similar proposals. Carey had carefully avoided calling for legislation, as Boulware had, as this would openly have contradicted the CIO position. Nevertheless, both had called for government investigation

43. Fitzgerald to Murray, July 18, 1952, IUE Carey Papers, A2.06/"UE 1952 I."

44. See CIO News, February 16, 1953, p. 9 for a summary of the subcommittee report.

of trade unions. The Humphrey hearings were not the only impetus for the increasing pressure on the "left led" unions in the next Congress, but the subcommittee's calls for closing of the Taft-Hartley "loopholes" helped pave the way for passage of the "Communist Control" Act the following year.[45]

Carey, in the meantime, continued to escalate his bid for outside support in his struggle with the UE. In October, barely a month before the Presidential election, the IUE president abruptly announced his resignation from the Public Advisory Board of the Mutual Security Administration to protest the continued awarding of defense contracts to General Electric, branding the company a security risk due to its continued recognition of the UE. Carey's immediate motivation could have been to put further pressure on the company, which was then aggravating already difficult negotiations by attempting to exploit the division between the two unions. In any case, such a sudden and dramatic move was hardly out of character for Carey.

Significantly, Carey appealed to the foreign policy question and evoked a response. In his wire to Harriman, he alleged that his union's "bitter struggle with the General Electric Company" was "not unlike the kind of struggle the MSA is concerned about in other parts of the world." The company had "entered into collusive arrangements with the Communist controlled" UE as part of its campaign of "vilification and deceit against the IUE-CIO." Calling the "contradiction in policy... intolerable to me," Carey charged that while "the MSA is committed to promoting free democratic trade unionism abroad and building up defenses against the Communist threat... in this country our government is closing its eyes to the fact that assignment of a vast amount of important, even secret, defense work goes to a company

45. For Boulware's testimony, see U.S. Senate, Communist Domination of Unions and National Security, 1952, pp. 391 ff. The NYT summarized his testimony July 9, 1952, p. 36.

which, in a cynical deal with a Communist controlled union, is seeking to destroy effective trade unionism in this country."[46]

Harriman's immediate reply indicated the weight that the foreign policy establishment attached to its relationship with the president of the IUE. While discreetly avoiding any direct comment on Carey's allegations, Harriman urged him to reconsider his decision to resign and cited the long, close working relationship the two had enjoyed since 1947. Harriman recalled Carey's support of the Marshall Plan, his participation on the MSA Public Advisory Board, and noted that "your consistent advice and support of our major foreign programs during these last five years have been invaluable."[47]

The Republican victory in November 1952 and Harriman's subsequent departure from the MSA the following January interrupted the connection between the labor leadership and the foreign policy apparatus. Although links were soon re-established, the relationship would never be as close as that under Truman and Acheson. The new environment forced the CIO leaders to take stock of their own situation and eventually to look more seriously at merger with the AFL.

During the first seven months of 1953, the MSA did not meet, but Congressional attention to GE's labor relations intensified. Two separate committees, the House Committee on Un-American Activities and the Senate Appropriations Subcommittee chaired by Joseph McCarthy, announced investigations during the second half of the year, and others prepared legislation to close the Taft-Hartley "loopholes."

In August, the direct labor foreign policy link was reactivated when the Mutual Security Administration was

---

46. Carey to Harriman, October 2, 1952, IUE Papers, A1.07/"UE October 1952."

47. Harriman to Carey, October 2, 1952, Ibid. Carey resigned simultaneously from two other government boards in protest: the Atomic Energy Plant Expansion Advisory Board and the President's Committee on Government Contract Compliance.

combined with three other agencies in the Foreign Operations Administration (FOA) and director Harold Stassen appointed a Labor Advisory Committee. This committee's composition and its relationship to the State Department suggested that, despite persisting differences of opinion and approach, labor leaders and the Eisenhower Administration desired an accommodation. The committee included CIO representatives Reuther, Carey, Jacob Potofsky of the Amalgamated Clothing Workers, and David McDonald of the Steelworkers. Also agreeing to participate were AFL president Meany, first vice president Matthew Woll, Ladies' Garment Workers president David Dubinsky, AFL international representative George Delaney, and two officers from the independent railroad brotherhoods, A.E. Lyon and N.E. Gilbert. While the labor representation on the committee was, therefore, considerable, the CIO representatives, especially Reuther and Carey, appear to have attended the most regularly.[48]

The FOA lasted two years and had minimal impact on United States foreign policy. However, the record of its Labor Committee suggests the determination of the most active labor leaders to find a role in the execution of the nation's policy abroad. It also suggests that the coming of the Cold War "consensus" in the mid-1950s did not solve the dilemma of the IUE's embattled president. The labor representatives did not hide their reluctance to associate officially with the Dulles State Department. When the Administration, in the spring of 1955, moved to bring the FOA directly into the Department, the labor leaders objected and argued for maintaining it as a separate agency.[49] The CIO representatives, in particular, frequently expressed dissatisfaction in the Committee with the State Department's outlook on a number of issues. Still sensitive regarding their treatment by professional diplomats, the CIO leaders contended that the Department ignored

48. "Summary Minutes" of Labor Committee meetings, January 25, 1955 and April 13, 1955, CIOST, Box 131/"FOA Labor Committee Memoranda."

49. Ibid., January 25, p. 2, April 13, p. 10.

their recommendations for personnel appointments to foreign service or labor advisory posts and had denied security clearance to a number of CIO nominees.[50]

The CIO leaders' frustration with the Administration involved more substantial issues as well. The organization had previously argued for increased economic aid to the nation's Western European allies and to developing nations, but when Stassen and the State Department urged liberalization of trade with Eastern Europe, the CIO was ambivalent. Its leaders were reluctant to alter their past position that the United States should lower its own trade barriers with Western Europe rather than encourage a renewal of the traditional trade patterns between the West and what had become, in the CIO view, the "iron curtain" countries of Eastern Europe.[51]

Whatever differences the CIO and the AFL had with the Republican Administration, and despite their reluctance to associate officially with John Foster Dulles, they never wavered from their commitment to participate in the world struggle against "Communist aggression." Indeed by 1955, it was becoming clear that the AFL-CIO merger would occur on a basis of participation in this Cold War "consensus," and the AFL and CIO leaders accepted the phasing out of the FOA as an independent agency by June of 1955.[52]

The approaching labor merger and the reaching of apparent national consensus on foreign policy masked disagreement in the ranks of labor and especially in electrical unionism. This meant problems for the IUE Carey leadership. Carey's standing in labor had depended in large part on his support from a Democratic administration and his relationship with the party's representatives

50. Reuther to Eisenhower, January 18, 1955; memo, "The Case of Svend Godfredsen, Val Bunati, and Alan Strachan," dated January 24, 1955, CIOST, Box 131/"FOA 1954-1955."

51. Confidential memo on East West Trade for CIO members of FOA Labor Advisory Committee, May 28, 1955, Ibid.

52. See Floyd Springer, Labor Committee Secretary, to Carey, June 23, 1955; June 30, 1955; also Labor Committee members to Springer expressing appreciation to Springer for his work with the Committee, August 1, 1955, Ibid.

in the foreign policy establishment. The IUE's patrons were out of power in Washington by 1955. Carey's position in labor now depended on his own ability to bring electrical workers together under his leadership. We will examine his attempts to do so in chapter V.

The position of the IUE leadership reflected in part that of leaders of other CIO unions. They also had to secure their positions as merger approached; the "arduous and expensive" campaign against the expelled unions had weakened the CIO. On the other hand, the AFL had, in part, adopted the CIO method of organizing on an industrial basis and had grown. While fears surfaced that the merger would amount to an AFL takeover, Carey found his position the most insecure because the electrical industry had seen the most determined resistance to the Cold War drive.

In summary, the leaders of the CIO had clung consistently to their foreign policy positions during the period of this chapter. They argued that the Cold War policy was justified and the State Department's view of the world accurate, but that the policy was flawed by failure to consider labor's views. The CIO took seriously the idea that it had a special role to play in winning the Cold War, and its leaders and foreign policy representatives became frustrated when official policy makers valued their support but not their input.

It remained for the labor "left" and the UE in particular to challenge the basis of the Cold War policy itself. The UE, like the CIO, would face hard decisions during the coming period, but its leaders and activists felt vindicated by the foreign policy developments of the early and mid-1950s. The criticism of the European Recovery Program by its own labor supporters and the disillusionment in the nation with the Korean War gave credibility to the UE positions. The UE argued that the frustration encountered by the CIO leaders in dealing with the foreign policy establishment inevitably resulted from the nature of the policy rather than from the policy's flawed execution. The CIO's foreign policy stance required a degree of cooperation with the representatives of the big business community that labor would not otherwise have contemplated. The resulting frustration on domestic issues could hardly be considered surprising.

The changes occurring by 1955 did not cause the UE leaders to abandon their positions. On the contrary, they reasoned that developments in the labor movement made the UE's voice as important as ever. An editorial in a small Pennsylvania newspaper which the *UE News* had reprinted in 1951 still seemed essentially valid. This editorial argued that the labor movement had "sacrificed almost all its objectives" on domestic issues because its leaders had refused to see that "these could be attained only if a larger objective, peace, was attained...." The editorial had continued, "No group in the U.S. is better situated to lead a constructive struggle for peace than the working people.... How much brighter the future of the world would seem if officials of labor unions in this country had so conducted themselves these past few years that they were ready to accept this leadership."[53]

The bruising arguments over responsibility for the Korean War and the aims of U.S. foreign policy during the early 1950s as well as the domestic hunt for potential domestic "security risks" exposed the largely theatrical nature of the "in house" debate. The party of Taft and McCarthy had become the party of Eisenhower and Dulles. The Republican isolationist wing found itself isolated as the party accepted the concept of global involvement in the "struggle" with "world communism." On the other hand, the party that had championed such involvement found itself simultaneously red-baited and saddled with responsibility for a distant war against the "reds" that had failed to gain broad public approval or support. The realignments of the mid-fifties, then, presented both possibilities and problems for the electrical unions. How they dealt with these will be addressed in the next two chapters.

---

53. York, Pennsylvania, Gazette and Daily editorial, reprinted in UE News, February 26, 1951.

CIO secretary-treasurer James Carey, center, with Soviet delegates at the London conference to organize a new international trade union federation, February 1945. At right is Vasily Kuznetsov, head of the All Union Central Council of Trade Unions. *UE Archives, University of Pittsburgh*

UE president Albert Fitzgerald, second from left with Hubert Humphrey, CIO-endorsed candidate for mayor of Minneapolis and other UE and CIO officials, probably fall 1945. The occasion is the gathering of hundreds of Minnesota CIO activists who came to hear Fitzgerald's report on the founding conference of the World Federation of Trade Unions (WFTU) in Paris in September. *UE Archives*

Seated L to R: Julius Emspak, James Matles, Russ Nixon n.d. (probably 1945). *UE Archives*

L to R: Emspak, Matles, Fitzgerald testifying against legislation soon to become the Taft-Hartley Act, probably March 1947. *UE Archives*

Local 155 business agent David Davis, n.d. *UE Archives*

Carey, right, stepping down after testifying before Congressman Kersten's subcommittee, September 1948; Fitzgerald, left, going up to offer opposing testimony. The back at far left is that of CIO Counsel Arthur Goldberg. The following week the hearings moved from Washington, DC to Schenectady. *UE Archives*

UE leaders, including defendants and supporters, following arraignment in U.S. District Court for contempt of Congress. Front row from L: Attorney David Scribner, James McLeish District 4, defendant Thomas Quinn District 6, Ernest DeMaio District 11, UE director of organization and defendant James Matles, John Gojack District 9, UE secretary-treasurer and defendant Julius Emspak. Back row at L: defendants Esther Tice and Thomas Fitzpatrick. *UE Archives*

The cover of the report on the UE national women's conference, 1953. *UE Archives*

Lula Stone, center, member of District 4 executive board and chair of Local 475 Fair Practices Committee before the district switched to the IUE, at the union's 1953 national women's conference. *UE Archives*

AFL-CIO merger convention: James Carey at left with George Meany, Eleanor Roosevelt, and Walter Reuther at the AFL-CIO founding convention, December 1955. *James Carey Papers, Special Collections and University Archives, Rutgers University Libraries; on line at www.gwu.edu/~erpapers/workers/workerpics/AFL-CIOmerger.html*

During the 1955-56 nationwide strike against Westinghouse, auto workers join the picket line in support of UE Local 107, Essington, Pennsylvania, February 1956. *UE Archives*

William Burch, District 11, at the UE 1967 convention. *UE Archives*

Thomas Quinn, Local 610, speaks at the National Labor Leadership Assembly for Peace, November 1967. *UE Archives*

District 1 field organizer James Hart, 1966. *UE News photo, courtesy Ellen Hart*

Chapter 5

The Schenectady Switch, 1953–1954

While the prospects for unity among electrical workers by late 1953 were decidedly mixed, the UE had sound reason to believe that it could survive as a major force in the industry and as a force on the national labor scene. It had survived four trying years in a hostile environment, had maintained its size since the split in 1950, and had continued its attempts to find a basis for reunifying the workers. It could claim to have been justified in its opposition to the Marshall Plan and its calls for peace in Korea.

At the same time, electrical workers were not alone in facing uncertainty. As layoffs in key manufacturing industries increased during the months following the truce in Korea, labor leaders voiced fears for the nation's future.[1] The question of whether the country could be simultaneously free of both war and depression reappeared to haunt employers and the Eisenhower Administration, as well as labor leaders and their members. In these conditions, the continuing strength of the UE, a large union in a basic industry that opposed large military expenditures and Administration foreign policy, presented a serious obstacle to the reaching of a national "consensus" in support of the Cold War. Under these circumstances, the UE would continue to face daunting

1. CIO News, January 11, 1954, editorial p. 4; UE News, February 8, 1954, p. 5; May 3, 1954, p. 5; UE Policy 1953-54, resolution on "Peace and Jobs," pp. 32-34, UE Archives PC 76.

pressure from several quarters during the pivotal middle years of the 1950s decade.

During the mid-1950s the UE's position eroded, but did not completely disintegrate. Both facts need to be remembered, because it soon appeared that the union's influence extended beyond its actual membership. How and why this change occurred is the subject of the next two chapters. The argument of the union's conservative and establishment opponents was that the membership, eager to return to the fold of "loyal American" trade unionism, deserted the leaders and "escaped" at the first opportunity. While this notion has been exposed as a gross oversimplification and generally wrong,[2] developments in electrical unionism during this period need more analysis. The next two chapters will argue that rank-and-file disagreement with the UE program was not the primary reason the union lost members during this period. In fact, members and local and district leaders frequently left the union in spite of agreement with the UE program. Outside pressures and attacks on the union generated by the Cold War intensified during late 1953 and early 1954. By 1955-1956, when the union's leaders felt that they had held their ground through the most trying times and were now poised to reassert their influence, the merger of the AFL and CIO on a Cold War basis added an additional dilemma for the UE and for workers in the industry.

This chapter will focus on the UE's largest local, Schenectady General Electric Local 301, where the union had won the widely publicized election victory over the IUE in 1951. In this local, a popular leadership, previously identified with the left in the labor movement, made an apparently tortured decision to leave the union and join the IUE in 1954. The switch resulted from intense outside pressures from government, employer, and the

2. See Filippelli and McColloch, Cold War in the Working Class, pp. 147-151, especially p. 151, "Neither red-baiting nor threats of job loss were generally enough to swing the vote to the IUE, so long as the officers stayed loyal." The Schenectady case demonstrates that point.

Catholic Church on the local's leaders and members. But, we are getting ahead of our story.

During the Korean War period, the UE's adversaries became increasingly frustrated with the union's persistent displays of staying power. The UE's strength forced a revision of the standard line that the organization consisted of a "loyal American" rank-and-file held prisoner by disloyal, manipulative leaders. In fact, Senator Joseph McCarthy had included the membership in his attacks as early as September 1950 when, following the union's convention, he charged that "when 200 to 250 thousand members continue to support the Matles-Emspak Communist machine in the UE, it is time to take another look at the alleged 'solid Americanism' of the rank-and-file."[3]

The continuing membership support for the UE during the early 1950s had resulted in new calls and proposals for tightening the legal restrictions on labor unions. If the existing laws failed to remove union organizations from "Communist" influence, the opponents of "left wing" unionism reasoned, then fault must lie in the law, which simply needed strengthening. The Taft-Hartley provision requiring union leaders and officials to sign non-Communist affidavits soon became a primary target of criticism. Critics noted that the signing of the affidavits had not altered the actions, or apparently the thinking, of the leaders of several of the unions expelled by the CIO.

In November 1952, a New York grand jury urged the National Labor Relations Board (NLRB) to decertify four independent unions, including the UE, charging that their continued existence constituted "a menace to national security."[4] The unions successfully resisted the move by going to court themselves, and in January 1953, they won a permanent injunction barring

---

3. Washington Evening Star, September 28, 1950, p. A22, clipping in IUE Papers, A2.05/"Communism and Right-Left Split 1941-1949."

4. NYT, November 26, 1952, clipping in IUE Papers, A2.06/"UE 1952 I"; Business Week, December 6, 1952, p. 153.

the NLRB from inquiring into the truth or falsity of the Taft-Hartley affidavits.[5]

Efforts to plug the legal loopholes soon surfaced in Congress. Legislation introduced by Senators Barry Goldwater of Arizona and John M. Butler of Maryland aimed at removing the perceived defects in existing laws, primarily the Taft-Hartley Act of 1947 and the Subversive Activities Control Act of 1950. The Butler Bill, first introduced in April of 1953, especially appealed to the forces most concerned with the seemingly intractable problem of workers choosing unacceptable leaders. This bill sought to deny NLRB certification to any union found to be "Communist dominated" by the Subversive Activities Control Board (SACB). The UE's opponents found this legislation attractive because it would not require proof that union officials actually belonged to the Communist Party. The SACB, which had been established by the act of 1950, would simply have to demonstrate that union leaders followed the "party line."[6]

By the spring and summer of 1953, legislative concern with the "loyalty" of American workers and their organizations had become so widespread that it is difficult to keep track of the investigations in progress. While William Jenner of Indiana announced that his Senate Internal Security Subcommittee would schedule hearings on the Butler Bill, the Senate Committee on Labor and Public Welfare had already started to work. Attempting to deal directly with the relationship of the electrical manufacturing industry to military production, the committee heard testimony from Westinghouse vice president Robert Blasier during the first week in April. Both his company and General Electric had taken criticism for continuing to recognize and negotiate with the UE, and Blasier took this opportunity to go on the

5. NYT, January 28, 1953; Washington Evening Star, January 28, 1953, both in IUE Papers, A2.06/"UE 1953 I."

6. NYT, June 27, 1953, Ibid.; for more about the 1950 legislation and its perceived weaknesses, see Report of the Subcommittee of the Senate Judiciary Committee, IUE Papers, Box 33 FF 5.

offensive. Citing the UE's five-month strike at the company's Nuttall gear plant in Western Pennsylvania the previous summer, he claimed that the union had disrupted work on jet engine parts and other vital defense work. The UE had argued that the Nuttall workers had struck against rate cuts and had postponed the strike several times at the urging of the national officers.[7] Nevertheless, Blasier obliged the Committee when he proposed that unions that refused to oust "Communist leaders" should be "outlawed."[8]

International events during the summer of 1953 probably intensified the concerns of the foreign policy establishment and the UE's opponents in Congress. Although the two sides in the Korean War reached a truce, the Cold War seemed to come closer to home with the renewal of widespread trade union militancy in Europe. In August, a near general strike involving three million workers occurred against the French Government's wage policy, a policy that was tied to continuing American aid to France. A notable feature of the strike was the expressed unity between the Socialist and Catholic-led unions on the one hand and the Communist-led unions on the other. French labor leaders stated that "the present movement was unmatched in the history of French labor because of its extensiveness and unanimity of feeling."[9] As Administration foreign policy had aimed to split the European labor movements since the late 1940s, the developments in France in August 1953 must doubtless caused policy makers concern.

Besides the setbacks regarding the French labor movement, the new Eisenhower Administration's policy toward Europe faced other problems. The reluctance of the French cabinet to accept the proposals of Secretary of State Dulles for the European Defense Community and

---

7. U.S. Senate, Committee on Labor and Public Welfare, Communist Domination of Unions and National Security, 1952, p. 492.

8. Pittsburgh Press, April 8, 1953, clipping in IUE Papers, A2.06/"UE 1953 I."

9. NYT, August 12, 1953, p. 12.

specifically for the rearmament of West Germany made headlines in December.[10] The tension between Dulles and the French government indicated the lukewarm support for Washington's Cold War policies in Europe. This situation, along with the uncertain future of the domestic economy, probably helped to focus attention on the "left led" union in the United States as potential obstacles to the consolidation of the nation behind the Cold War.[11]

By early 1954, in any case, the pressure had clearly increased on the UE as the largest of the unions expelled from the CIO. The union's convincing victory in the NLRB election at the Westinghouse Lester, Pennsylvania plant in mid-January demonstrated indicated the inaccuracy of predictions of the Use's early demise. However, the month of March brought a dramatic setback. The sudden defection of the union's largest local, GE Schenectady 301, to the IUE underscored the UE's increasingly difficult position. The Schenectady local's move certainly appeared to tip the balance in the ongoing rivalry in favor of the IUE. However, the manner in which it occurred reveals much about the forces aligned against the UE as well as the difficult choices workers had to make in the mid-1950s. A brief look at the background of the local will be helpful.

The Schenectady local's history and character reflected, in a sense, those of the larger union. During most of the local's early years and during World War II, the left-wing character of the leadership actually placed Schenectady 301 in the mainstream of the movement for American industrial unionism. The local's publication, the *301 Electrical Union News,* printed editorials with titles such as "The Union Way is the American Way" and commented favorably on a statement by the Catholic Bishops that "wages take precedence over profits."

---

10. Ibid., December 16, 1953.

11. In 1953, Dulles attended the conventions of both the AFL and CIO. See correspondence in John Foster Dulles Papers, Box 72/"Meany George 1953," and Box 74/"Reuther, Walter P. 1953."

In 1940, the paper projected the idea that the employers were the ones "with-holding [the] abundance" of the United States from the nation's working people.[12]

During World War II, when the CIO unions all supported the no-strike pledge, the *EU News* continued to argue that the working people were the most loyal Americans. In March of 1942, the local's paper responded to an editorial in the New York *World Telegram* that had implied that workers' insistence on "thinking in terms of less work for more money" was preventing the nation from achieving its full war production potential. The *301 News* charged that, on the contrary, American industrialists were on a "sit-down strike," had failed to put sufficient capital into new plants and were "geared to depression level" production. The paper noted that a special conference of the union's District 3, which included Schenectady, had called for expanded production, urging plants to operate full time with three full shifts, or even four six-hour shifts seven days a week where possible.[13]

After the war, the local continued to show the same qualities. Not only did the leaders continue actively to support the program of the UE nationally, but they also appeared to enjoy widespread support from the membership. The life of the local included not only regular attention to trade union and political matters but also social activities including union members and their families as well. The *301 News* frequently printed pictures of groups such as the 301 women's basketball team and parties at the union hall sponsored by one or another of the union committees in the plant's numerous buildings and departments. Chief Steward William Mastriani missed a day of work, the *News* chuckled, after he suffered an accidental injury while refereeing a wrestling match at the local's annual field day in July 1948.[14]

---

12. Local 301 Electrical Union News, March 27, 1940, pp. 2-3, UE Archives, D/3-236.

13. Ibid., March 24, 1942, pp. 1,4, UE Archives, D/3-2236.

14. Ibid., July 16, 1948, p. 4, UE Archives, D/3-239.

The evident support enjoyed by the leadership of the local during the early Cold War years attracted the attention of Congressional investigators from 1948 onwards. Local 301 first became a target during September of that year when the Atomic Energy Commission instructed GE not to recognize the UE as bargaining agent for the workers at the company's Knolls Atomic Power Laboratory near Schenectady. While the number of workers seemed small compared to the 15,000-member local, the issues in the case were ominous for the UE. The Commission based its action "upon the information available... of alleged Communist affiliation or association of various officers of UE," and stated that its instructions were merely "a first step in improving the situation at Schenectady."[15]

On the heels of the AEC decision came another problem. A subcommittee of the House Committee on Un-American Activities called the UE's national leaders to Washington and, a week later, traveled to Schenectady and called in leaders—and members—of the UE's largest local. This first instance of outside pressure had little immediate effect on the political or leadership situation in local 301. The subcommittee received no cooperation from most of the witnesses, and the audience, sympathizing with the witnesses, repeatedly interrupted the proceedings. The chairman, Charles Kersten of Wisconsin, attempted to target the clause in the UE constitution that opened the union to all workers without regard to political belief. Before hearing witnesses' testimony, we should consider the basis for the subcommittee's line of questioning.

Kersten introduced a "friendly witness," Salvatore Vottis, who had served as treasurer of the local during the 1930s and early 1940s and allegedly been a member of a Communist Party "fraction" in the Schenectady plant. Vottis's testimony is difficult to assess, wavering as it did

---

15. Saturday Evening Post, October 18, 1952, p. 20; AEC Chairman David Lilienthal to Fitzgerald, October 6, 1948, UE Archives, D/1-751.

between apparently credible statements, unclear memories, and one charge that appeared fantastic, about which more will be said below. Even if taken totally at face value, however, his testimony was, with that one exception, notable for its lack of damaging evidence. He claimed, for example, that during the mid and late 1930s, there had been "about 15" active Communists in the Schenectady works, and that they had included some of the leaders of the local. He alleged that longtime business agent Leo Jandreau and been in the party "for a period of about two or three years" despite the fact that "he had had some trouble at home" due to the disapproval of his wife. According to Vottis, the Emspak brothers, Frank and Julius, and James Matles had also been part of the group.[16]

This witness drew a picture of an active, but hardly dominant or controlling group. He claimed that, although he had left the party in 1939 "due to disagreements on foreign policies," he had remained friendly for the next five years. During that time, he told the subcommittee, "There was a tacit agreement between the party and myself that we were to fight all questions on the basis of merit.... In other words, if a proposal was made, I was free to fight the thing on the basis of whether I thought it was good for the union or not."[17]

Vottis testified that the group supported non-Communist union or political leaders on the same basis, the merit of their positions. He claimed, for instance, that Jandreau "was considered a good officer in the union...

16. U.S. House of Representatives, Committee on Education and Labor, Communist Infiltration of UERMWA, 1948, pp. 201-203. The influence of Jandreau's personal life on his union activity is a matter of speculation. It became an issue during the 1950s after he had remarried. His second wife was Ruth The Young, who had previously been a left-wing activist and officer in the union's District 4. Jandreau, a Catholic, was thus attacked, not only for marrying a second time, but also for marrying a Communist as well. At least one source felt that the pressure from the Church on Jandreau to leave the UE increased after his marriage to Ruth. Harry Block thought that he "saw the hand of the Catholic Church" attempting to influence the Schenectady local during the early 1950s. Block interview, March 17, 1987.

17. U.S. House, Communist Infiltration of UE, p. 203.

even at the time he was not a member of the party." At one point, Vottis caught Kersten off-guard by stating that, in 1942, at the initiative of the party, the regional CIO council had endorsed Republican Bernard Kearney for Congress. He produced a letter of appreciation, which Kearney had written after his election, thanking the council for its support. The letter, addressed to Vottis, said, "Especially in Schenectady did the vote show the results of this endorsement."[18]

The one charge Vottis made that, if true, would have provided hard evidence of dishonest trade unionism was that the UE activists had, in 1936, forged 3,000 union cards in order to force a labor board election and win union recognition. This charge was vigorously disputed by at least one credible source. The election had pitted the UE against the company-sponsored "Works Council." Local 301 vice president William Hodges challenged Vottis's claim, arguing that it was widely known that supporters of the Council at the time, including Hodges himself, had personally satisfied themselves that the election "was perfectly all right."[19] In any case, even if we assume the worst and that the charge were true, the UE would still have had to win the NLRB supervised election.

Other witnesses were vocal, but not on the subject that interested the Congressmen: the politics of leaders of local 301. When Kersten asked the local's recording secretary, Helen Quirini, for instance, what type of work women did in the plant, she answered:

> They do all kinds of work.... A lot of women are doing men's jobs, and we have to fight like hell to give them men's wages, and we are terrifically battling down there to give them an equal break.

Kersten, however, showed more interest in whether witnesses believed that the local should be able to bar

18. Ibid., pp. 204, 211-212.
19. Ibid., p. 283.

Communists from holding office. When Quirini answered that the party was legal and on the ballot in New York State, Kersten tried again.

Mr. Kersten: That is what I say. There is no law presently making it a crime to belong to this worldwide party here—this worldwide conspiracy. There is no law against it as yet. So I am just wondering why you stand on the Constitutional ground that it might tend to incriminate you.

Miss Quirini: I didn't say that, Mr. Kersten.

Mr. Kersten: I may have misunderstood you.

Miss Quirini: Don't forget this. When you became a Congressman, you took an oath to uphold the Constitution. When I became an officer, I took an oath to uphold our constitution, and I will not co-operate with violating your oath or my oath....

Mr. Kersten: Do you share the view that to expose communists in local 301 would result in the union being busted?

Miss Quirini: I believe very strongly in our Constitution; because you are starting with Communism, tomorrow it will be married women; next day, Jews; next day, Negroes; next day, Italians; next day, Poles....[20]

Another witness, Albert Lenta, a machine repairman and former steward in the control division refused to answer the Congressman's question whether he was a Communist Party member.

Mr. Kersten: In other words, you refuse to answer that on Constitutional grounds.

Mr. Lenta: On Constitutional grounds; that is right. I like my Constitution.... I answered the one. The inner thoughts I answer to Jehovah God....

Mr. Kersten: Should the Communist Party use the Constitution to set up Communism in this country?

Mr. Lenta:... Why this bogy about Communism? I am not afraid of the Communists taking over. And if they fail in

20. Ibid., pp. 261, 263, 265.

> the trade union—if they are crooked, we fire them out. The rank-and-file will fire them out. They don't have to stay in there. If they don't do a job, we kick them out.[21]

Lenta's testimony was as close as any witness came to addressing the concerns of the subcommittee. Frank Emspak, a past president of local 301, denied knowing anything about the party and called Vottis a liar. Jandreau referred to Vottis as a "degraded rat around this community."[22] The president at the time, Andrew Peterson, was no more helpful.

> Mr. Kersten:...How can you say that your members have no right to inquire, for example, as to whether you are a member of this Communist Party?
>
> Mr. Peterson: Well, my members have a right to inquire.... I don't think anyone else has a right to inquire.... I don't think my members are inquiring. You are the only one that is inquiring.
>
> Mr. Kersten: We are trying to find out how many members of the Communist Party are in this union....
>
> Mr. Peterson: You are in Schenectady to bust up this union and you know that.
>
> Mr. Kersten: We are in Schenectady to try to help the members bust up the Communist hold on 301....
>
> Mr. Peterson: I suppose you are for organized labor.
>
> Mr. Kersten: Definitely.
>
> Mr. Peterson: Your record in Congress doesn't show that. You voted for the Taft-Hartley Law. You voted for the Mundt Bill. You voted against housing.[23]

The testimony of Peterson and Hodges carried weight beyond the content of their remarks. They demonstrated a crucial characteristic of the local leadership. This consisted of a coalition of the left and the center in terms of

---

21. Ibid., p. 297.
22. Ibid., pp. 269, 291, 293.
23. Ibid., pp. 258-259.

the politics of the labor movement. The leading activists in the local prominently included people identified with the left: Jandreau, Quirini, Mastriani, William Kelly, James Cognetta, and Joseph Saccocio. They had been joined by forces who were originally skeptical of the CIO and of industrial unionism, but who had joined the UE after it had won bargaining rights, become active in the local, and could now be counted on to defend the union against outside interference. Hodges and Peterson were two of these.

While this first Congressional incursion had little immediate impact in the local, it proved only the first of a series of events that influenced it from outside. During the first IUE campaign in 1949-50, the newly elected president of 301, Frank Kriss, broke with the executive board and the shop stewards and invited James Carey to speak at a meeting of the local at a nearby high school. The local executive board refused to endorse the meeting, charging that Kriss had called it and secured the meeting hall—obviously intended for a large crowd—on his own without the proper authority.[24] The UE won the labor election in the spring of 1950, and when the IUE petitioned for a second election in September 1951, the UE won more convincingly in the election discussed in chapter III.

The UE's continuing dominance in Schenectady had, therefore, frustrated the union's opponents for the better part of a decade. Especially since the widely publicized 1951 election, the local's leaders had been under pressure to prove their patriotism. Within a week after the 1951 vote, Secretary of Labor Maurice Tobin had told the IUE national convention that he felt "profound disappointment... that the Schenectady plant is still in the hands of a union with Un-American leadership," and offered to appear personally in Schenectady as he had done at Lynn.[25]

---

24. Electrical Union News, September 9, 1949, p. 1, UE Archives, D/3-240.

25. Pittsburgh Press, September 21, 1951; Schenectady Union Star, September 21, 1951; clippings in UE pamphlet, The Schenectady Story, p. s41, IUE Papers, Box 31 FF 5.

The following year saw the appearance of the influential article "Red Pipeline Into Our Defense Plants" in the *Saturday Evening Post.* The article highlighted the Schenectady local, and a picture of 301 business agent Jandreau before the House subcommittee appeared next to the headline. A cursory glance at this article would certainly have reinforced the impression created by Congressional committees, by the IUE's Carey and other UE opponents: UE leaders were dictatorial union bosses and probably traitors to their country as well.

However, a close reading of the entire article revealed a different picture. The author noted Jandreau's claim that the leadership dealt with every grievance, no matter how insignificant it seemed. He seemed surprised and confounded by the level of rank-and-file support enjoyed by the 301 leaders. Large numbers of Schenectady workers appeared to regard the "Communist" issue as insignificant or a diversion. One self-described Catholic worker told him, "The more the Church and the press are against our union, the more we're for it." In short, the article concluded, to get the UE out of Schenectady, the government would have to intervene, because it could not be "blasted out" by a rival union.[26]

During the second half of 1953, with legislation such as the Butler Bill pending, the pressure on UE local 301 intensified. In mid-July, HUAC chairman Velde announced that a subcommittee would again hold a hearing in upstate New York to determine "the extent of Communist influence" in defense industries in the area. The chairman stated that the GE Schenectady situation would receive special attention, and that Congressman Kearney, whose district included the city, would chair the three-member panel.[27]

---

26. Saturday Evening Post, October 18, 1952, pp. 19-20, 110 ff. The tone of the Post article by Lester Velie was less strident than that of an article by Congressman Kersten in Reader's Digest, January 27, 1953, pp. 27-31, entitled "We Are Protecting Spies in Defense Plants," which argued that Matles and Emspak controlled the union with an "iron fist."

27. AP Ticker printout, n.d. in IUE Papers, A2.06/"UE 1953 I."

The fall brought further signs that government and company officials were accelerating the drive to alter the labor situation at the General Electric Company's home plant. The remarks of GE president Ralph Cordiner at the company's 75th anniversary dinner in Schenectady in October indicated the corporation's desire to free itself of the UE's brand of trade unionism. Cordiner touched on issues of great interest to the labor movement, but his words held little encouragement for workers. The company could not provide a guaranteed annual wage to workers in "our free competitive economy where each of us is at risk." He appeared to send a double message when he predicted new growth and investment in research and manufacturing due to the expected large increases in demand for electrical machinery but at the same time warned of cutbacks in the workforce in the post-Korean War period.[28]

Cordiner had provided barely a hint of what was to come, however. In November, Senator Joseph McCarthy brought his subcommittee to Schenectady and called GE workers to testify at a closed hearing with plant manager A.C. Stevens and other company personnel attending. The *301 Electrical Union News* blasted the hearings and the company's cooperation in them, and the paper published statements by six of the workers who had been called to testify. While the tone of their statements indicated that witnesses had not cooperated with the investigation, the proceedings clearly increased the pressure on the union and its members. GE's Stevens provided reinforcement after the two-day hearings, predicting that they would "prove helpful in solving this problem with which we have been so long concerned."[29]

The closed nature of the hearings and the reports of witnesses added to the atmosphere of intimidation. Chief Steward Mastriani related that McCarthy had told

---

28. NYT, October 7, 1953, p. 46.

29. Electrical Union News, November 20, 1953, p. 4, UE Archives, General Electric Conference Board 865.

him, "I hate you from the pit of my stomach. I'm going to send you up." Harold Rollins, shop steward on the third shift in Building 19, described his session in the following terms:

> It was a stacked deck. They bring you in like a criminal with about 25 people sitting around staring at you and nobody says a word. After a while McCarthy comes in; by that time you're pretty nervous. They asked me if I'm on classified work, which I am not. Where I am it's just plain pound your head off on piecework.

Likewise, Robert Northrup, second-shift shop steward in Building 17, said McCarthy "asked me all about my duties as steward. They were trying to make it seem that stewards are spies."[30]

Barely two weeks later, the Department of Defense ratcheted up the pressure by suddenly "declassifying" a list of 100 plants involved in military-related work in which the UE held bargaining rights. A spokesman stated that the Department was "most anxious to have the situation corrected" but had no authority to act as long as the UE was certified by the National Labor Relations Board. The list was released to the press by Wisconsin's Congressman Kersten, who had questioned GE workers in Schenectady five years earlier. General Electric and Westinghouse appeared near the beginning of the long list of firms.[31]

Five days later, GE president Cordiner turned up the heat still farther. On December 9, he made headlines when he announced what became the notorious GE security policy or Cordiner policy. Any employee who refused to answer questions—or had refused within the previous six months—regarding espionage or sabotage activities or political affiliations in public government

30. Ibid.

31. Labor Press Associated Memo, Vol V, No. 14, December 4, 1953, IUE Papers, A2.06/"UE 1953 II."

hearings would be suspended, given 90 days to prove their innocence, and, failing that, discharged. Cordiner's statement indicated that the policy reached beyond the personal political views of GE workers. People "who might be subject to pressure due to relatives behind the Iron Curtain" also presented possible "security risks." Cordiner conceded in his statement that security regulations already existed for employees working on classified government contracts, but he alleged that this was not "fully adequate in the present condition of world affairs." General Electric and other private organizations should have the "authoritative aid of Government in identifying suspected subversives." While Senator McCarthy commended the company for its "fine" new policy, the IUE's Carey allowed that the new GE move would hit "rank-and-file dupes" but would miss the "Communist" UE organizers and their officers.[32]

What was going on inside local 301 by this time remains a puzzle. Outwardly, the Jandreau group responded aggressively to Cordiner's announcement. In a letter to the GE president, Jandreau labeled the new policy "Un-American and anti-labor" and charged that the announcement was timed to influence the representation election at the company's Lynn, Massachusetts plant on December 10. The company was certainly aware, he continued, that no UE officer or member had "ever been legally charged, much less tried and convicted" of sabotage, espionage, or "any such illegal conduct," and

32. NYT, December 10, 1953, p. 1. One worker of Eastern European origin dismissed from the Lynn GE works after hearings in November 1953 was Alexander Gregory, for example. IUE local 201 handled his case. Gregory, born in Bulgaria, was not asked whether he was a Communist, and his work was not classified. However, when McCarthy asked him for the names of Communists that he knew, he refused to answer. One of the Senator's questions was "...if you would care to... give us the names of the Communists...that would be of considerable help to your adopted country," thus letting Gregory know that his place of birth was a consideration at the hearings. For Gregory's testimony, see U.S. Senate, Permanent Subcommittee on Investigations of the Committee on Government Operations, Subversion and Espionage in Defense Establishments and Industry, 1954, pp. 63-66; for the IUE's grievance, see UE Archives, D/2-161.

that "the members alone determine the policy of our union." He further expressed confidence that the local and the international union would act to protect the job security of all GE workers.[33] While other evidence would later suggest that the local leadership was in turmoil by this time, their quick response to GE's announcement gave no such indication.

The UE and UE members took action to protect the job security of the union's members at GE. The McCarthy subcommittee again descended on upstate New York during late February of 1954. The two-day proceedings, public this time, featured the presence of GE executives observing in front-row seats with an audience of workers, mobilized by the union, seated behind them.

While it certainly appears in retrospect that the Cordiner policy supported by the McCarthy proceedings chilled trade union activism in Schenectady, this was not readily apparent at the time. The hearings occurred in an atmosphere more like a circus than a serious investigation. UE members and supporters from Schenectady were joined by delegations from Buffalo, Elmira, Rome, Fort Edward, Tonawanda, and New York City. The union estimated that 200 people actually managed to enter the hearing room, but an overflow crowd of undetermined size remained outside. The subcommittee's "friendly witness" this time was not an ex-officer of the local, but a young man, Jean Arsenault, who claimed to have been in the Communist Party from 1949 until 1953 and to have worked for the FBI. The subcommittee called eight other witnesses, including activists such as executive board member Sidney Friedlander, shop steward Robert Northrup, and a former trustee of the national union, Arthur Owens.

Despite the threat of firing, the witnesses refused to cooperate with the subcommittee, and some tried to explain their reasons. Owens, one of the relatively few

33. NYT, December 11, 1953, p. 23.

African American workers in the Schenectady plant, had this exchange with the investigators:

Mr. Anastos (staff investigator): Is it true that you attended meetings, Communist Party meetings, at your home?
Mr. Owens: I certainly would like to answer that question... the way it should be answered. But I realize that I am not before a good American democratic committee. I am before a Ku Klux Klan outfit. So because of that, I must use the privilege of the first and fifth amendments....
The Chairman: Mr. Marshall, do not worry about the Communists clapping in this room.... It is a public hearing. I had been warned previously that they would try and load this hearing room.[34]

Two of the witnesses protested at the end of the session that the subcommittee had manipulated the testimony by asking only questions about their political affiliations, which they had refused to answer. They claimed that in the executive, or closed, sessions held previously, they were asked whether they had committed espionage or sabotage, and that they had answered negatively. The hearings closed with the following exchange:

The Chairman: I will hear no further witnesses this morning.
Mr. Belgrave: We testified against espionage and sabotage. We have a right to say so in public.
The Chairman: Officer, remove this other fifth amendment Communist.[35]

Some UE observers later noted that two of the local's top leaders, Jandreau and Mastriani, who had testified at the closed November sessions, and who had received subpoenas in February, were never called in the open

34. U.S. Senate, Subversion and Espionage in Defense Establishments, pp. 86-87.
35. Ibid., p. 115.

hearings, suggesting that they had already struck the deal to lead the local out of the UE.

Still, the leaders of local 301 gave no public indication that they were starting to buckle under the strain of repeated outside intervention. Indeed, the beginning of March appeared to bring them support and encouragement from the international union. Over 300 UE delegates attended the union's legislative conference in Washington and spent three days visiting legislators and lobbying for the UE program, including action on unemployment, conversion to a peace time economy, and opposition to the Butler Bill and other similar legislation before the Congress. The size and tone of the conference appeared to indicate that the UE was alive and active, despite harassment and attacks. The media covered the gathering as the first lobbying effort by a major labor organization that year and quoted president Fitzgerald's direct reference to the General Electric situation: "Our union is going to protect every individual who stands up and tells McCarthy and the General Electric Company to go to hell."[36]

Yet, within a week after the Washington conference came the bad news from Schenectady that the leadership of the UE's largest local intended to bolt. Leo Jandreau formally notified the UE in a letter to Fitzgerald dated March 9. He wrote that the officers of local 301 had received "a forthright and unqualified proposition from the IUE-CIO." Jandreau noted that the plan to transfer the local's union affiliation had, at the time, been approved only by the officers, but that they intended to recommend it to the full membership. He gave as the "most important" reason the local officers' desire to unite with the 78,000 GE workers already represented by the IUE and urged Fitzgerald and all UE members to follow their lead.[37]

---

36. Washington Daily News, March 1, 1954, clipping in IUE Carey Papers, A2.06/"UE Clippings 1954."

37. Jandreau to Fitzgerald, March 9, 1954, reprinted as an IUE leaflet, IUE Papers, Box 23 "UE Local and District Files of Presidential Assistant Les Finnegan" /Folder 4 "UE Local 301 1953-1955."

While the developments in Schenectady came suddenly, they probably did not take the UE's national leaders totally by surprise. They had suspected for over a year that Jandreau wanted to move and would try to persuade other 301 leaders to agree. In fact, a small group consisting of Jandreau, Mastriani, Joseph Saccocio, and the local's attorney, Leon Novak, had met with the IUE's Carey and Harry Block as early as December 1952 soon after the appearance of the *Saturday Evening Post* article. This meeting produced no agreement and only took place after Jandreau had persuaded the local's current president James Cognetta and chief Steward Mastriani, who "objected violently" to the entire project.[38] Jandreau later claimed that he intended the meeting only to reach agreement on common objectives in bargaining with General Electric, a goal the UE had long sought on a national level. Nevertheless, rumors circulated that the Schenectady local had asked to affiliate with the IUE.[39]

The circumstances surrounding the actual decision of local 301 to secede from the UE suggest that the motivation came from the leadership's response to the pressure from outside the union. Jandreau's personal reaction, while not the only factor, certainly played a major role. Jandreau's picture had appeared next to the provocative headline in the Post article; he was the one the media implicitly held responsible for the reputed left-wing character of local 301. In addition to the influence of the press, company and political figures, the Catholic Church also played its role, as it had in other UE locals. On February 28, soon after Jandreau had reached his tormented decision to lead the local out of the UE, Father Joseph Lamanna, a Schenectady labor

38. "Chronology of Carey Meeting with Jandreau," unsigned memo, IUE Papers, Box 23/ Folder 6 "Local 301 Affiliation with IUE Jandreau and Carey 1954."

39. Joseph Saccocio to Carey, February 2, 1953, Ibid.; Saccocio, a UE 301 activist close to the Jandreau leadership, blamed the rumors on "some IUE representative in Philadelphia saying that UE local 301 came to you asking for affiliation." He continued, "...Please be advised that such an idea does not have the chance of a 'snowball in Hell.'"

priest, told Carey that "he has been dealing with Jandreau on a more frequent basis in the last three months and spent all night with him last night. Jandreau says he is bowing to Carey."[40]

However, persuading Jandreau was only part of the job. Bringing the rest of the leadership on board took longer. Once the veteran business agent had decided, around February 28, he moved cautiously, acutely aware of his tenuous position and hoping to prevent the UE national leaders from hearing the news prematurely. After securing the approval of the other top officers, including Cognetta and Mastriani—now more agreeable after several visits from Congressional investigating committees, the announcement of the Cordiner policy and the imminent passage of draconian labor legislation—Jandreau arranged meetings with the 605 shop stewards in groups of 35 to100 in order to persuade them to accept the plan. His personal stature in the local meant that his opinion would carry considerable weight, and he succeeded in gaining the approval of almost all of the stewards.[41]

Of course, it may be argued that a majority of the members had already changed their minds as a result of the years of intensifying pressure on the local, desired now to leave the UE, and realization of this change caused Jandreau and the other leader to follow along. Indeed, the *Electrical Union News* mentioned reports of a petition circulating in the plant calling for disaffiliation from the UE during February. But the 301 leadership pointedly belittled this activity and "those of our people who unconsciously have been duped by the IUE," even after the McCarthy visit. A week earlier, on the

---

40. Unsigned memo apparently written by Carey, February 28, 1954, Ibid. In addition to dealing directly with Jandreau, priests spoke from the pulpit urging opposition to the UE. This presented loyal UE members and their families with painful choices. Helen Quirini told the author in September 2005 that, after one such Sunday experience, one woman was upset enough to tell her: "I felt as bad that day as the day my daughter was laid out."

41. "Chronology of Carey Meeting with Jandreau." Ibid.

eve of the hearings, thousands of workers had left the plant during their lunch period to hear their leaders, Cognetta, Mastriani, Kelly, and others blast the McCarthy subcommittee.[42]

While the outside factors had certainly caused the members concern, the attitude of the leaders was decisive. In the past, a majority of the local members had generally responded to the resolute stands and actions of Jandreau and the other local officers. When the resolve of the leaders weakened, as it did by early March of 1954, the members faced a situation previously unknown in the history of local 301.

Therefore, Jandreau's caution was understandable. Despite his personal standing in the local, the years of civil warfare in the industry had not made the IUE popular in Schenectady. Opposition to the secession appeared quickly among Schenectady workers, as UE loyalists, faced with the loss of many of their long-time leaders, attempted to organize themselves. The national UE officers, once alerted to the events in upstate New York, also acted to prevent the move. Arguing that no election had taken place and that the UE still held bargaining rights at the plant, UE went to court to prevent the 301 secession leaders from withdrawing the local's funds from the UE 301 account. The UE national office succeeded in securing a restraining order against the Jandreau group on March 12, but by that time, the secession move had gained momentum, and funds had already been withdrawn from the local treasury.

The high stakes involved in the struggle to control local 301 dictated that neither side would surrender easily. Carey, after years of frustration and defeat in Schenectady and never one to underestimate a situation's dramatic potential, preserved this moment of apparent success for posterity. The reports he received from his

42. Electrical Union News, February 19, 1954, p. 1; February 26, 1954, p. 1, UE Archives, GECB/866.

representatives on the scene provide an idea of the tense atmosphere in the local:

March 8—Jandreau went to Father Lamanna's home last night and told him the following:
--He (Jandreau) has been meeting with his Executive Board in groups of 10 and 5.
--There are 38 on the Board; they have voted 34 to 4 for disaffiliation with UE and affiliation with IUE-CIO.
--Jandreau is working particularly on Helen Quirini, a member of the Board, who presumably voted no. She left headquarters crying, but said she admires Jandreau so much she will think it over and let him know today....
--Jandreau has removed a great deal of money from the local treasury and turned it over to various trusted lieutenants in 301 for safekeeping.
--Both Matles and Emspak are in Schenectady prepared to take over the local if they can.
--However, Jandreau has trusted guards posted at the door to the 301 with instructions to bar Matles, Emspak, or anyone else representing the national UE.
--Brandt, assistant police chief, has a 24-hour guard on Jandreau.[43]

The unsettled situation in the plant continued until a representation election was finally held on June 30. During the intervening four-month period, the UE supporters attempted to function as the bargaining agent for the plant workers, held numerous meetings, and

43. "Running Report on UE Local 301," March 8, 1954, based on reports Carey received from IUE supporters in Schenectady, Ray Hansen or Frank Fiorillo, IUE Papers, 23/6. In a poignant e-mail to the author, December 14, 2006, Quirini showed that the memory was still vivid after half a century when she elaborated, "I had been out in the field fighting against the IUE. I had no idea what was going on locally.... When Jandreau hit me with the news, I was shocked. I think I started to cry... I asked him about the fact that as newly elected officers we had raised our right hand and swore to live up to our Constitution.... He muttered something.... I know that I touched Billy [Mastriani] because he was supposed to drive me home and they wouldn't let him.... I had lost a very valuable friend."

produced literature on conditions in the factory. They were, however, involved in an uphill campaign against the Jandreau group that had now become the leadership of IUE-CIO local 301 and issued their own publication: *IUE-CIO News*. The UE group elected Ernest Kopper acting president and included people, such as William Hodges, who had originally opposed the coming of industrial unionism to Schenectady in the 1930s.[44]

During the period leading up to the June 30 election, the two sides engaged in the not unexpected battle of printed literature. The argument in local 301 went forward as a disagreement over how best to achieve unity in the industry. Significantly, the Jandreau group, well aware of the local's history of rejecting red-baiting, steered clear of the "Communist issue." By joining the IUE, they argued, local 301 would contribute to the re-unification of GE workers. They said nothing in support of the IUE's Cold War positions, and they did not attack the UE's program. In fact, they took pains to distance themselves from the Carey leadership. Jandreau wrote to Fitzgerald that "the proposal of the IUE-CIO assures the members of local 301 that we shall have full and complete Local Autonomy in our new parent union." He cited as the "most important reason for our selection of IUE-CIO" the fact that it would "put the members of Local 301 and the overwhelming majority of all GE production workers back in the strong collective bargaining position they enjoyed in 1948 when the Company... smacked us to pieces and split our ranks."[45]

The UE side, for its part, charged that GE used the IUE disruption to accelerate its drive to eradicate gains the local members had made during their nearly two decades of industrial union activity. The UE literature noted that the company had stated publicly that, since its contract was with the United Electrical Workers, it would refuse to

---

44. Electrical Union News, April 1, 1954, p. 3; June 29, 1954, UE Archives, D/3-241, GECB/866.

45. Jandreau to Fitzgerald, March 9, 1954, IUE Carey Papers, 23/4.

deal with the Jandreau leadership. With the union thus weakened, General Electric had "stepped up its program of seniority violations and rate cuts, [and] has tried to provoke turbine workers into disorganized actions."[46] The UE further charged that GE had actually financed the secession move by advancing Jandreau $40,000 in dues funds once he had decided to join the IUE.[47] Since this would have represented an advance of several weeks' dues payments, this suspicion particularly angered the UE activists, who remembered that the company had previously made a practice of withholding dues payments from the UE as soon as the IUE filed for an election.

In assessing the Jandreau argument, we must take account of the figures and recall the background of the situation. Before the secession of local 301, the UE represented approximately 70,000 GE workers to the IUE's 78,000. As recently as December 1953, the UE had almost regained bargaining rights at the Lynn GE plants, where an election victory would have reunited the three largest GE locals in the UE. As of February 1954, therefore, the UE appeared to retain a strong position in the largest GE plants. On the other hand, Jandreau was correct that the UE had failed to organize any new GE plants during the 1950s, as he observed in his letter to Fitzgerald. However, in the case of one of the newer General Electric facilities, the "appliance park" in Louisville, the UE charged that the IUE had won the election by appealing to racism because the president of the UE's Ohio-Kentucky district 7, Sterling Neal, was African American.[48] Given the background and the circumstances, the UE found it difficult to take seriously Jandreau's formula for achieving unity.

In the representation election in June, the IUE's 9,005 to 5,179 victory indicated the change in the local since

46. UE Local 301 leaflet, UE Archives, D/3-352.

47. UE News, March 22, 1954, p. 7.

48. Confidential Report on the 18th UE Convention by George F. McCray, Trustee, CIO Editors Association of Illinois, p. 6, IUE Papers, Box 32 FF 14.

1951, but the UE's vote did not go unnoticed. The press comment on the end of the "Battle of Schenectady" included this from a source favorable to the IUE: "It was a measure of the hold which UE had on its members that, despite the action of their leaders and for reasons which are still a subject of speculation in union circles, the old union polled a substantial vote."[49]

The situation in electrical manufacturing for the rest of 1954 reflected the contradictory trends in national politics. The UE's situation grew increasingly difficult, and its locals continued to suffer raids by other unions. By the time of the union's national convention in September, the mood in the union differed markedly from the previous year. Matles told the delegates that the UE faced "dark days" and reported that the union now represented less than 300,000 workers, a decline of 20,000 from the previous year.[50]

The most ominous development of the year was the passage of legislation known as the Communist Control Act, or alternatively the Brownell-Butler Law or the Humphrey-Brownell Law. This law represented the culmination of the efforts of the conservative critics of Taft-Hartley with the active support of many Congressional liberals. The law threatened any union cited, after an investigation, as "Communist controlled" with loss of collective bargaining rights and NLRB recognition. While the law was not formally invoked by the Attorney General in regard to the UE until December of 1955, and would never result in the union's loss of bargaining rights, its presence hung over electrical workers until 1959 and

49. America, July 17, 1954, p. 390.

50. Business Week, October 9, 1954, p.171. Matles reported a drop from 316,000 to 294,000 during the preceding year. BW claimed the UE's financial report showed dues payments from only 166,000 members. Leo Troy's Trade Union Membership lists UE's 1954 membership as 182,000, down 21,000 from 1953. The loss of Schenectady local 301 would have accounted for most of this decline. See table 1.

provided another potential obstacle to the UE's continued viability and influence.[51]

Also during 1954, the Eisenhower Administration appeared to move to a new level of Cold War foreign policy when Secretary of State John Foster Dulles introduced the concept of "massive retaliation." The term raised the possibility of the actual use of the new "super bomb" or hydrogen bomb, and its introduction suggested the Secretary's lack of confidence in the policy of regional alliances.

On the other hand, the year brought signs that the most intense features of the Cold War had outlived their usefulness, and the UE had reason to believe that its years of strenuous activity had produced some results. Not only had the AFL and the CIO belatedly joined in the opposition to the Brownell Law, but also, no sooner had the law passed then criticism came from diverse sources including the *Wall Street Journal*. The *Journal* took issue with the bill's hurried passage by Congress and noted that the bill had received more attention after the President had signed it than before. The *New York Times* reported that the final text of the law was not available to the press, and the *UE News* charged that the President had actually signed a text different than the one Congress had passed.[52]

In another dramatic sign of shifting political winds, the Army-McCarthy hearings began in April and signaled the beginning of the end for the Wisconsin Senator. The UE leaders recognized the significance of the hearings but remained guarded in their optimism. The union's Washington correspondent, Russ Nixon, wrote that the political argument in progress in Washington was over how best to advance the Administration's big business oriented program, and that the Senate opposition to McCarthy represented merely the belief that McCarthy's

51. NYT, March 22, 1959, p. 73, reported that the Justice Department was dropping attempts to have UE classified as a "Communist infiltrated" organization.

52. Wall Street Journal editorial, August 27, 1954; for the labor opposition, see UE News, June 28, 1954, p. 5.

methods had served their purpose.[53] However, the election results in November, which saw the Democrats regain control of Congress, and the Senate vote censuring McCarthy, did seem to indicate that the bleakest days of the Cold War might have passed.

It even appeared that other forces in the labor movement might join the UE on some international matters. The *UE News* reprinted several articles from union publications indicating that the Dulles policy had aroused widespread concern and doubt. The CIO's radio commentator and columnist, John Vander Cooke, had labeled the Dulles policy "massive nonsense" and asked "what government on earth could be composed of such maniacs?" The Amalgamated Clothing Workers (CIO) noted that the apparent contradiction between the President's talk of peace and the Secretary of State's "saber rattling" had caused the rest of the world to "view us with suspicion."[54]

The independent United Mine Workers published two editorials opposing the Administration's foreign policy and went beyond criticism of "massive retaliation." The *UMW Journal*, arguing that the "matter of eliminating war as a method of settling disputes" was "too big to be left in the hands of a few who make policy at the top of governments," called on "the peoples of the big nations to make another desperate try" at finding alternatives to war. In another issue, the UMW specifically addressed the issue of Indochina when it stated, "we wonder if labor is going to dog along at the heels of Dulles as he pursues his evident policy of involving us in every border incident and revolt in the jungles and deserts against colonial rule."[55] While these voices still represented a minority of the organized labor movement, they indicated that the UE might find itself less isolated than in the recent past.

But the combination of contradictory trends posed intractable problems for the UE and for the rebuilding of

---

53. UE News, May 3, 1954, p. 7.
54. CIO News, April 12, 1954, p. 5; UE News, April 19, 1954, p. 3.
55. UE News, April 12, 1954, p. 9; May 31, 1954, p. 9.

unity among electrical workers in the mid-fifties. While the legal machinery of potential repression and the threat of being declared an "outlaw" hung over the union until at least 1959, the downfall of McCarthy and other indications of the weakening of the Cold War made the UE's continued independence seem less urgent to some. As a large union in a key industry, the union rightly claimed in 1955 to have played a role in blunting the extreme manifestations of the Cold War at home and abroad. Cold Warriors had made the UE a special target, however, and the years of strenuous activity with few allies had taken their toll.

A number of observations can be made about the Schenectady situation in 1954. It was McCarthy's last victory. In the spring, the Army hearings began to erode his support. It seems almost that he became expendable after having finally achieved the removal of the Schenectady local from the UE and the firing of union activists as suspected subversives.

For local 301, the switch to the IUE did not solve the problems of the leadership. Within three years, the entire group, with the exception of Jandreau who narrowly escaped, was defeated by an insurgent slate.[56] The local's relations with the national leadership, never smooth, ruptured during the IUE's strike against GE in 1960. For the UE, the loss of Schenectady was a major blow after four years of holding its own. While, on the one hand, it resulted from the most extreme and protracted Cold War attacks on the union, it also suggested that another process was gathering momentum. This was the intensified search for renewed unity in the industry and a place in the larger labor movement.

How important was it, in the changing conditions of 1954–1956, to maintain the UE's independent existence? If the Cold War was moderating and the barriers could now be overcome, then why risk continuing ostracism in the labor movement by adhering to rigid positions?

---

56. UE News, December 24, 1956, p. 2.

These questions confronted electrical workers during the coming year, 1955, when serious movement for the merger of the AFL and CIO developed. Could the UE afford to remain outside the "mainstream" of the labor movement simply because of its refusal to abandon or modify positions that appeared likely to become outdated? The developments in local 301 demonstrated the power both of the external pressures on the union and of the desire for unity in the electrical industry a year before the AFL-CIO merger became an issue.

This situation presented the union with complex and formidable choices. How much should the union now compromise, when it finally appeared that it could claim some vindication for the stands it had taken? The UE had always sought unity, but on what basis could electrical workers achieve it? The UE national officers argued against major concessions. Albert Fitzgerald expressed this point of view to the union's District One annual convention in Philadelphia in October 1954, saying:

> There is a turn in the tide. Who would have believed six months ago that McCarthy would be silenced during the election campaign as he is today? Or that the big business regime in Congress would be on the way out?
>
> ... We can't lose unless we lose courage and try to run. Today there is less point than ever in doing that. In the first place, there's nowhere to run to, and secondly, it is foolish to try to run now when we've been through so much and victory is in sight.[57]

One may wonder in retrospect whether Fitzgerald's optimism was warranted, but his words demonstrated the resolve of the union's leaders to adhere to their program. The period immediately ahead would see the union face decisions at least as difficult as those of 1949.

---

57. UE District 1 Second Constitutional Convention, Minutes, October 16, 1954, p. 3, UE Archives, D/1-90A.

Chapter 6

Hard Choices: The Electrical Unions and the AFL-CIO 1955–1956

The years 1955–1956 saw the climax of a decade-long campaign to impose political conformity on the labor movement and to bring it safely into the Cold War fold. The AFL-CIO merger, based on acceptance and active support of the Cold War, demonstrated the apparent success of this effort. The outlook of the new organization's leadership temporarily dominated organized labor, at least on the surface. Our story, however, shows a more complicated picture. "Consensus" around a Cold War program was never reached in the electrical industry, and the experience of electrical workers suggests that the same could be said of the broader labor movement.[1]

Because the UE suffered major losses in membership, especially during 1956, it is tempting to assume that the union then became an ineffective splinter group. We have argued so far that this was not the case for the period up to 1954, but what are we to make of the next two years? Had electrical workers finally had enough of Cold War arguments and did they yearn to return to pure and simple trade unionism? This is an intriguing question. Electrical workers appear to have badly wanted unity, but on what terms? Despite the challenges and the decline in the union's size, during 1955–1956, the

---

1. Godfrey Hodgson in America in Our Time places the arrival of political "consensus" in the United States in September 1955. See his chapter 4, "The Ideology of the Liberal Consensus," especially p. 74.

UE and its supporters already in the IUE continued to play a key role in electrical unionism. At the beginning of 1955, the UE was still a large union, although much reduced from the peak of the late 1940s. By the end of 1956, it had lost approximately one-third of its 1954 membership, but the record shows that these losses did not occur because of disagreement with the UE program and did not result in a total loss of influence in the labor movement.

The year began with two events that foreshadowed future developments in labor's house. The first was President Eisenhower's State of the Union address, in which he hinted at a shift in the emphasis of Administration foreign policy. The President indicated his acceptance of what he termed "world stalemate" as the relationship between the United States and the Soviet Union. The *UE News* specifically noted this foreign policy shift as one positive element in a program that otherwise had little to offer labor. In a program that called for a minimum wage of 90 cents an hour, tax breaks on foreign income, and generally emphasized "more military, more armaments," and peacetime conscription, the "less virulent" language in foreign policy provided an important bright spot.

The *UE News* pointed out that both the AFL and CIO had criticized the failure of the address to deal with labor's concerns: jobs, plants moving to lower wage areas (the term "runaway shop" was already in use), or a higher minimum wage. On the other hand, both Meany and Reuther had generally approved of the "military aspects" of the speech. The paper commented that they were "apparently still unable to realize that the policy of the preservation of the Cold War at all costs—which they approve—provides the basic reason, inspiration, and excuse for the domestic policies they deplore."[2]

The second event followed within three weeks of Eisenhower's speech. On February 9, George Meany and Walter Reuther announced the merger agreement that

2. UE News, January 17, 1955, pp. 6-7.

would unite the major sections of the labor movement in a single organization. The announcement sparked a flurry of press coverage that suggested substantial disagreements remained to be resolved before the merger occurred. Apprehension and resistance surfaced in several CIO unions, which reportedly feared that the new organization would lack the "fighting spirit" and the commitment to progress in civil rights that had marked the CIO during much of its existence.[3]

Indeed, uncertainty about how the two bodies would mesh and what the nature and influence of the new organization would be marked the ten-month period between the announcement and the consummation of the merger. In the labor movement, the presidents of many AFL unions reportedly opposed the whole idea but kept their objections private; mineworkers' president John L. Lewis expressed skepticism. Outside the movement, the National Association of Manufacturers voiced fears that the AFL-CIO would unduly influence national politics and stifle the "freedom of choice" of its members.[4] The proposed merger, in short, generated widespread interest and attention.

On one issue, however, the leaders of both the AFL and CIO left little doubt about their position. The new organization would not tolerate "Communists" at home or compromise with "Communism" abroad. AFL president Meany warned labor leaders that the "Communist-led" unions were attempting to merge with AFL unions as a "shield" to escape the 1954 Communist Control Act, and he served notice that standards would be set to prevent such action.

---

3. NYT, February 10, 1955, p. 1, for the merger announcement; February 14, 1955, p. 1 for the CIO reservations; also see Political Affairs, March 1955, pp. 32-35, "The AFL-CIO Merger," by George Morris for a discussion of the differences of opinion aired at the CIO Convention just held.

4. NYT, August 2, 1955, p. 13; August 12, 1955, p. 9, for the views of AFL union presidents; September 2, 1955, p. 26, "UMW President Lewis Sees Merger Dissolving like Rope of Sand"; December 2, 1955, p. 20, "Reuther Denies Merger is Funeral for CIO"; December 7, 1955, p. 43 and December 10, 1955, p. 1 for the NAM reaction.

Within days after the merger announcement, the CIO expressed similar sentiments. Its General Counsel Arthur Goldberg sent notices to CIO affiliates warning against "Communist infiltration." In May, a joint committee of the AFL and CIO presented a proposed constitution for the merged organization that specifically included provisions barring "Communist dominated" unions. By the fall, specific references to foreign affairs appeared in the form of speculation about the influence of the new AFL-CIO International Affairs Department and a statement from Meany that the AFL-CIO planned "to expand its worldwide anti-communist program." The AFL-CIO founding convention passed a resolution pledging to oust unions "tainted with racketeering or Communism" thus formally establishing the Cold War character of the merger.[5]

Faced with the probability that the merger would occur on a basis of excluding the "left wing" unions, the UE leadership had difficult decisions to make. On the one hand, the union had consistently called for united labor action on concrete issues and had attempted to find a basis for such action. On the other hand, the UE had refused to abandon its positions on politics and foreign policy that the AFL and CIO leaders had rejected. That is, the union would not agree to exclude people on political grounds or to support the Cold War. How could the union, in the circumstances of 1955, contribute to its long-stated goal of labor unity and still uphold its positions? While the Eisenhower Administration's foreign policy appeared to be moderating in the face of global realities, the leadership of the "mainstream" labor organizations adhered to their hard-line stance.[6]

5. Ibid., February 3, 1955, p. 17, for Meany on attempts of left unions to enter AFL; February 16, 1955, p. 17, for Goldberg's note; May 3, 1955, p. 1, for account of proposed constitution; December 4, 1955, Section VI, p. 11, for Meany statement on worldwide anti-Communist activity; December 8, 1955, p. 1, for Convention resolution.

6. Differences existed between the AFL and CIO positions on foreign policy; see for example Political Affairs, January 1956, p. 55, "The Labor Merger" by Hal Simon. In a victory for the AFL's "free trade union" agenda, it appeared that its harder line stance was prevailing.

The resulting disagreements in the UE were sharp, but they were not about the union's program; they involved deciding how best to advance that program under the unfavorable circumstances of the period.

The UE general executive board at its February meeting attempted to forge a position that would guide the union through the period ahead. It issued a statement emphasizing the objective of reuniting the workers in the industry and urged "the development of a united parallel action among the rank and file of our Union with all other unions."[7] The Board's statement reflected the fear that leaders of other unions aimed to annex sections of the UE on a piecemeal basis and dismember the largest of the unions expelled from the CIO. Two months later, the GEB amended its position to include the four points that would be so often repeated, widely debated in the union, and difficult to adhere to over the next eighteen months. These points indicated the widespread conviction in the union that the UE should itself attempt to merge with another union in the industry, but not sacrifice its principles. Their dilemma, of course, had confronted the union since 1949 and continued now: The most logical merger would be with the IUE, whose differences with UE policy had caused the original split and whose leaders still vigorously rejected any cooperation between the two unions. The points on which the UE leaders proposed to discuss unity or merger with other unions were:

1. The unions proposing merger must agree to "discontinue any raids upon each other."
2. Discussions "must be conducted in good faith" with "full information to the memberships of the respective organizations."
3. "The principle issues of autonomy, democracy, membership rights, program, policies, and administration must be resolved prior to any discussion

7. UE News, February 28, 1955, p. 5.

of who holds what jobs or occupies what position in such unified organization."

4. "Efforts to achieve unity in our industry should be accompanied by simultaneous cooperation and united action on wage and contract negotiations between the respective organizations wherever possible."[8]

The board's concern with other unions besides the IUE sprang from the fact that the UE had also competed with the AFL's International Association of Machinists (IAM) as in the Westinghouse 107 election in chapter III, the International Brotherhood of Electrical Workers (IBEW), and with the CIO United Auto Workers (UAW) in the International Harvester chain in the Midwest. This concern seemed justified, when in March, the seven remaining International Harvester locals seceded from the UE and joined the UAW. While these locals represented an unusual case in some respects and did not mean that the union was unraveling, their move had obvious broader implications for the UE. This secession, led by former UE international representative Milt Burns, confirmed the danger that other unions could attempt to annex entire chunks of the UE at one time.[9]

With all signs indicating that the AFL-CIO merger would occur on a Cold War basis, UE leaders set a priority on keeping their own union intact, but they had no illusions about the difficulties ahead. Matles, in a March 11 letter to UE field representatives, expressed this thinking:

> During the recent weeks we find that the officials of the AFL and CIO unions in our industry have not only solicited

8. UE News, April 11, 1955, p. 3.

9. Matles to UE International Representatives and Field Organizers re: International Harvester, March 21, 1955, IUE Papers, Box 32 FF 23. Originally part of the Farm Equipment Workers (FE), these locals had been ordered by Philip Murray to merge with the UAW five years earlier. Their decision not to do so had left them vulnerable and unsupported by the CIO during a hard-fought three-month strike during the fall of 1952. See UE bulletin "The Louisville Story," IUE Papers, A2.06/"UE Convention 1953 II."

> UE local leaders, but they have solicited UE District leaders and UE Conference Board leaders, making them all kinds of "attractive" offers if only they will agree to bring in their respective...set ups to any one of these unions. After years of the most intensive red-baiting attacks made against these same UE Local and District leaders, these AFL and CIO officials are ready to break bread with them, if they will only agree to dismember our organization. Our union cannot permit the real and urgent desires of our membership, and that of the other unions, for unity to be reduced to dickering for petty deals and accommodations on a local, district, or any other fragmentary basis.
>
> The International Union will leave nothing undone to fully exploit every opportunity for unity.[10]

Tough relations with other unions presented one obstacle. In the fluid conditions of mid-1955, however, pressures on the union and on electrical workers continued to originate outside the labor movement. During the summer, workers in electrical manufacturing received a strong indication of what the Cold War "consensus" might mean in economic terms. In both major chains, serious collective bargaining problems loomed as companies sought changes in job classifications and wage rates and asked for long-term, multi-year contracts.[11] The "crisis in collective bargaining" accompanied the imposition of political "consensus" on the labor movement. The episode deserves attention because it illustrates not only how the Cold War-inspired division in the industry aggravated the "crisis," but also that influential leadership at this time came from the UE, despite its numerically smaller size. Also, James Carey

---

10. Matles to UE IR's and Field Organizers, Circular letter 165, March 11, 1955, IUE Papers, Box 32 FF 23.

11. For a detailed discussion of the changes sought by the companies, see Schatz, The Electrical Workers, pp. 237-238; Mark McCulloch, "The Shop Floor Dimension of Union Rivalry" in The CIO's Left-Led Unions, Steve Rosswurm, ed., pp. 183-199; Fortune, December 1955, pp. 57 ff. On the Westinghouse situation, and pp. 110 ff., "The Overhaul of General Electric," by William B. Harris.

apparently missed most of the GE negotiations due to an extended hospital stay following his return from the ICFTU congress in Vienna.[12]

In July, the IUE announced that it would seek a "full guaranteed annual wage" in talks with General Electric. After considerable media buildup around the union's militant bargaining stance, the IUE negotiators quickly accepted a five-year contract without the annual wage provision. While the agreement did provide for annual wage increases and Carey called it the "best contract ever," indications quickly surfaced that the GE agreement would not bring settled conditions in the industry.[13]

On August 18, a week after the IUE's acceptance, the UE rejected a similar offer from the company. On August 25, the IUE GE conference board ratified the contract, despite what the UE labeled an "outburst of membership sentiment" against it. The UE charged that the company had had to help the IUE leadership win acceptance of the agreement and that a contract of such long duration amounted to a wage freeze.[14] The UE also claimed that the widespread objections to the GE offer and its own initial refusal to ratify had led GE to withdraw the most controversial "management rights" provisions. Reports in the national press tended to support the impression that General Electric had won a quick victory. The IUE had failed to win the guaranteed annual wage and reached an early settlement, one account alleged, due to the "superior" skill of the company negotiators and the union's "lack of organization and will to strike."[15]

The GE agreement escalated existing tension in the Westinghouse chain. Traditionally sensitive as the number-two firm in the industry, Westinghouse desired a settlement along the lines of the GE contract, but the company faced an increasingly apprehensive workforce.

---

12. IUE News, June 20, 1955; August 1, 1955, photo of Carey with Reuther and caption, p. 6.

13. NYT, July 19, 1955, p. 21; August 12, 1955, p. 1.

14. UE News, August 29, 1955, pp. 1, 6, 7.

15. NYT, August 16, 1955, p. 21; August 17, 1955, p. 1.

The company's use of "time studies" and attempts to shift jobs from incentive to straight-time pay had already strained relations with its workers, who saw gains they had made in wages and working conditions threatened. These policies along with company plans to transfer work to new plants in the south where unions had not organized loomed as part of a general attack on the gains made by industrial unionism. These issues and the perception that the IUE leaders had not dealt with them in negotiations led to the restless mood of GE and Westinghouse workers by 1955.[16]

The response to the GE contract put pressure on the IUE president to deliver more in the Westinghouse negotiations. By 1955, his reputation as a negotiator already dramatically distinguished him from his UE counterparts, political differences aside. As an article in the *Wall Street Journal* related two years earlier, management negotiators had "repeatedly" said off the record that:

> UE runs a much more orderly union than the rival CIO Electrical Workers and that negotiations with UE are far more businesslike than with the CIO outfit. With General Electric, for one, negotiations between Vice President Lemuel Boulware and CIO Electrical Workers President James Carey are generally carried on through the newspapers, while talks with UE are carried on in more orderly fashion in the conference room.[17]

---

16. The companies made elimination of incentive pay a priority during the mid-1950s. See Schatz, The Electrical Workers, pp. 237-238, and the Fortune articles in n. 12. For the Westinghouse situation, see McColloch, "Union Rivalry" in Rosswurm, The CIO's Left Led Unions, pp. 190-192.

17. Wall Street Journal, August 21, 1953, "Three Unions Rip the Tough Red Tinted Electrical Workers." One UE activist had this to say about the IUE leader's relations with the employers: "The company knows exactly what the IUE-CIO stands for and what Carey stands for. They are not concerned about his publicity statements. They know that the policy of the IUE is based solely on McCarthyism in collaboration with the boss," UE Field Organizer Thomas Quinn to "Dear East Pittsburgh Worker," September 27, 1954, UE Archives, CB/W 1097.

During the late summer of 1955, Carey's individual negotiating style apparently aggravated an already difficult situation. During August and September, the workers at the Westinghouse home plant in East Pittsburgh were on strike for six weeks against the company's use of time studies for non-incentive workers. Although the plant had voted narrowly for the IUE in 1950, and again in 1952, the national IUE had never consolidated its ties to local 601, and the local still included a core of pro-UE activists. One local newspaper, perhaps exaggerating, had blamed the strike on "UE die-hards" in the plant.[18] When Carey, negotiating individually, reached an agreement, the IUE local 601 executive board rejected it, arguing that the document appeared to bind not only 601 but all Westinghouse locals to the company policy.[19] A three-day strike by twenty-nine other Westinghouse plants followed.

A leading business magazine labeled these events the first "automation strike," noting that employment at the East Pittsburgh plant had declined by 25 percent during the previous four years and that only workers with thirteen years seniority or more were currently employed there. The strike ended when, after three days, the company agreed to postpone further time studies and to discuss "ground rules" for time studies in general contract negotiations.[20]

Tough choices thus confronted the UE when the delegates gathered in Cleveland during the last week of September for the annual convention. The major employers pressed for drastic and unpopular contractual changes. The AFL and CIO proceeded with plans for merger on a basis that would freeze out the UE at the very moment that it appeared that only the UE could provide the leadership needed and sought by electrical

---

18. Quinn to Matles, September 2, 1955. Quinn said the charge was made by the Wilkinsburg Gazette, published by former HUAC member John McDowell. UE Archives, CB/W 1098.

19. IUE-CIO News, September 26, 1955, p. 10.

20. Fortune, December 1955, pp. 58 ff.

workers. With the exception of the Eisenhower Administration's moderation in foreign policy, the future seemed to hold only intensifying pressure on the UE and on electrical workers generally.

Fitzgerald's opening remarks reflected this assessment. He charged that the Republican Party, in its domestic policy, had "demonstrated again it is the Party of big business in America," while the Democrats remained under the "control of dominant leaders who have compromised and double-talked on basic labor legislation...." However, he credited the Administration with adjusting "some of its policies to the people's compelling demand for peace" by shifting the trend away from the Cold War toward "the new spirit of Geneva."[21] In addition to Fitzgerald's remarks, the lead article in the convention of the *UE News* observed that "finally some of the greatest causes for which the UE has long fought and for which it has been most bitterly attacked are winning the widest support—notably the cause of peace and the settlement of world differences by negotiation." The paper also claimed among the "major contributions" of the UE in the recent period the "collapse of McCarthy and the new tide of decisions upholding the Bill of Rights, sparked by the UE fight in the Quinn and Emspak cases."[22]

The apparent moderation of aspects of the Cold War seemed, ironically, only to make the UE's decisions about its future more difficult. The union's leaders and activists continued to believe that the AFL and CIO ties to official foreign policy hampered labor's ability to confront domestic issues. The convention's major debate addressed the issue of labor unity. Every speaker expressed support for the general executive board position adopted in April: The union should seek unity and merger but should not surrender its principles. Unlike the contentious debates of the late '40s, this was a

21. Cleveland Plain Dealer, September 21, 1955, p. 6.
22. UE News, September 26, 1955, p. 1.

sober and probing discussion to which several local and district leaders contributed, as well as two of the top officers, Matles and Fitzgerald.

The resolution under discussion reaffirmed the union's position and directed the GEB "to implement, in every possible way, our policy to reunite the workers in our industry in one union." While every speaker supported the resolution, differences in emphasis were obvious; some speakers emphasized 'unity' while others stressed the importance of standing by the UE program. For instance, James Lustig of local 437 argued that UE members in District 4 (New York City and Northern New Jersey) had achieved unity on a local and district level with many shops that had joined the IUE. He implied that clinging rigidly to abstract concepts would prevent the "day in and day out" work necessary to reunited electrical workers. Lustig argued that the GE "sell out contract" would not have been accepted by GE workers if the contact and cooperation between the two unions in District 4 had existed elsewhere. He pointed out that the IUE District 4 executive board had almost unanimously opposed the contract.[23]

On the other hand, Carl Gray, president of Westinghouse local 107, emphasized the importance of upholding the UE program in any merger, stating, "To me this resolution says that we will not exchange labor leadership for labor bosses.... We have fought for years to establish a set of principles... we are willing to unite... but we certainly do not intend to give up any of those principles—not one." Gray related that his local had also spearheaded a drive for labor unity in the Philadelphia area based on the UE program and formed the Labor Policy Committee, "which has practically taken over the Democratic Party in Delaware County."[24]

---

23. See UE Policy 1955-1956, pp. 10-12 for the resolution; 1955 UE Convention Proceedings, pp. 150-175 for the discussion; p. 160 for Lustig's remarks.

24. 1955 UE Convention Proceedings, p. 159.

While the discussion demonstrated the delegates' desire to re-enter the "mainstream" of the labor movement, the general officers warned that their meetings with other union leaders had not showed promise. Fitzgerald reported that attempts to reach agreement with the IUE and the IAM had run up against the old question: the "Communist issue." The other unions would accept UE locals one at a time and would accept only local officers who could satisfy the new union's constitutional requirements that barred alleged Communists from office. The UE president reported on two meetings with IUE leaders. At one, Carey had told him that "he was afraid if we had a merger that the General Electric Company would red bait him." At the other, secretary-treasurer Al Hartnett and vice president Harry Block had named names: "... this one and that one and this leader and that member were reds" whom they would never accept in the IUE. They had finally agreed to establish a joint subcommittee but not to stop raiding, thus failing to satisfy the first of the UE's four points.[25]

The convention adopted the resolution, but the discussion showed that disagreements persisted. During the next year, the UE would face a national strike against the Westinghouse Company and a difficult search for a home in the "mainstream" of the labor movement. While a level of rank-and-file cooperation would be built during the five-month strike, the leadership differences with the IUE would prove impossible to bridge. When in the spring of 1956 it appeared that unity efforts of the national UE leadership would not succeed, the tactical disagreement suggested by the remarks of Gray and Lustig at the convention would re-emerge as some UE districts left the union on their own.

Before proceeding, we should note that the goal of unity did not seem out of reach in 1955. Despite the Cold War obstacles, the overall situation in the industry placed

---

25. Ibid., pp. 175-179.

strong pressures on the IUE leadership to take a more flexible stance than their public statements showed.

The Carey leadership had not succeeded in welding a unified organization out of the locals it had won from the UE and those it had organized on its own. From the moment of its creation, the union had known internal discord and strife; in November 1949, supporters of Frederick Kelly of Lynn local 201 had objected to Carey and put his leadership in doubt.[26]

The IUE's uncertain first two years demonstrated Carey's inability to attract sufficient support to sustain a viable organization, and dissatisfaction with his personal style of leadership constantly plagued the new union. In March of 1952, Mike Fitzpatrick, leader of the IUE forces at East Pittsburgh in 1950 and an original member of the "Committee of Ten," resigned as chairman of the union's Westinghouse conference board, charging that Carey's habit of negotiating with management on his own had undercut the board and the interests of Westinghouse workers. Refusing to be a "party to Carey's irresponsible acts" that had earned the resentment of conference board members, Fitzpatrick charged that the IUE program had been drawn up in the Washington office by people "who know nothing of our problems with the company."[27]

When we recall that not only the largest Westinghouse local, but also the two largest GE locals, Schenectady 301 and Lynn 201, all in the IUE by 1955, included large and active pro-UE forces, it is not surprising that the IUE leadership's rapid acceptance of the GE five-year contract had generated immediate protest in both major chains. The possible designs of the IAM or the IBEW

---

26. Cleveland Press, November 4, 1949, clipping in IUE Papers, A2.05/"Communism and Left-Right Split 1941-1949."

27. UE News, March 17, 1952, p. 3; for other reports of dissatisfaction with Carey's leadership, see the Daily Worker, October 13, 1952, "Expensive Raids on UE Help Beat Carey on Dues Hike," and the Minneapolis Tribune, August 30, 1951, "12,000 May Bolt CIO-IUE in Three States," clippings in IUE Papers A2.05, A2.06.

on parts of the IUE's jurisdiction added to the potential problems. Under these circumstances, Carey could not simply ignore the UE and its insistent calls for concrete steps toward reunification of electrical workers. He realized as well as did the UE leaders that the future and the strength of electrical unionism were at stake.[28]

Therefore, communication between the two unions did occur during this period. During the week of the UE convention, Carey and Fitzgerald fired telegrams back and forth. The day the UE delegates passed their "unity" resolution, Carey wired Fitzgerald a proposal for the "immediate affiliation of all UE locals under the banner of the IUE-CIO, such affiliation to be completed by December 1, 1955."[29] Fitzgerald, certainly realizing that this proposal would eliminate the UE and bring electrical workers together under Cold War leadership just in time for the AFL-CIO merger, responded with a proposal of his own on the Westinghouse situation: "A committee of the Westinghouse Conference Board of UE stands ready to meet immediately with a committee of the IUE-CIO Westinghouse Conference Board to arrange for cooperation in negotiations with the Company."[30]

Carey persisted. Immediately after the UE Convention, he tried again to gain acceptance of the IUE position, wiring the UE president that "you and the delegates to your Convention are fully aware that the IUE-CIO is the only union capable of striking such giant corporations as Westinghouse on a national basis." He added that the IUE top officers—vice president Block, secretary-treasurer Al Hartnett, and Carey—were prepared to meet with the UE executive board to present "this program for genuine, democratic unity."[31] When Fitzgerald received the second telegram, he had already

---

28. See Matles circular letter 165, March 11, 1955, p. 2, for analysis of Carey's position, IUE Papers, 33/6 "Unity Communications between UE and IUE following Convention."

29. Carey to Fitzgerald, September 22, 1955, Ibid.

30. Fitzgerald to Carey, September 23, 1955, Ibid.

31. Carey to Fitzgerald, September 26, 1955, Ibid.

written to Carey repeating his proposal for joint committee meetings on the Westinghouse negotiations and, in addition, suggesting a joint meeting of the general executive boards of the two unions to discuss the more general matter of reunification. He wrote, "Despite our failure to secure the cooperation of your union in the recent GE negotiations, we again call your attention to our proposal of September 23rd for an immediate meeting of committees representing the Westinghouse Conference Boards of UE and IUE-CIO. Obviously, to achieve the best results, no time should be lost in establishing cooperation in the current Westinghouse negotiations." The UE president also commented that the IUE proposal "received at the end of the fourth day of the UE Convention did not present a serious approach" to the problem of reuniting electrical workers."[32]

The urgent tone of Fitzgerald's communications did not produce a positive response, but informal contacts did occur. Neither union made progress in talks with the company, and by mid-October, a strike appeared inevitable. The strike, which lasted five months nationally, and ten months at the UE's largest local, showed the readiness of rank-and-file electrical workers to build unity by their actions.

Unable to win agreement from its workers for desired changes, the Westinghouse Company refused to extend the old contract and notified the unions that changes would be made unilaterally. At the Steam Turbine Division in Essington, the company locked the gates at midnight before the morning of October 15. Three days later, over 40,000 IUE members at twenty-nine plants met the same situation. Finally, on October 25, the thirteen additional plants represented by the UE were shut down.[33]

---

32. Fitzgerald to Carey, September 26, 1955, Ibid.

33. NYT, October 16, 1955, p. 60; October 17, 1955, p. 1; October 26, 1955, p. 6. UE local 107, representing the workers at the Lester plant, referred in its literature to the stoppage as a "lockout," arguing that, if an employer offers less than what was contracted for in the previous contract,

While the IUE leadership continued to eschew any public cooperation or even contact, local actions went forward, encouraged by the UE. Fitzgerald told the delegates to the union's District 1 Convention in Philadelphia on October 22, at the beginning of the strike, that rank-and-file and local contacts held the only real chance for common action with the IUE or any other union in the industry. "The only way it can come about is if we make up our minds as individual leaders to get out and work with local unions of other internationals and work with the rank and file of these unions and try to win them over to fight for the same kind of policies that we fight for in this union." He argued that resentment in the IUE at the GE settlement had forced Carey to take a more militant stance with Westinghouse, and that Carey would "not have it as easy as he did with GE. We have had some contact with some of his locals, and there is some desire on their part to take on the company. We are going to do everything to see that these contacts are maintained."[34]

Such contact did continue throughout the strike with tangible results. At the Jersey City elevator plant, for instance, the 350 salaried workers in the IUE and the 950 UE production workers opened joint strike headquarters. When the strike ended in late March, the IUE members respected UE picket lines that were still up pending local ratification of the agreement by UE local 456. The most notable example of such activity occurred in the case of local 107 where the strike continued over local issues for more than four additional months. Twenty-six of the local's leaders spent nineteen days at the Delaware County prison farm for defying

a lockout exists under Pennsylvania state law. The state courts agreed with this interpretation. See local 107 publication, "The Westinghouse Lockout at Lester," p. 8, entry for February 17, 1956. For more on the topic, see Roy Weed, "The Westinghouse-UE Strike at Lester 1955-1956," Master's Thesis, Temple University, 1961.

34. Minutes, UE District One Third Constitutional Convention, October 22, 1955, pp. 4, 6, UE Archives D/1-91.

an injunction against picketing. The local rallied wide support from the AFL-CIO unions in the area, from communities around the plant and from local politicians.[35] Indeed, the wide recognition the local received provided the strongest of the numerous indications that the UE's Cold War isolation could be ending at this time. Westinghouse workers had, in effect, conducted a major national strike and forced the company to compromise, despite the lack of cooperation between the two unions at the national level and the specific refusal of the leadership of the largest electrical union to join forces.[36]

The issues of merger and reunification remained unsettled, however. In November, the UE executive board invited Carey to meet with them face to face to explain his conditions. On November 30, the IUE president came to UE headquarters in New York. The IUE's typed summary of the two-hour meeting suggests that Carey wanted nothing on paper that indicated a change in his stance. He restated the IUE position: no formal cooperation or contact with the UE leadership; no "tampering" with "the protection we have against infiltration... under our constitution you cannot be an officer if you're a Communist or a Fascist or some other kind of totalitarian."

However, the summary also hinted that Carey realized that his situation demanded more flexibility behind the scenes. He conceded that "...the informal meetings can continue." The meeting also included sober give and take on the serious trade union issues in the Westinghouse strike. The UE leaders, critical of the GE settlement, suggested that the IUE's quick acceptance of the GE terms had, by encouraging Westinghouse to take an aggressive bargaining position, in large part caused the strike then

---

35. See UE News, October 31, 1955, p. 5 for Jersey City; local 107 pamphlet "The Westinghouse Lockout at Lester," entries for December 12, 1955; March 8, 1956; March 30, 1956; July 21, 1956; August 3, 1956.

36. Mark McColloch, "Union Rivalry" in Rosswurm, The CIO's Left Led Unions, pp. 191-192, says the contracts "presented a mixed picture" but the UE took a tougher stance on the company's demands for a productivity clause.

in progress. Carey responded that Westinghouse "was now worse than GE. They had been doing these things—time studies, rate cutting, and job slashing—long before the GE negotiations." The UE side did not seem convinced, and in any case, the discussion of "pure and simple" union issues did not change the IUE's official position on merger.[37]

Following the AFL-CIO merger, electrical workers received a sharp reminder of the continuing impact of the Cold War and that they faced broader forces than a single employer. On December 20, Attorney General Brownell filed a petition under the 1954 Communist Control Act requesting the Subversive Activities Control Board (SACB) to declare the UE a "Communist infiltrated" organization. Such a declaration by the SACB would mean the loss of the union's collective bargaining rights and an end to its recognition by the National Labor Relations Board. The IUE had regularly used this possibility as a campaign issue against the UE.

The UE's charge that the petition aimed to disrupt the growing unity among Westinghouse workers and undermine the strike gained credibility the next day with the IUE's public response. While more strident in tone, this press release reinforced the substance of Carey's statements to the UE executive board three weeks earlier. "IUE has always made it clear that it would never consider a merger with UE. The CIO expelled the UE in 1949 because it found that the UE was Communist dominated." This statement was triggered by Brownell's mention in the petition that some UE locals had already left the UE and "merged" with the IUE. While the Attorney General may have intended to illustrate his point that "the great majority of members of UE and all trade unions are good Americans," and that the purpose of the petition was "to aid the rank and file

37. Summary of Meeting of IUE-CIO President James Carey and Vice President Harry Block with UE General Executive Board at UE Headquarters, November 30, 1955, written by Les Finnegan, IUE Carey Papers, 33/6, "Unity Communications between UE and IUE Following Convention."

members of this union clear their organization of Communist dictators," Carey feared that Brownell's example might also taint the IUE as a "Communist dominated" organization.[38]

Carey's public repudiation of any merger talks showed that Cold War politics still trumped joint action in dealing with employers. While thousands of Westinghouse workers and the UE leadership objectively acted in concert in the first major electrical strike in a decade, the leaders of the largest electrical union emphasized that, for them, the Cold War issue overrode all others.

Despite Carey's vehement public stand, informal meetings between the two unions continued during and after the strike. The UE leadership had a mandate from the union's convention to seek unity, and Carey, for his part, understood that his stature in the new AFL-CIO Industrial Union Department depended on his ability to represent all electrical workers. In the absence of extensive documentation for much of this period, the skeletal written records plus the memories of participants provide a basis for historical speculation. First, the written record appears straightforward as suggested by the following summary.

At the last meeting on April 21, the UE officers presented a memorandum, at Carey's request, containing the UE conditions for merger. The irreconcilable differences boiled down to two: The UE sought assurances that their policy of no "political discrimination" would be respected, as would their practice of allowing rank-and-file members in the shops to decide on the "calling and settling of strikes." On the first point, for instance, the UE proposed that "anyone who complies with the Taft-Hartley Law and signs the affidavits... is in full and complete compliance with the UE constitution." The UE

38. A copy of the petition; Fitzgerald's response in NYT, December 21, 1955, p. 18 and UE News, December 26, 1955, p. 1; copy of the IUE press release. IUE Carey Papers 33/5 "Subversive Activities Control Board."

also asked for assurances that the AFL-CIO would not "set aside or interfere in any understanding that may be reached between the IUE and the UE."[39]

The point regarding "political discrimination" remained a major sticking point. Both sides understood that the issue was whether or not many of the most effective UE organizers and elected leaders would keep their positions in a merged organization. According to the summary, the IUE countered with its own proposal: The UE "should provide a list of individuals whom the UE would like to see placed, the IUE would in turn check such a list, advise UE how many and who on the list would be acceptable, and that this procedure would resolve all matters between the two organizations and... dispose of the problem of raiding and cooperation." In other words, the IUE would screen UE applicants for jobs. IUE vice president Harry Block put it more succinctly in a 1987 interview: "We didn't want any Commies on staff."[40]

The public IUE rejection did not appear until three weeks later in an uncompromising statement accusing the UE leadership of "colossal arrogance" and refusing to make "any concession whatsoever to the power-hungry UE leaders. The IUE statement rejected the UE's proposal to regard the Taft-Hartley affidavits as satisfying the IUE's constitutional bar against 'Communists.' Since only a very small part of the national staff is required to file such affidavits, this would mean that the anti-Communist constitutional provisions would have to be waived with regard to those members of the staff who do not file Taft-Hartley affidavits."[41]

Although the IUE did not issue its public rejection until May 9, a strongly worded and revealing internal

---

39. Summary of positions of UE and IUE presented to IUE officers by UE officers, April 21, 1956, Washington, D.C., IUE Carey Papers, 33/8, "Unity Meeting April 21, 1956."

40. Ibid.; quote is from Harry Block interview, March 17, 1987.

41. "The Programs of the IUE and UE in Regard to Unity in the Electrical Industry," IUE statement, May, 1956, Ibid.

document, dated April 20, suggested the leadership's thinking, even before the April 21 meeting with the UE. This memo, entitled "Unity Yes! Merger No!" and apparently written by the top officers—Carey, Block, and Hartnett—is a major Cold War statement from right-wing electrical union leaders presenting the rationale for their position. The thrust of this statement was that, since the IUE had justified its existence and built its image by attacking Communism in the labor movement, it would be suicidal to merge with, or even recognize the UE. Since the IUE enjoyed a national and indeed "worldwide reputation as a prime destroyer of Communist unionism," a UE-IUE merger would ruin the union's relations with its allies inside and outside of the labor movement. Such a move "would gravely affect the IUE's prestige:

1. with the rest of the democratic labor movement;
2. with government agencies and Congress;
3. with the press and clergy;
4. with employers."

This document specifically mentioned that the "preferential treatment" accorded the IUE by the Labor Relations Board officials "would end forever" in the case of merger with the UE, as would the "courtesy" with which president Carey was generally received by Congressional committees. "Any merger or amalgamation of the IUE and UE could be made ridiculous to the world" by the publication of past IUE statements and leaflets regarding the UE.

Carey's gravest apprehension, however, could well have been the last point in the section entitled "The Effect of Merger on the IUE Internally." While allowing that right-wing opposition to the merger would likely appear in the union, the memorandum also grimly observed that merger "would raise the long-range prospect of UE holding the balance of power in IUE, with the entering UE elements combining with malcontents and unreconstructed Party boys."[42] In other words, the Carey leadership suspected that, despite the surface changes in the landscape of electrical trade unionism, so painstakingly wrought by years of attacks on the left-center coalition, the underlying political situation in the industry still resembled the 1940s. At that time, the coalition had successfully prevented the right-wing forces from gaining power in the UE. Reunification of the UE and the IUE would risk the loss of Carey's crucial allies outside the union and could strengthen the opposition to his leadership inside it.

Given the thinking of the IUE leaders, it hardly seems surprising that reunification, merger, or any form of public cooperation on a national basis did not occur during Carey's presidency. Within weeks of the failure of the merger talks, however, it appeared that Carey's effort at urging UE locals or districts to affiliate with his union independently was bearing fruit. The UE's District 4, once the mainstay of support for the national leadership, voted to leave the UE and affiliate with the IUE-AFL-CIO. On May 10, the district leadership issued a press release bringing the news that the UE now faced its leanest days thus far.

To get a sense of what happened in District 4, we must go beyond the written record and test the memories of participants. The District 4 story merits attention not simply because the district's change of affiliation meant a serious setback for the UE, which, of course, it did. The story also tells us much about the underlying resistance among electrical workers to the Cold War policies of the right-wing leaders in their industry and to Cold War policies generally. The events of April and May 1956 left acute disappointment on both sides: those who remained in the UE and those who left. But a look at the deeper meaning of that period yields a less negative estimate. The evidence indicates, for instance, that the fear expressed by the IUE leaders in their memo was

42. "Unity Yes! Merger No!" IUE memo, April 20, 1956, Ibid.

justified and reasonable. Indeed, it appears to have been the real possibility of major UE influence in a merged organization that made the failure of the merger negotiations so disappointing. With these points in mind, we can proceed with the story of District 4.

The District, once the UE's largest, had already suffered losses before 1956. During the summer of 1953, for instance, the officers of the 3,000-member local 426 at the Westinghouse meter division in Newark had led the local into the IUE. UE activists had noted that this event coincided exactly with the unsuccessful attempts of Francis Bradley and others to steer Westinghouse local 107 in Lester, Pennsylvania, in the same direction. Nevertheless the district continued as an influential force in the union, the home district of organization director Matles, and traditionally one of the most outspoken in opposing Cold War policies at home and abroad. Despite the losses, the UE still claimed 35 locals in the area to the IUE's 68.[43]

While the two unions competed during the early 1950s, activists there noted that another process gathered momentum as the decade reached its midpoint. In specific situations, opportunities arose for common or united action at the local level. District 4 delegates to the UE 1955 national convention spoke with pride of their success in pursuing the union's policy of building rank-and-file unity whenever possible. District president James McLeish credited such efforts with the ability of the International Projector Company's 350-member UE shop in Bloomfield, New Jersey, to wage a successful six-month strike that year. The community around the shop and the IUE locals in the area had given crucial support.[44]

By the spring of 1956, many members in District 4 were impatient with the failure of the union's national

43. NYT, May 13, 1956, p. 78; May 15, 1956, p. 22.

44. 1955 UE Convention Proceedings, p. 161; also interview with David Montgomery, former shop chairman in UE local 475, July 29, 1987.

officers to accomplish on a national level what they had in the district. Anxious to become a part of the newly united labor movement and believing that their experience showed that Cold War barriers could be surmounted, they felt the national officers were being stubborn in their refusal to modify positions that they knew the Carey group would not publicly accept. The district leaders believed that the IUE leadership, acutely aware of its own precarious position in the industry and in the AFL-CIO and eager to enlist the UE's organizing experience, had made concessions not suggested by their public pronouncements. According to one former member of the UE national staff, the IUE group made a "substantial offer" including major UE influence on both the GE and Westinghouse conference boards and in the editing of the newspaper of the new merged organization.[45] A UE district president and member of the UE subcommittee assigned the task of negotiating merger, who opposed the District 4 move when it came, also suggested that negotiations were more substantial than the IUE public positions indicated.[46]

Believing that a merger under the conditions offered could pave the way for the UE to reassert its influence in the industry (as the Carey group feared), District 4 and its leaders, James McLeish and Archer Cole, favored going ahead in April 1956. When no merger occurred nationally, District 4, hoping that the move would open the way for other UE districts to merge, proceeded on its own.[47] At a meeting of representatives from the locals in the district, the decision was made to recommend immediate affiliation with the IUE. The UE local representatives based their recommendation

---

45. Interview with former UE International Representative Benjamin Riskin, May 20, 1987.

46. Interview with former UE District 11 President Ernest De Maio, October 2, 1986.

47. Pro-merger leaders of local 475 projected this idea. Montgomery interview; also interview with Ed Weise, president local 456, by Ruth Prago, April 24, 1981, Tamiment Library, Oral History of the American Left.

on a fourteen-point agreement with the IUE leaders in the area. In their press release, they stated that "workers must unite" because "employers all over the country are stepping up attacks against all unions and against the wages and conditions of their employees."

The statement included a hint of the old UE pride when it predicted that the affiliation would "combine the strength and know-how of our locals with the strength of IUE locals...." It blamed the national officers for failing to reach a national agreement: "Unfortunately, after 12 months, we find that the National Officers have spent more time throwing obstacles in the way of this unity than in actually trying to unify the industry. They have placed their own personal feelings and antagonisms above the needs and interests of our members."[48]

How are we to assess the merit of the District 4 charges? We have no way of knowing whether national merger talks might still have succeeded when the district leaders reached an agreement with their counterparts in the IUE. In the opinion of Ernest DeMaio, who participated in the national meetings, an agreement was still possible when "District 4 broke ranks. It's like having a strike and your biggest local going back to work."

On the other hand, DeMaio's words also suggest the great reluctance of the national leaders of both unions to take the step that would have reunited the workers in one union:

> ...it was obvious that two guys weren't too happy about the idea. Carey was not happy about taking in the UE. Matles was not happy about going in. And they had personal reasons.... Matles saw the handwriting on the wall. There was no place for him in that kind of unity. Carey was opposed to it because he feared us. He feared that we

48. UE District 4 Executive Board Statement, "District 4 Locals Vote to Recommend Affiliation with IUE AFL-CIO," IUE Carey Papers, 33/9, "UE-IUE Unity."

> had the loyalty of the people, and we had the ability and we would be able to take the union away from him....[49]

The District 4 charges may sound harsh, but for their part, the UE national officers made charges of their own. They drew an exaggerated image of a District 4 leadership attempting to drag their members into the IUE. The *UE News* argued that "all the fire for secession was in the [district] leadership," and that membership meetings called to vote on secession had generally been "small and gloomy."[50] However, in Matles's home local 475, a "packed meeting" of shop stewards and rank-and-file members, after hearing Matles personally urge the local to wait, had voted to support immediate merger with the IUE.[51]

Hearing the words of a UE local leader in the district gives an idea of the strength of the "fire" for unity at the time. In the words of Pat Barile, president of local 428:

> Practically every day of my life, we would have to be—the local leadership—getting out leaflets, explaining what was going on in the world: the Cold War, red-baiting, what it was: lies about the UE, what the split was...over and over and over again....
>
> You finish [dealing with] one raid, negotiate a contract, there would be another raid... and not only in my shop... We were consuming people and we were consuming money and worker rights in the struggle, and it had to come to an end.... It was always our opinion that the UE leadership and the UE contract was superior, and given the merger situation we could hold our own with anybody and eventually... whatever the union was called would be a better union.[52]

---

49. DeMaio interview.
50. UE News, May 28, 1956, p. 8.
51. Montgomery interview.
52. Interview with former president of local 428 Pat Barile, August 14, 2001.

Based on their experience in such instances as the Bloomfield and Westinghouse strikes, their confidence in their ability to influence the course of a merged organization, and their belief that the IUE leadership in the district desired to oust Carey and would welcome their help, members and leaders in UE District 4 were ready to merge.

In fairness to the national UE officers, the IUE leadership in District 4 had apparently made concessions that Carey had resisted on the national level. Publicly district president Milton Weihrauch continued to echo the national position. The IUE press release stated that "the workers still trapped in the discredited Communist-dominated UE in District 4 have initiated action to bolt from UE" and rejoin their fellow workers in a "non-Communist American trade union." It continued that the UE locals would "be governed by the IUE-AFL-CIO Constitution that forbids from holding local, district, or international office any individual who is a Communist Party member or who consistently pursues policies and activities directed toward the achievement of the program" of the party.[53]

However, the actual 14-point agreement that the two sides in District 4 had reached included very different language. In this district, the IUE leadership had apparently relaxed the most restrictive Cold War barriers in order to reach terms acceptable to the UE. For example, all locals were guaranteed the right to elect officers, stewards, and business agents with no mention of the ban on "Communists." Especially significant was point number 5:

> All present UE members will become good standing members of the IUE. In locals which previously went IUE, where some UE members have been barred, District

53. Draft of IUE District 4 press release, n.d., IUE Carey Papers, 33/9 "UE-IUE Unity."

> Officers of IUE will urge these few locals to admit all former UE members into membership.[54]

Also point 11 assured the new members that IUE members and staff who use the Fifth Amendment are not to be deprived of their livelihood by companies or the Union for availing themselves of their constitutional rights."[55] Thus, IUE District 4 leaders committed themselves to support members fired for refusing to answer questions under conditions such as the Cordiner policy. In short, the agreement included language that appeared to soften the IUE's national Cold War positions. The efforts of UE District 4 to build bridges between their locals and those now in the IUE had enabled it to bargain for conditions more favorable than those the national IUE leaders had been willing to concede.

During the next five months, several other entire districts left the UE. Having been unable to build the local relationships characteristic of District 4, they did not for the most part go into the IUE, but instead divided among the other unions with which the UE had competed. District 3 in upstate New York, Districts 8 and 9 in the Midwest, and the Ohio-Kentucky District 7 had all left by the time of the UE's next national convention in September 1956. The case of District 7, which only left less than a month before the convention, especially disappointed the national leaders. That district, after serious division during the 1949-50 split, had reorganized by early 1951 and continued under leaders such as Sterling Neal of the International Harvester local 236F in Louisville and Marie Reed of local 735 in Cleveland.

The districts aggressive program on civil rights had been the topic of reports in the *UE News*. When the District 7 council meeting convened in Louisville in April 1954 in racially integrated facilities, the district and

54. UE District 4 Executive Board Statement, "District 4 Locals Recommend Affiliation with IUE."

55. Ibid.

national leadership considered it a major breakthrough in the union's work.[56] When the Harvester locals had joined the UAW in March 1955, district president Neal had divorced himself from the move, counseling patience while the national leaders sought merger for the entire union.[57] However, during the weeks immediately before the convention, District 7 seceded and joined the IAM.

It has been suggested that, because the districts that left the UE in 1956 included those in which the left forces and the Communist Party had the most influence, the secessions resulted from a Party decision to "liquidate" the union.[58] There are problems with this interpretation. The Party had always urged the building of unity and participation in the "mainstream" labor movement whenever possible, but there is not evidence that it had, or claimed, the ability to "liquidate" unions. Rather, evidence suggests that disagreement existed and was at least implicitly acknowledged in the party on trade union issues under the adverse circumstances of 1955–56.[59] While it is true that the seceding districts included those where the party had the most influence, such as Districts 4 and 7, parts of the UE which remained, such

---

56. UE News, May 31, 1954, p. 9; District Council 7 Minutes, April 24-25, 1954, UE Archives, D/7-20.

57. UE District Council 7 Minutes, April 23-24, 1955, UE Archives, D/7-21.

58. Ronald Schatz, The Electrical Workers, p. 230, writes that the party's "decision to liquidate the left-wing union [was] the ultimate blow." Here, Schatz appears to make assumptions about the party's influence and intentions that he does not make in his previous discussion. He notes, for example, that the UE did not always follow the advice of the Communist press, p. 185. When discussing the attacks that did come from sources outside the union, such as employers, Congressional committees, the press, and the Church, Schatz argues that factionalism was not "solely" the result of external factors. When discussing the split of the mid-1950s, he appears to assume the opposite.

59. For Communist Party discussion on the issue of labor unity during this period, see Political Affairs, July 1953, pp. 33-42, "The Left and the Struggle for Labor Unity" by John Swift; August 1953, pp. 37-50, "The Left Unions and Labor Unity II" also by Swift; March 1955, pp. 30-40, "The AFL-CIO Merger" by George Morris; January 1956, pp. 51-65, "The Labor Merger" by Hal Simon; and February 1957, pp. 49-58, "Some Concepts of Our Trade Union Work" also by Simon.

as District 11 (Illinois, Wisconsin, and Minnesota) and Districts 1 and 6 in Pennsylvania had also shown strong left influence.

A more significant overall assessment of the developments of 1955–56 would be that 1) the UE districts made their decisions based on their own particular circumstances and 2) the disagreement was not over the basics of the UE program, but was rather a tactical one over how best to move that program forward under the existing conditions. In District 4, the UE leadership and activists felt that their work in building rank-and-file unity with the IUE had created possibilities in that union and in the AFL-CIO. In District 1, on the other hand, the large local 107 had played a central role in forging unity during the Westinghouse strike while itself remaining outside the AFL-CIO. No one could predict what the results of these decisions would be—that for instance, the officers of District 7 would find themselves investigated and barred from office in the IAM or that the UE District 4 would eventually play an influential role in the IUE.[60]

Would UE members and activists have preferred to find a way to remain in a unified organization? Listen again to local 428's Pat Barile:

> ...If the whole union had done it, then what would have come into play is this group of... UE people in the IUE shops. We would have been shaking hands with them again and seeing them at meetings again, organizing the work together again.... It didn't happen around the

60. For local 107 leadership's thinking, see Carl Gray's statement in "The Westinghouse Lockout at Lester," p. 29. On the other hand, Archer Cole, former international representative in UE District 4, in a telephone conversation on February 27, 1987, stated that he was the only UE member who was barred from office after the district merged with the IUE, and that he was reinstated after Carey's defeat in 1965. As of that conversation, Cole was the IUE director of organization and remained positive about the results of the District 4 decision to merge, saying that "he was proud of having helped build the IUE into a strong progressive organization."

> country; it happened only... in District 4, and we lived with it the best we could....[61]

How fared the UE in its new situation? The union's 1956 convention delegates, fewer than the previous year, gathered in New York City in September in a grim mood. The question of labor unity continued to occupy their attention, and the discussion indicated that they had lost none of their commitment, although they clearly resented the treatment they had received from leaders of other unions. Secretary-treasurer Julius Emspak captured the tone of the discussion when he asked:

> Is there any unity in the AFL-CIO? The answer is no.... Is there a union of eight or nine hundred thousand now in the industry which we could have been? Did we split or did we fight against it?[62]

Delegates also leveled criticism at the district leaders who had departed the UE during the previous months, but one speaker, DeMaio, took a more restrained and reflective view. Arguing that those who had left the union were "honorable men" and that "one day longer than necessary to achieve unity in the UE is too long," he urged an end to name-calling.[63]

Emspak observed that, in fact, several unions now competed for members in the industry and that many workers remained unorganized. The convention adopted a program for "reuniting" the workers in the industry that called on the AFL-CIO to grant the UE a charter as an "autonomous international union" and on the other unions in the electrical industry, the IAM, IBEW, UAW, and IUE to join UE in establishing a committee in order to assure cooperation in collective bargaining, in organizing, and in planning for the "reunification of the

61. Barile interview.

62. UE News, October 1, 1956, pp. 2, 10.

63. Ray Hansen to Carey, UE Convention Report, IUE Carey Papers, 33/9; IUE-CIO News, October 1, 1956, p. 9

workers in our industry."[64] While more than a decade would pass before the UE's proposal would find a positive response from a new IUE leadership, this position, nonetheless, provided a guideline for the union's activity during the coming years.

At the end of 1956, the UE, despite its losses, still enjoyed certain advantages and was not without influence. In certain places, the union retained significant membership. For example, it still claimed 40,000 members in Pennsylvania alone. During the 1956 election campaign, UE's District 1 (eastern) and District 6 (western) actively supported former Philadelphia Mayor Joseph Clark in his campaign for the United States Senate. Clark, reflecting the changes outside the labor movement since 1953, sought the union's endorsement, and the UE claimed a share of the credit when Clark succeeded against the "Eisenhower tide."[65] Besides Pennsylvania, the union's membership was now concentrated in New England (District 2), Canada (District 5), parts of the Midwest (District 11), and the West Coast (District 12).

However, this accounting does not fully reflect the extent of support for the UE's program among electrical workers. The Westinghouse strike suggested the extent to which the actions of the UE leadership reflected the sentiments of Westinghouse workers. Also, the secessions of the mid-1950s, in upstate New York and in District 4, had not resulted from disagreements with the union's principle policies. Rather, electrical union leaders and activists had disagreed over how most effectively to promote the UE program in the labor movement. Finally, when we recall that the IUE leaders themselves feared that the UE forces might actually regain leadership in a merged union, it appears that even the UE's harshest critics in the labor movement believed that the union's influence exceeded its formal membership.

---

64. UE Policy, 1956-1957, pp. 8-10.
65. UE News, October 29, 1956, p. 1; November 12, 1956, p. 1.

On the other hand, while the UE's influence and reputation went beyond its own membership, the union's continued existence as an independent organization was also of considerable significance. While the left-center coalition had suffered reeling setbacks, it was still on its feet. Some of the more familiar left-wing speakers would from now on be missing from UE conventions: John Gojack of District 9, Neal and Reed of District 7, McLeish and Lustig, and others of District 4. But others remained: DeMaio of District 11 continued to serve as chair of the resolutions committee, and Max Helfand of local 155 chaired the credentials committee; George Bobich of District 6 and William Burch of District 11 would still be heard at conventions. Along with the other surviving unions expelled from the CIO, notably the west coast longshoreman and the western miners ("mine-mill" which by the mid-1960s would merge with the United Steelworkers), the UE provided an alternative labor voice during the period of the Cold War "consensus."

For instance, the union's conventions would consistently address the growing issue of atmospheric testing of atomic and nuclear weapons. The 1956 convention also continued the policy of addressing the military budget, which would again become a burning issue a decade later. The 1956 delegates adopted a resolution repudiating "the assumption of some AFL-CIO officials that it is only possible to keep America at work by maintaining the fear and danger of war."[66] The existence of the independent unions, which after 1958 included the teamsters, provided a reminder of the fragile nature of the consensus in the labor movement.

Finally, any accurate assessment of organized labor's position after the AFL-CIO merger must include an accounting of the political contradictions. While the leadership of the AFL-CIO had ridden the Cold War wave into power and showed no signs of changing, dominant sections of the U.S. ruling class now appeared to

---

66. UE Policy, 1956-1957, pp. 25-26.

moderate their rhetoric and grudgingly to accept "world stalemate." The UE had noted the significance of the Geneva summit the previous year, and the events of 1956, while not fulfilling the hopes that the summit had raised, tended to blur the lines of debate over the Cold War. Eisenhower's role in reining in the colonial powers during the Suez crisis appeared to match the urging of the UE resolution that "In every case the influence of the United States should be put on the side of the anti-colonial forces throughout the world seeking freedom from old imperial dominations."[67]

The uneasy "Cold War consensus" would be temporary. One historian has suggested that by the fall of 1955 "consensus was settling like snow over U.S. politics,"[68] but the record shows that the labor movement found no such settlement. The storm ebbed somewhat, but the snow never settled. When the consensus in the country unraveled during the mid-1960s, the significance of the UE's role and its program would again become clear.

---

67. Ibid.

68. Hodgson, American in Our Time, p. 74.

Chapter 7

Shoulder to Shoulder? The Electrical Unions and the Consensus 1956–1965

The IUE's national president, speaking to the union's District 1 Council in September 1963, explained why the district boundaries had been redrawn. With the reconstituted District 1 expanding to include western Pennsylvania as well as the eastern part, the IUE could focus its efforts on rooting out the last UE strongholds at both ends of the state, and, he believed, "If the UE is wiped out in Pennsylvania, it is finished in the United States."[1] Carey's assessment showed how far removed from trade union realities he had become. Within two years, the IUE's founding leader would find himself forced from office after a Labor Department investigation overturned his 1964 election.

The decade following the AFL-CIO merger exposed the remarkable failure of the Cold War leadership to bring electrical workers into their fold. On the other hand, the UE and pro-unity forces in the IUE would re-emerge as the stabilizing influence in the industry at the same time as the UE became one of the first organizations to oppose United States policy in Southeast Asia. The UE's staying power and renewed growth combined with the IUE's problems and Carey's eventual defeat would open the way for renewed cooperation between the two unions

1. Harry Block Papers, Box 1 Folder 1963, Temple University Paley Library Urban Archives.

in collective bargaining. By the end of the 1960s, the first chain-wide united bargaining with GE and Westinghouse in two decades would occur.

While the developments of the 1960s demonstrated the lack of consensus in the labor movement, they also showed the deep and lasting effects the Cold War would have on labor. The coordination between the two major electrical unions would reconfigure the collective bargaining situation in the industry; it would show the increasing pressures from below for change in the leadership of the IUE; and the breakdown in labor's "consensus" would be a factor in the eroding support for the Vietnam War. All these changes would not, however, lead to any change in the rigid Cold War stance of the AFL-CIO leadership. This period roughly falls into two parts: 1) the decade of the "consensus" when the quarantine of the "left" unions" and the dominance of the AFL international posture held sway, and 2) the period of the erosion of the consensus from 1965 onwards.[2]

During the decade following the AFL-CIO merger, the fortunes of the UE and the IUE were always linked. After District 4 left the UE, IUE leaders continued to show their acute awareness of their precarious position. If an anonymous FBI informant is considered a reliable source, at least one more meeting took place in August with both Carey and Fitzgerald present. This report suggests that Carey pressed desperately for a merger along the lines of the agreements reached with Schenectady or District 4, but that Fitzgerald resisted because those agreements threatened "membership rights and representation." So, the old roadblocks remained and stalled any further progress.[3] In September, three days before the opening

2. See Hodgson, America in Our Time, chapters 13 and 14, for a general discussion of the breakdown of the "liberal consensus."

3. UE Archives, FBI New York file, Box 26, 100-13644, section 97, SAC Newark to Director, FBI (10026912) 2/1/57. According to this memo, "CAREY mentioned that EMSPAK, MATLES, and DE MAIO were out as far as some IUE people were concerned." [upper case in original] IUE representatives had taken a similar stance at meetings the previous summer. See the same file, Box 28, subfile A-1, SAC Albany (to) Director, FBI (100-3-89) 8/19/55.

of the IUE convention in St. Louis, Carey invited Fitzgerald to speak as a guest if Carey could address the UE's gathering in New York the following week.[4]

The lateness of the invitation meant that Fitzgerald's own convention preparations prevented him from attending, but three UE representatives, including Matles and District 11 president DeMaio, did travel to St. Louis. They met twice with Carey on the convention's third day, but that was as far as the IUE president was willing to go. The UE members spoke informally to IUE delegates outside the convention hall, but they left St. Louis without making a formal presentation to the entire convention.

This episode characterized the complex relationship between the two unions during much of the next decade: lack of formal productive contact despite general understanding that the division in the industry damaged both. Each union reported its own version of the failed convention exchange. The IUE claimed that the presence of Matles in St. Louis had torpedoed any possibility of success, and that the UE leaders must have known this ahead of time. According to Carey, had he let Matles address the convention, the delegates "would have ripped him limb from limb," and that one delegate had threatened, "If that red SOB ever comes in here, there will be hell to pay."[5] The response Matles met, the IUE version went, relieved the UE leadership of any obligation to reciprocate and invite Carey to its own convention in New York. The UE, on the other hand, contended that its representatives had been well received by IUE delegates in the hotel lobby and that the IUE leaders "seemed surprised and uneasy that their invitation had been accepted," and that, due to the UE members' presence in St. Louis, "the convention corridors buzzed with speculation."[6]

---

4. UE News, September 17, 1956, p. 1; IUE News, October 1, 1956, p. 9.

5. IUE News, October 1, 1956, p. 9. The St. Louis Post Dispatch also reported on Matles's visit, September 12, 1956, p. 13A, clipping in IUE Carey Papers 33/10.

6. UE News, September 17, 1956, p. 1.

Carey's invitation to Fitzgerald suggested that he still considered the smaller union a force to be reckoned with, but his response to Matles's arrival shows that he was uncertain how to do so. The 700 IUE delegates included representatives of sharply divergent strains of opinion, and what response Matles or DeMaio could have expected was anyone's guess. Carey may have feared that inviting them to speak would have antagonized his right-wing supporters; on the other hand, he may have feared that a UE unity proposal would have proved popular with many of the delegates newly arrived from the UE. While this flirtation yielded no concrete results, it demonstrated that the loss of UE District 4 had not eliminated the UE as a factor in the industry. In fact, during the period of the Cold War "consensus," the UE seems never to have faced the danger of total elimination. Even at its lowest point in the late 1950s and early 1960s, it was always a going concern.

It was true, however, that the union still had to expend much time and energy fighting legal battles at least through the remainder of the 1950s. The highest profile case was the effort to deport James Matles. By 1959, Matles had faced legal proceedings for a decade. In December 1949, the House Committee on Un-American Activities had subpoenaed Matles and Julius Emspak, charging that the two had falsely denied membership in the Communist Party when filing their Taft-Hartley affidavits. Their refusal to cooperate with the Committee resulted in contempt of Congress charges against both. Emspak had been convicted, but the Supreme Court overturned the conviction in March of 1955. Although Matles was acquitted in March 1951, his legal problems continued.[7]

7. See UE News, October 17, 1955, pp. 6-7, for summary of the Matles case; also "Matles Case Manual," UE Archives, Series PA, file 330; UE News, March 12, 1951, p. 1, for Matles's acquittal. For the Emspak case, see UE News, March 11, 1955, p. 3 and June 6, 1955, pp. 1, 5-9, and the St. Louis Post Dispatch, May 29, 1955, clipping in IUE Papers A 2.06, FF"UE 1955 I."

In December of the following year, the Attorney General's office filed a petition in federal court in Brooklyn asking the court to deprive Matles of his U.S. citizenship. The Government charged that Matles had falsified his citizenship application almost 20 years earlier when he denied membership in the Communist Party. Therefore, in 1958 when the Supreme Court denied the Justice Department's petition, it marked the end of a long legal battle for the union.[8] The decision also signaled that the most nefarious Cold War assumptions were losing their clout. Matles, born a Rumanian Jew, had attended night school classes in New York to learn English, had become an American citizen in 1934, and had enlisted and served two years in the Army during World War II. Within a few years, he had found himself more than holding his own before Congressional investigators. His detractors and political opponents had, on occasion, resorted to egregious stereotypes when called upon to account for his leadership performance. For example, in 1948 before the deportation proceedings had begun, a "research specialist" had advised Congressman Kersten's subcommittee:

> James Matles is not an American by any reasonable definition, neither by birth nor present citizenship nor ideological attachment. He is a Hungarian born alien Communist, and as such in his union capacity, he exercises a dominant influence in the lives of 2,000,000 Americans.... It may be time to reopen the status of citizenship of union leaders who possess such extraordinary powers in the union movement.[9]

---

8. A biography of Matles, as told to editor Tom Wright, was serialized in the UE News during the winter of 1955-56 after Attorney General Herbert Brownell resurrected the suit following a period of relative inactivity. For the Supreme Court's decision, see UE News, April 14, 1958, p. 1 and NYT, April 8, 1955.

9. U.S. House of Representatives, Subcommittee of the Committee on Education and Labor, Investigation of Communist Infiltration of the United Electrical, Radio and Machine Workers of America, 80th Congress, 2nd Session, 1948, p. 168, testimony of Dr. Joseph B. Matthews.

During the decade since Congress heard this assessment, the UE had seen much of its formal membership stripped away, the circulation of the *UE News* and its other publications drop as a result, and its measurable influence, perhaps, decline, but Matles would remain a citizen and a trade union leader.

The union, as an organization, continued to face legal issues. Since December 1955, the UE had faced the threat of decertification by the Subversive Activities Control Board as a result of the Attorney General's petition filed during the Westinghouse strike. In March 1959, the Justice Department, now under William Rogers, requested that the SACB abandon the proceedings that had aimed to cite the union as a "Communist infiltrated organization." The Department gave as its reasons for dropping the case the unavailability of key witnesses or their withdrawal from the union, a likely reference to the old UE District 4. The union, on the other hand, saw the Department's decision as proof that the Government had never had a case in the first place. While this in no way marked the end of the union's problems with investigating agencies, the UE did see it as a tacit admission by the Government that the effort to unearth some evidence of the subversive intentions of the union's leaders or members had failed.[10]

In fact, the UE had more on its plate than the legal problems of its top leaders or the union as a whole. Of the 28 General Electric employees dismissed under the company's "Cordiner policy" or "security policy," the

---

10. NYT, March 25, 1959, p. 8; April 1, 1959, p. 29; UE News, March 30, 1959, p. 1; April 13, 1959, p. 1, for the Justice Department decision to drop the case. However, the issue was still alive as late as 1962 when J. Edgar Hoover responded to a request for information about the UE from an "unnamed person" who had contacted the FBI during a representation vote between the UE and the Steelworkers. Fitzgerald protested in a letter to Hoover that Hoover's response left "a false inference that this private accusation has some sort of official status," but that in fact "the files of the FBI were combed" and no evidence for the charge of "Communist infiltration" of the union was ever found. Fitzgerald to Hoover, February 8, 1962, UE Archives, UE Staff FBI files, Box 26, File 122-199.

most widely publicized was that of John Nelson, president of the Erie local. The forty-year-old activist died in 1960 with his court case still pending. Less well-known cases included that of John Killian of local 1111 at the Allen Bradley Company in Milwaukee. A World War II veteran, Killian had gone to work at Allen Bradley after attending the University of Wisconsin. In 1952, he had served the last four months of an unexpired term in a vacated post as a trustee of the local. In November 1955, the Justice Department charged him with having filed a false Taft-Hartley affidavit when he assumed the position. More than two years later, after his second trial, Killian was sentenced to a five-year prison term in May 1958.[11]

Some former UE activists who had left the union also faced prosecution. For instance, Marie Reed Haug, her husband Fred Haug, and five other former District 7 activists who had left the UE were sentenced to 18-month jail terms and fined $2,500 each for allegedly conspiring to file false Taft-Hartley affidavits during the time they belonged to the union in Ohio. The contempt of Congress's conviction of John Gojack, former president of UE District 9 who had gone into the IAM, was finally overturned by the Supreme Court in 1966.[12]

While the UE persisted in its legal battles, its experience showed that the union could survive as an independent organization and that it was never totally isolated. Following the expulsion of the Teamsters from the AFL-CIO in 1958 on grounds of corruption, the UE gave sympathetic coverage to the Teamsters' position and reprinted articles from other labor publications, questioning the AFL-CIO action and comparing it to the CIO expulsions of nearly a decade earlier. The Cleveland Federation of Labor recalled that, during the late 1940s

---

11. Nelson's case has been covered by Matles and Higgins, Them and Us, pp. 221-223 and by Ronald Schatz, The Electrical Workers, pp. 241-242. For the Killian case, see NYT, November 18, 1955, p. 1; November 30, 1956, p. 16; May 14, 1958, p. 14; and the UE News, November 28, 1955, p. 5.

12. NYT, February 20, 1958, p. 18; June 14, 1966, p. 25.

"backed up by loud howls of anguish in the nation's daily press, businessmen convinced the general public that labor in America was getting its orders from the Kremlin" and suggested that a similar campaign was being waged against the Teamsters, this time using the issue of internal corruption.[13] By the early 1960s, a loose relationship appeared to develop among independent unions, including the UE. According to one report, a "close working alliance" was the topic of discussions between the Teamsters and other unions including the UE. In April 1963, Teamster president Jimmy Hoffa and the UE's Fitzgerald both addressed the "Mine Mill" convention where Hoffa told the delegates that "the hope of the American labor movement rests on such unions as Mine Mill, the International Longshoremen and Warehousemen, United Electrical Workers, Teamsters and certain other independent unions."[14]

By the mid-1960s, the UE showed signs of renewed organizational success, including the regaining of some shops lost during the 1950s. For instance, in September 1964, the 700 workers at the GHR foundry in Dayton, Ohio, voted to return to the UE after eight years in the United Steel Workers. The union claimed that the plant, whose workforce was sixty percent African American, would have come back sooner had its adversaries not succeeded in exploiting racial tensions among the workers. In 1959, the Labor Board had needed three elections to determine the USW the winner. At the 1964 UE convention, new organization director Robert Kirkwood reported that, during the previous year, the union had suffered no losses due to raids, had won elections covering 4,000 workers, and was engaged in sixteen

---

13. UE News, June 6, 1958, p. 9, quoted the Cleveland Citizen, publication of the Cleveland Federation of Labor.

14. The report of the "working alliance" appeared in the Montreal Star, May 6, 1959, and was featured in a critical article in the IUE News on June 28, 1962, in which the IUE accused the Teamsters of "fronting for the UE at Lynn GE" after some Lynn workers signed Teamsters' cards. For the Hoffa quote, see UE News, April 22, 1963, p.1.

major organizing drives. At the 1965 convention, Kirkwood reported that only the UE had won any major labor board elections against General Electric during the previous year.[15]

During this period, the union never abandoned its commitment to seeking alternatives to the nation's foreign policy. At the 1958 convention, the delegates heard retired Brigadier General Hugh Hester urge productive negotiations between the United States and the Soviet Union. The *UE News* printed excerpts from Hester's speech that directly addressed the issue of American ideas about the USSR. Reporting on his recent 12,000-mile journey through the Soviet Union, Hester said, "Neither the Russian people nor the Russian leaders want war with the United States. They have had it. They want peaceful co-existence and want it badly." Hester illustrated the cost of the arms race to Americans in terms of domestic social programs and challenged the notion that "Stalin's intransigence caused the Cold War while the West was perfectly willing to have a co-operative effort," adding, "I submit that is simply not true."[16]

Four years later, when Fitzgerald addressed the convention of the west coast longshoremen (ILWU), he mentioned the expanding role of the AFL-CIO in foreign affairs. The American Institute for Free Labor Development (AIFLD) had been chartered by the AFL-CIO in 1961 as a private nonprofit corporation ostensibly for the purpose of supporting "the development of free, democratic trade union structures in Latin America through labor training centers and social development programs...." Fitzgerald, however, voiced suspicion of the AFL-CIO's relationship to official United States policy and referred specifically to Walther Reuther's reported willingness to participate in foreign policy-related activity. Noting

---

15. UE News, September 21, 1964, p. 9; October 5, 1964, p. 1; September 27, 1965, p. 6.

16. UE News, September 29, 1958, p. 5. See also Hester to Russ Nixon, UE Archives, RG 1, Nixon, Box 1/FF 1. Nixon had worked with Hester during his time in the Army during WWII. See his bio in Appendix B.

Table 2
Membership of Selected AFL-CIO and Independent Unions 1955–1983

Union	1955	1960	1962	1965	1970	1973	1980	1983
Auto UAW*	1,329,000	1,136,000	1,074,000	-	1,486,000	1,502,000	1,356,000	1,026,000
Steel USW	1,015,000	945,000	879,000	-	1,091,000	1,248,000	966,000	694,000
Electrical								
UE**	133,000	59,000	55,000	-	-	90,000***	89,000	54,000
IUE	284,000	271,000	270,000	-	309,000	296,000	224,000	172,000
IBEW	601,000	689,000	706,000	736,000	831,000	854,000	940,000	869,000
Machinists								
IAM	-	687,000	667,000	-	842,000	743,000	754,000	540,000
Clothing & Textile	274,000	273,000	269,000	-	287,000	264,000	306,000	251,000

* independent after 1968

**independent 1955-1983

Sources: Leo Troy, Trade Union Membership 1897-1962, National Bureau of Economic Research, Occasional Paper 92, 1965, pp. A-20 through A-27, A-37.

Troy and Neil Shefflin, Union Source Book, West Orange, New Jersey, 1985, pp. 3-6, 3-7, 3-16, 6-5, 6-21, B-4.

*** The UE figures for 1973, 1980, and 1983 are the author's estimates based on Troy's statement that the figures in the Union Source Book, pp. 6-21, specifically undercounted the UE because that union's Canadian membership had been subtracted twice—once by the union and once by Troy. The UE claimed higher figures, 160,000, by the late 1960s. The UE figures presented here could also be an underestimate due to the union's unusual method of collecting dues. Employers holding UE contracts did not send dues receipts directly to the national office as was the case in other unions, but to the locals, who, in turn, paid per capita dues to the national union. Troy used the national dues reports to compute membership.

that Reuther was then traveling to Japan and that the Administration was "going to use him in the South American countries in the near future," the UE president asked, "Is the main purpose of the AFL-CIO to send representatives around the world to take the fight out of these people? If it is, then they better tell them to stay the hell home where they belong." While the union had previously published articles on the cost of high military budgets and the need for a nuclear test ban treaty, in 1964, it began reporting speeches and statements by members of Congress, such as Senators Wayne Morse and William Fulbright, who were warning against American military involvement in Southeast Asia.[17]

During this period, the UE continued to insist that its brand of "bread and butter" unionism, unencumbered by ties to big business dominated foreign policies, could benefit American workers and that AFL-CIO leaders frequently refused to confront substantive union issues. For example, the union criticized that UAW leadership for not responding to demands in the auto workers' union to mount a campaign for a shorter workweek during the recession of 1957–58. The UE claimed that a shorter workweek at forty hours pay would create 40,000 jobs at GE and Westinghouse alone, and Fitzgerald wrote to other unions in the major electrical chains urging a campaign on the issue. The proposal of the UE's 1958 convention to forego a wage increase in exchange for a reduction in the hours worked received national press attention, but no sympathetic response from employers or AFL-CIO union leaders.[18]

The union never gave up its active efforts to influence legislation, reduced in size though it was. In June of 1958, 150 UE members brought 100,000 signatures to

---

17. For discussion of the AIFLD, see Ronald Radosh, American Labor and United States Foreign Policy, pp. 415 ff. For Fitzgerald's remarks, see UE News, April 22, 1963, p. 1; for reports on Congressional statements, see UE News, April 6, 1964m, p. 9; June 15, 1964, p. 9.

18. UE News, July 21, 1958, p. 2; September 15, 1958, p. 1; September 29, 1958, p. 1; NYT September 4, 1958, p. 43.

Washington to urge Congressional action on the issues of unemployment compensation and high taxes on workers' earnings.[19] Although the number of delegates was only half the number that had attended the legislative conference four years earlier at the peak of the McCarthy hearings in March 1954, the effort nevertheless demonstrated the union's continuing ability to mobilize members around political issues.

Circumstances forced the UE to show its staying power in one other area during this period. The sudden death of Julius Emspak in 1962 meant the loss of one of the union's most influential leaders and brought the first change in top leadership since Carey's defeat in 1941. Emspak had been one of the "young fellows" that the older activists had encouraged to take leadership in organizing the Schenectady local during the 1930s and had served as the union's secretary-treasurer since its founding. One obituary described him as "quiet and studious," and Matles, his longtime colleague in leadership, later remembered him as a "true worker intellectual."[20] At the time of his death, Emspak was developing his thinking on the rising issue of the displacement of workers by automation. He saw corporations reaping the benefits of new technology, such as the "electronic computing machine," and he argued that, because the research was supported by public funding, workers had a "social claim" to a share of the benefits.[21] After Emspak's death, Matles changed jobs and became the union's next secretary-treasurer, and the convention elected veteran organizer Robert Kirkwood to the post of director of organization. This change occurred as the

---

19. UE News, July 9, 1958, pp. 1-7.

20. Lynn, Massachusetts Daily Evening Item, April 27, 1962, clipping in UE Archives, RG 1.2, Box "Emspak, Julius correspondence 1936-62, FF "1962 Death." James Matles interview by Ronald Filippelli, May 6, 1968, transcript in Penn State Labor History Archives.

21. Emspak to Dr. Dirk Struik, UE Archives, "Emspak correspondence 1936-62" FF "1961-62."

UE's fortunes were improving and would test the continuity of its leadership.

While the UE struggled to survive outside the Cold War fold, the IUE wrestled with its own problems of a different nature. Disunity and rancor at the highest levels continued to plague the nation's largest electrical manufacturing union. Its leaders attempted to function as heads of a trade union in the traditional sense, and some local leaders showed the benefit of their earlier experience in the UE. The union's publication, the *IUE News*, reported on contract negotiations and published informative articles sharply critical of the major electrical employers when they were indicted on charges of collusion and rigged bidding. The IUE held an annual "Citizenship Conference" that featured leading political figures, generally members of Congress, as featured speakers. Photographs of the conferences show racially integrated groups of men and women union members working and socializing together.[22]

The reality of the IUE's situation remained more complicated, however. Its original leaders—Carey, Al Hartnett, and Harry Block—never succeeded in unifying the organization or in winning the confidence of a clear majority of the membership. Having sowed division in the industry for so long, they now confronted the task of effectively representing a large diverse constituency including many politically aware and militant members, while at the same time holding their position in the Cold War fold of the AFL-CIO. District 4 presented special challenges. The IUE's success in bringing in the UE's New York-north Jersey district presented awkward problems elsewhere in the union. At the 1956 IUE convention, when the leadership, arguing that the long Westinghouse strike had depleted the strike fund, proposed a dues increase, opposition surfaced. The dues

22. IUE News, June 20, 1960, p. 1; July 4, 1960, p. 1; February 22, 1962, p. 1; also photographs in IUE Papers Photos Box 1.

increase eventually passed, but the basis of the opposition exposed the leadership's precarious position.

The opposition originated with leaders of local 755 in Dayton, who doubted the given reasons for the increase and suspected that the leadership intended to use the money to hire "Communist organizers" from the former UE District 4. The opponents, taking a page from Carey's own previous activity, took the step of announcing the formation of the "IUE Committee for Democratic Constitutional Action" and circulated their complaints to numerous other locals.[23]

The affiliation of UE District 4 with the IUE also brought unwelcome attention from outside the union. In August 1957, the Senate Internal Security Subcommittee, in a move reminiscent of the earlier part of the decade, claimed to have identified 16 IUE officials as "one time Communists." The chairman, Nebraska's Roman Hruska, noting Carey's record as an anti-Communist, asked for his help in eliciting testimony from the sixteen. Carey adhered to his usual public posture, charging that the subcommittee had "smeared a great international union that prides itself on its anti-Communist record" whose success in its Cold War endeavors had "become one of the most brilliant chapters in American labor history." He continued that the IUE would conduct its own internal investigation as authorized by its executive board.[24]

In fact, on the ground inside District 4, the merger seems to have gone forward in an atmosphere of uncertainty and with both sides feeling their way ahead. Evidence suggests both attempted to honor the deal as they saw it, although their interpretations of the terms did not always match. They spoke only in the most

23. Report to IUE locals and district councils on the referendum results and constitutional changes, November 14, 1956; Report of regular membership meeting of Delco local 755, Dayton, Ohio, September 23, 1956, attached to letter from E.J. Kraft to Carey, September 27, 1956, IUE Papers A1.01 FF "IUE Committee for Democratic Constitutional Action."

24. NYT, January 25, 1957, p. 1; August 7, 1957, p. 55.

guarded terms when questioned by the press or politicians. At least some former UE staff members went on the IUE payroll and continued to function as organizers.[25] But the past still hovered over the district. Two of its members, James McLeish and Archer Cole, had appeared before the House Committee on UnAmerican Activities (HUAC) in May 1955 when they were still in the UE. They had not been cooperative witnesses.[26] When in the spring of 1957, reporters asked whether the two former UE leaders who had "taken the 5th" were on the IUE payroll, they received only noncommittal answers from all sources.

For example, former UE District 4 president McLeish told a reporter only that "I'm a member of the IUE rank and file." Former UE organizer Cole was no more forthcoming, saying, "I'm an organizer and can't comment on whether I'm paid or not." IUE District 4 president Milton Weihrauch commented to the press, "Under my watchful eye they are following [the] policies" they agreed to follow. And Les Finnegan, executive assistant to James Carey allowed that "we can exercise forgiveness... just like the Church does."[27] While sticking to their part of the bargain, the former UE activists now in the IUE appear to have felt strongly that they had opened the way for their old union to fold itself into the larger organization and exercise substantial influence. One former local president in District 4 later told an interviewer, "I had a lot of people that agreed with me, except Matles.... I always told him that if he had made the change when we made

---

25. Letter from IUE District 4 director of organization Matthew Miller to Al Hartnett, May 16, 1956, regarding 10 former UE staff members being employed by IUE; typed memo "Conference Between President Carey, James McLeish, Clifford Cameron and Charles Fay," May 16, 1957, IUE Papers, Box 23 FF 8; also Pat Barile interview.

26. House of Representatives, Committee on Un-American Activities, Eighty-Fourth Congress, Investigation of Communist Activities in the Newark, New Jersey Area, Part I, pp. 1087-1126.

27. Newark Star Ledger, April 7 and 8, 1957, clippings in IUE Papers 33/11.

the change, even as late as '57, you could have been the [word here is unclear on the tape] within two years...."[28]

Despite the internal stresses in his own union and the problems facing workers in the industry, these years saw Carey briefly blossom as a leading spokesman for the cause of anti-Communist unionism on the world stage. With the newly merged AFL-CIO as his springboard, he pursued his interest in international matters and his efforts to advance the cause of "free trade unionism" outside the United States. Following the announcement of the AFL and CIO merger plans, Carey had joined other leaders from both groups at the ICFTU Congress in Vienna in June 1955. This meeting, for the purpose of launching a "grass roots organizing campaign" in developing countries around the world, aimed to establish the international body as a force for raising living standards and "strengthening democracy against the threat of totalitarianism." The *IUE News* carried pictures of Carey with leaders of the American steel, textile, and transport unions at the Vienna meeting.[29]

After the merger, Carey stepped energetically into the role of anti-Communist labor statesman. In November 1957, he and Irving Brown attended the ICFTU executive board meeting in Brussels. As a vice president of the AFL-CIO, Carey seemed to relish activity in the international arena, but representing American labor abroad placed him in an increasingly uncomfortable position. The Meany leadership of the AFL-CIO faced criticism for bypassing or ignoring the ICFTU in specific areas and countries. Carey, who seemed often to have agreed with the criticism, apparently felt strongly enough to take the step of resigning from the AFL-CIO International Affairs Committee, but he continued his international travel on behalf of the organization. He showed sensitivity and a grasp of issues when he called in March 1958

---

28. Interview with Ed Wiese, former president of UE local 456, by Ruth Prago, April 24, 1981, New York University, Tamiment Library, Oral History of the American Left.

29. IUE News, June 20, 1955.

for Congress to pass an "anti-recession" program to combat unemployment in the electrical and other industries in the United States as "the Russians were making marked propaganda advances based on the sliding U.S. economy."[30]

During this tenuous period of persisting division in the industry, Carey also maintained his relationship with members of the foreign policy establishment in the Democratic Party. In September 1957, he accepted an invitation to join the Foreign Policy Advisory Committee of the Democratic National Committee. The twenty-eight member FPAC, chaired by Dean Acheson and Paul Nitze, was charged with establishing an alternative to the "indecisive and inconsistent...weak and wavering... military and moral posture" that the Eisenhower Administration presented to the world. The IUE president also continued to carry the anti-Communist message to the entire planet in his numerous speeches and press conferences broadcast over Voice of America.[31] Thus, the late '50s saw Carey's career pattern continue: cultivating support from sources in the foreign policy establishment while encountering resistance in the union.

The process that resulted in Carey's defeat and an eventual change in the relationship between the two electrical unions accelerated beginning in 1960. Several events of that year exposed the insecurity of the IUE's original leadership. In March, the continuing strength of the UE forces surfaced at the Lynn GE plant, now IUE local 201. Anxiety about job security persisted as a key issue here, as in the other older plants. At Lynn and the nearby Everett plants, total employment had declined from a peak of 25,000 in 1953 to 16,000 by 1958. When the UE, after more than six years, filed for a labor board

---

30. IUE Papers, Box 71 "International Affairs Files of President James B. Carey 1957-62," FF 1, 9. Carey frequently had the Soviets on his mind. During the 1956 presidential campaign, he hosted a Soviet delegation including L.N. Solovyev, chair of the AUCCTU, at IUE headquarters in an attempt to "show Russians freedom." IUE News, October 29, 1956.

31. IUE Papers Box 2 FF 53; Box 3 FF 52, 55 for VOA Broadcasts.

election, the IUE dusted off the charge that plants represented by the UE risked losing military orders. The UE, noting the sharp decline in employment at Lynn during the IUE's tenure, ridiculed the charge. In fact, the government appeared to give careful consideration to dividing the work between the two major electrical firms. Two weeks before the scheduled election, both the Lynn plant and the Westinghouse plant in Essington, still UE local 107, received large orders for atomic submarine propulsion equipment. In addition, the Army had recently a Polaris submarine contract from GE's IUE Fort Wayne plant to the company's Erie works, where the workers were still represented by UE local 506.[32]

To counter the UE arguments, the IUE called on former allies who were now presidential hopefuls. The day before the election, the IUE issued statements of support from Senators Hubert Humphrey and John Kennedy. Humphrey echoed his subcommittee report of six years earlier, warning that he would question the award of any contracts to plants whose workers were represented by an organization whose "record leaves doubt as to its first allegiance.... The UE leadership leaves considerable doubt." The Kennedy statement was also apparently not new. According to Filippelli and McColloch, his endorsement was actually a seven-year-old re-issued statement that the Senator declined to repudiate. The next day, the IUE won another narrow victory at the Lynn plant.[33]

In a surprising move less than a week after the IUE's victory at Lynn, Carey endorsed Missouri Senator Stuart Symington, another Democrat, for President. Symington had not involved himself in the Lynn election, but his relationship with Carey went back two decades to his time as president of Emerson Electric Company in

---

32. UE News, April 4, 1960, pp. 2-3. On the other hand, when the UE petitioned for an election at the Westinghouse Air Arm Division in Baltimore the same year, the Senate and the Senate Internal Security Subcommittee openly intervened. Matles and Higgins, Them and Us, pp. 224-226.

33. Ibid. Also Filippelli and McColloch, Cold War in the Working Class, p. 170.

St. Louis, and Carey's statement recalled the "model contracts" the firm had signed at that time. The endorsement received considerable press coverage, but the reports had an incredulous tone, and one suggested that Symington had asked Carey for a quick endorsement in an attempt to "head off a Kennedy stampede in labor." Although the IUE president got a warm expression of gratitude from Symington, this episode could only have added to his reputation for erratic behavior.

The contract negotiations with General Electric that year, however, most clearly demonstrated Carey's vulnerability in the union. With the widespread pattern of declining employment in the large electrical plants, the decade of the "consensus" generated numerous local work stoppages over interpretations of the contract, job description and classification, and layoffs.[34] Unable to make progress and with the company calling for further changes, including elimination of the cost of living adjustment clause, the IUE called a nationwide strike in October. GE clearly intended to maintain the initiative gained during a decade of dealing with a divided workforce, and the company's aggressive tactics aroused widespread comment in the press and from local politicians. Philadelphia Mayor Richardson Dilworth charged after the strike that the company had attempted to "blackmail" 135 communities by threatening to relocate operations if local authorities failed to keep plants open.[35]

In the fall of 1960, the IUE leadership reaped the consequences of a decade and a half of union cannibalism. While the IUE bargained for 90,000 of the 150,000 GE workers across the nation, the others were divided

34. See Schatz, The Electrical Workers, pp. 233-234, for the pattern of declining employment; David Noble, Forces of Production, pp. 270-276 and IUE News, February 29, 1960, p. 1, for accounts of unrest specifically at Lynn.

35. On the GE strike, see NYT, October 25, 1960, p. 31; Lynn Sunday Post, October 19, 1960, p. 1; IUE News, October 18, 1960, p. 1; November, 1960, p. 7.

among several unions, with the largest single group in the UE. Many plants now continued to operate and even in the plants on strike support for the union was tentative. The conduct and the outcome of the strike at the Schenectady plant underlined the tepid support for the Carey leadership. The veteran business agent Leo Jandreau was at best a reluctant Carey ally, and was the only member of the former left-wing leadership of local 301 still in office. The Schenectady local waited three days and joined the strike only on October 4. By the middle of October, Jandreau publicly broke with the national leadership and the entire local returned to work. On October 22, with other shops returning to work, the IUE called off the strike and accepted terms virtually the same as those the company had originally offered.[36]

The strike's outcome embarrassed the IUE leadership, demonstrated Carey's lack of support in the union, and insured that he would face increased opposition in the future. As the *IUE News* reported that the settlement and the "firings and suspensions" of strike activists had "embittered" GE employees toward the company, Jandreau blasted the new contract and called on Carey to resign.[37] Although Jandreau and Carey attempted to repair their relationship at a meeting in December,[38] it soon appeared that Jandreau's initial response to the settlement had reflected a growing sentiment in the union. While this would take time to develop since Carey had been re-elected to a four-year term in September, his standing in the union, always tenuous, was now in irreversible decline.

---

36. NYT covered the strike extensively. For a more detailed account of Carey's role, see Herbert Northrup, Boulwarism, pp. 81-84, 165-173.

37. IUE News, November 7, 1960, p. 3; for Jandreau's statement, see NYT, October 24, 1960, p. 17; NYT, October 25, 1960, p. 31 for A.H. Raskin's estimate that the GE settlement was the worst setback for a major union since 1945.

38. See two-page memo, "The Carey Jandreau Meeting," December 28, 1960, in IUE Papers A1.01.

Given the roots of Carey's predicament, the chaotic situation in the IUE in the early 1960s comes as no surprise. The original IUE has been described as "an inherently unstable aggregation [of] religiously motivated Catholics, secular socialists and Trotskyists, and discontented 'pork choppers'...lacking a commitment to each other and a shared vision of labor's future."[39] His reputation outside the union and outside the labor movement had made Carey the figure around whom these groups rallied. But, the IUE had also included from the beginning considerable numbers of UE supporters in workplaces where the IUE had won elections. The realignments of the mid-1950s had added increased numbers of former UE loyalists to this equation. While the opposition to Carey in the early 1960s stemmed primarily from his performance on "pure and simple" trade union issues and did not overtly call for an end to Cold War politics and red-baiting, his fate would show that appeals to anti-Communism no longer sufficed as a basis for union leadership. Forced to rely on his own leadership abilities and his record in the union, he proved unable to sustain his position.

The IUE's 1962 convention witnessed an open break between Carey and secretary-treasurer Al Hartnett, who had held office since the union's founding in 1950. After "tumultuous debate," the convention voted four-to-one to support Carey and suspend Hartnett from his post. This "victory" for Carey came at the cost of removing one of the president's key sources of support and left him in a still more vulnerable position.[40] At the next convention in 1964, the position of the union's original Cold War leader unraveled completely. The challenge this time came from supporters of Paul Jennings of the New

---

39. Schatz, The Electrical Workers, pp. 226-227.

40. IUE News, September 27, 1962, pp. 1, 3, for the convention vote and debate summary. The executive board voted 25-5 to sustain the convention decision, and Hartnett was finally ousted by a recall vote with 434 locals opposing him and 20 in support. IUE News, December 20, 1962, p. 1; December 31, 1963, p. 1.

York-northern New Jersey district, now re-designated District 3. The convention witnessed shouting matches, raucous delays, and one wrestling match involving Carey personally at the front of the hall. On the last day, the Washington, D.C. police escorted Carey from the platform as a protective measure. Despite its unsettled internal politics, the union remained the one preferred by the Democratic Party. On Wednesday, the convention's midpoint, the delegates came to order to hear an address by President Johnson and to endorse the Johnson-Humphrey ticket in the coming election.[41]

The outcome of the struggle for leadership of the IUE was finally decided in April 1965 after the U.S. Department of Labor subpoenaed the ballots cast in the election between Carey and Jennings. The investigation concluded that the union's election committee had undercounted the vote for Jennings by 25,000 out of the 130,000 ballots cast. The IUE trustees had reported inaccurate results from many locals including the largest and Carey had been decisively defeated in Schenectady local 301, Lynn local 201, and East Pittsburgh local 601.[42]

The IUE's problems did not go unnoticed by other union leaders. In February, auto workers' president Walter Reuther wrote to Carey formally proposing that the IUE merge with the UAW. Reuther noted that the two unions shared many coinciding jurisdictions, but the proposal did not strike a responsive chord with electrical union leaders. The IUE executive board rejected the offer saying that "it took us completely by surprise."

---

41. IUE News, October 8, 1964, p. 6 and UE News, October 5, 1964, pp. 2,9, for the IUE convention summary. Both the UE and the IUE endorsed the Democratic ticket in 1964. In so doing, the UE, citing the danger of the Goldwater candidacy, broke its "no endorsement" tradition of the four previous elections.

42. Report of Labor Secretary Willard Wirtz to George Meany, James Carey, and Paul Jennings, April 5, 1965. The turnaround was especially marked in local 601 where Carey's vote dropped from 2,817 to 517 and Jennings increased from 718 to 3,107. The IUE News published all the local vote totals on April 15, 1965, pp. 2, 11.

The UE's Fitzgerald commented that the more than one million workers in the electrical industry "need a union of their own and are entitled to a union of their own."[43] The IUE would remain an independent organization, but with new leadership.

The UE responded to these developments with guarded optimism. The *UE News* registered agreement as it quoted the Jennings charges against the IUE's first president:

> Carey's failure to organize contributes to his failure to negotiate better contracts.
>
> Carey has given up the cost of living. He has given up annual wage increases. He has given up the right to arbitration. Carey's failures at GE have made it difficult to push ahead at other corporations.[44]

The paper went on to argue, however, that Jennings had not yet confronted the root cause of the crisis facing their industry. Contending that the unity that had existed in electrical unionism in the 1940s had been "deliberately smashed by a conspiracy of the corporations, corrupt and ambitious labor union officials, and politicians," it suggested that Jennings bore a share of the responsibility. The paper charged that "Paul Jennings, as he brags elsewhere in his campaign literature, was a prominent leader in the conspiracy that set the IUE on foot and led to the very mess he now complains of."[45] The Philadelphia-based District 1 issued a press release suggesting that Carey's defeat would improve the outlook for electrical workers: "The UE offers a united organization of electrical workers in this area that can bring together all the people in our industry and end the confusion and weakness that have plagued them since

---

43. UE News, February 22, 1965, for the text of the Reuther proposal and the IUE and UE responses.

44. Ibid., November 16, 1964, p. 2.

45. Ibid.

the split originally brought about in our ranks by Carey in the 1950s."[46]

As Carey exited the stage of public life, he left a decidedly mixed legacy. It is tempting to rate him harshly when we recall his prominent role in splitting the industrial union movement at a critical juncture in its history. Neither the style nor the substance of his leadership won the confidence of electrical workers or brought them together to confront the challenges they faced in America after World War II. Those who have written about his career use terms such as "mercurial" and "cavalier" to describe his behavior and his treatment of the people who worked for him and with him. He richly deserves this judgment. But, Carey had other qualities that surface upon closer examination and are also part of the record. Some of the early lessons he learned in the UE stayed with him. For instance, his commitment to civil rights and racial justice influenced his union work. One of his longest lasting professional relationships was with his assistant George Weaver, an African American activist who had come out of the Brotherhood of Sleeping Car Porters and had served during the War as director of the national CIO Committee to Abolish Discrimination. In fact, Carey's last picture on the front page of the *IUE News* in March 1965, immediately before his ouster, shows him among young African-American marchers in Selma, Alabama.[47] As we consider the ironies and paradoxes of his career, Carey looks more and more like a tragic figure who missed one opportunity after another to follow a path that would have ended in a more favorable historical light.

Carey's removal from office did not immediately change the political or international outlook of the IUE leadership. Jennings told an IUE District 3 conference in Atlantic City in June that his campaign to bring unity

46. This April press release was in the personal file of former UE local 107 secretary Edward Boehner for 1965.

47. IUE Papers Box 7 FF 5 "Qualifications of George Weaver" probably written "for Jim" Carey by Les Finnegan; IUE News, March 5, 1965, p. 1.

to the industry would exclude the UE "whose whole philosophy and programs are foreign to American workers." However, there were signs that rigid adherence to Cold War positions would meet increasing challenges in the IUE. According to an internal UE report, opposition to Jennings's position was openly expressed at this conference. A delegate who had called for acceptance of the UE offer to join forces in collective bargaining had received "a good round of applause from roughly one-third of the delegates present."[48] Because Carey's position resulted from and depended on his role in supporting the Cold War, his departure created new conditions in electrical unionism.

The early months of 1965 brought two nearly simultaneous developments. In an eerie reversal of the events of a decade earlier, United States foreign policy and the industrial union movement underwent significant changes. In early 1955, President Eisenhower had raised the possibility of relaxing Cold War tensions as the AFL and CIO announced that they would show no such flexibility and that their merger would occur on the basis of a continuing quarantine of Communists at home and abroad. In early 1965, President Johnson escalated American involvement in Southeast Asia as a key industrial union took a step in the opposite direction and rejected one of its original and most active Cold War spokesmen.

48. Matles to UE General Executive Board Members, International Representatives and Field Organizers, July 8, 1965, "Situation in IUE," in Ed Boehner personal file 1965.

Chapter 8

The Collapse of the Consensus, 1966–1973

In September 1965, three months short of a decade after the AFL-CIO merger, *Time Magazine* ran a remarkable editorial that at first glance seems like wishful thinking on the part of corporate America. Labor's most important task in the near future, the editors proposed, would be to cooperate with management in order to share in the abundance that the 1960s had brought to the nation. This "common share of America's affluence" was keeping labor and management "marching along shoulder to shoulder."[1] Further consideration, however, suggests that the editors might have been more perceptive than we at first thought. Perhaps they realized that the "consensus" so carefully manufactured by the commercial media rested on increasingly uncertain ground and that labor needed a reminder in order to stay in the fold. The coming years would witness upheaval and change in the labor movement and produce three significant developments relevant to electrical unionism and its political outlook.

First, workers in the industry achieved a measure of concerted action made possible by the UE's re-emergence as a force and the renewed recognition accorded the union inside and outside the labor movement. A second development accompanied the first: the appearance of

1. Time, September 19, 1965, pp. 42-43, "Union Labor: Less Militant, More Affluent."

increasingly vocal opposition in labor to official United States foreign policy and to the AFL-CIO leadership's support of that policy, especially regarding Vietnam. Third, by 1972, labor leaders began to address the increasingly troubling issue of American-based corporations relocating operations to areas outside the United States where "labor costs" were lower. All of these developments indicated that pressures were forcing leaders of American unions away from Cold War positions and toward more serious consideration of those advocated by the UE.

On the other hand, the top leadership, the International Affairs Department, and other forces in the AFL-CIO stiffened their resistance to any such changes. These contradictory trends leave us with the mixed picture of organized labor prevailing by 1973. The Cold War consensus had disintegrated, but the forces in labor responsible for imposing it in the first place showed no signs of willingness to change. Thus, while the AFL-CIO leadership remained committed to Cold War at home and abroad, it could no longer be argued that the policy had anything like unanimous support from American workers, or even a clear majority of them.[2]

The dramatic developments and potential changes represented by James Carey's defeat brought no change in the AFL-CIO's international stance, and the executive board continued to back the Johnson Administration's escalation of the war in Vietnam. The significance that the Administration attached to ensuring this support was driven home at the AFL-CIO convention in December 1965. The leadership made Vietnam the first major order of business and devoted the better part of two days to the issue. After a telephone address by President Johnson, the delegates heard speeches by Vice

---

2. See George Gallup, The Gallup Poll: Public Opinion 1935-1971, Gallup Opinion Index, Report number 40, October 1968, and number 49, July 1969. See tables 3-A and 3-B. For labor and business viewpoints on the role of multinational corporations, see NYT, February 15, 1972, p. 43, and for the IUE's position, see NYT, February 19, 1972, p. 30.

President Humphrey, Secretary of State Dean Rusk, and AFL-CIO President Meany himself, supporting Administration policy in Southeast Asia.[3]

This approach succeeded in gaining the unanimous approval of the 928 delegates for the resolution in support of the Administration's conduct of the war, but signs pointed to discontent among some labor leaders. Although only three delegates raised questions during the floor discussion, published reports indicated that some had privately expressed their doubts, and the war was not an issue that generated enthusiasm. Rather, it appeared as an uncomfortable matter to be disposed of as expeditiously as possible without offending the Johnson Administration. No one appealed to patriotism or "flag waving," and one delegate who questioned the Vietnam policy, UAW vice president Emil Mazey, seemed to capture the mood of many of those present when he said:

> I recognize that foreign policy is probably the most difficult single subject to discuss, because any time you criticize or challenge or question a policy of the government, your policy is immediately equated with treason, appeasement, maybe even charged with being soft on Communism or even being charged with disloyalty.[4]

The resolution was a compromise agreed to in advance by Meany and Reuther, the latter having urged inclusion of a statement favoring negotiations as a way to end the war. Meany had agreed to the change after Vice President Humphrey "indicated to union leaders... that the Johnson Administration would not like to see a divisive

---

3. AFL-CIO, Sixth Constitutional Convention Proceedings, pp. 126-133, for Rusk's address; pp. 142-155 for Humphrey's.

4. Ibid., pp. 562-575, for the floor discussion on the resolution. For other accounts of the convention, see Edmund F. Wehrle, Between a River and a Mountain; The AFL-CIO and The Vietnam War (Ann Arbor: University of Michigan Press, 2005) pp. 110-112; Philip Foner, American Labor and the Indo-China War, pp. 32-33; and Ronald Radosh, American Labor and United States Foreign Policy, pp. 443-444.

controversy erupt on the floor."[5] Since the resolution contended that seeking negotiations was already a policy of the Administration, the AFL-CIO went on record in support of "all measures the Administration might deem necessary to halt Communist aggression and secure a just and lasting peace."[6]

Despite the efforts of the Administration and the hopes of the editors of *Time*, changes were brewing in the labor movement. Within a year, as the GE and Westinghouse contracts expired, reports surfaced of a new militant mood among workers and of challenges to established leaders in several unions. Carey's defeat in the IUE provided one example. I.W. Abel had recently replaced David McDonald as president of the steelworkers, and the leadership of the rubber workers also faced a serious challenge.[7] During the previous year, workers had rejected over one thousand agreements negotiated by their leaders, or one in every seven.[8]

Several factors contributed to the unrest among American workers. Some union leaders cited the Landrum-Griffin Act, which, they noted, employers had supported in order to weaken the "control" of union leaders over their members, and which was now having an unintended result. Other sources suggested the coming of age of a younger post-World War II generation of workers, the atmosphere generated by the Civil Rights movement, and the increasingly harsh and oppressive conditions of industrial labor in the nation.[9] While the internal challenges generally did not explicitly target

---

5. NYT, December 16, 1965, p. 2.

6. AFL-CIO, Sixth Constitutional Convention Proceedings, pp. 560-562.

7. Business Week, September 17, 1966, pp. 71-73, "Winds of Change Ruffle Unions' Top Executives"; and September 24, 1966, "The Mood Is Militant," pp. 47-49.

8. Monthly Labor Review, July 1969, p. 22; also see David Brody, Workers in Industrial America, p. 209. For more on rank-and-file militance in labor during this period, see Gil Green, What's Happening to Labor (New York: International Publishers, 1976), chapters 15 through 19.

9. A study by the University Research Center in Chicago of 141 companies in twenty-six industries indicated that "pressure from heavy overtime

Cold War policies, the Cold War era leaders of several AFL-CIO unions, recently secure in power during the period of the "consensus," now felt threatened by the new situation.[10]

The UE leaders, on the other hand, appeared to feel no threat. Instead, they saw the rise of rank-and-file militancy as a vindication of the positions that they had taken during the preceding two decades. They had continued to claim that the independence enjoyed by the UE districts and locals, the annual conventions, and the modest salaries that UE leaders received had distinguished the leadership method of their union from those of many others and of the AFL-CIO itself. They viewed the new militant mood as a legitimate response to the style of leadership and the policies of the AFL-CIO since the formation of the organization a decade earlier.

As in the past, the UE drew a connection between the labor's support of the Cold War and the passive attitude of many labor leaders on domestic issues. In his 1963 address to the west coast longshoremen, Fitzgerald had, in addition to mentioning Walter Reuther's journeys abroad, sharply criticized the Meany leadership on issues such as unemployment, civil rights, and labor legislation. Charging that this leadership was "tied hand and foot to the Administration in Washington" and therefore unable to pursue an independent course, he urged the leaders of the AFL-CIO to learn from the struggles of people in other countries and from African-Americans. Urging a return to a more activist style of leadership, the UE president exclaimed:

> What a lift it would be if George Meany got out of his golf cart or McDonald took a few days off from Palm Beach to go down in the state of Mississippi and walked with their

---

schedules" was a major factor in the "current labor unrest." Business Week, August 6, 1966, p. 122.

10. Ibid., August 6, 1966, p. 122; September 24, 1966, p. 49; Brody, Workers in Industrial America, p. 209.

> Negro brothers. It would shake the country to its roots and move that struggle ahead by ten years if they had the guts to do it.[11]

While Meany remained in office, I.W. Abel had replaced McDonald by 1965.

The developments of the mid-1960s did not surprise many UE activists. The discussion at the union's 1965 convention provided a remarkable contrast to the *Time* essay on labor's affluence that would appear the following week. During the discussion on organizing, local 610's George Bobich referred to the recent developments in other unions and placed them in the context of the Cold War, arguing that, "Since 1943 or '46 when Winston Churchill said something in Fulton, Missouri, the working people of our country have been paying through the nose...." He contended that the discontent among industrial workers and its causes had been evident for several years:

> About three or four years ago I told Jim [Matles] that Abel was going to run against McDonald, and he said, "You're nuts." Am I right, Jim [apparently to Matles at the front of the hall]? And he asked "How do you deduce that?" I was talking with a lot of steel workers and you can sense the resentment. I know. I talk to steelworkers every day.... All of us do.
>
> When we tell these workers that we have a steward for every fifty men and every fraction thereof on each shift, it is unbelievable.... When we say the dues checkoff comes

---

11. UE News, April 22, 1963, p. 1. Four years later when the NYT, January 3, 1967, reported that Labor Secretary Willard Wirtz had expressed "deep concern" about the increasing tendency of union members to reject contracts proposed by their leaders, and that Wirtz considered this development "very dangerous for collective bargaining," Fitzgerald wrote to the Secretary objecting and asking, "What possible danger can there be in the free expression of the majority of the rank and file members of a union?" He continued, "The real danger, it seems to me, is the suppression of that free expression...." UE News, January 9, 1967, p. 3.

> to the local and we send the per capita to the international union, they say it is unbelievable....
>
> Isn't it odd that Abel, who had a plush job, a sweet job with good pay—what made him decide to run against McDonald? He sensed the rank-and-file unrest and tried to reflect it, and that is what he did. Why do you think Carey got defeated?[12]

The UE was certainly not immune to the problems raised by the new attitudes so widely observed among workers and did not always find the results easy to deal with. One UE local leader, business agent Tom Quinn of local 610, blamed the "employer-oriented press" for printing misleading information about unions which influenced young workers lacking a background in trade unionism. Believing that unions were all powerful, these workers "expect us to pick up the phone and say to management, 'OK, you take care of us.'"[13]

Generally, however, UE leaders and activists, believing that their approach to trade unionism gave them an advantage in relating to the rank-and-file mood, did not shrink from discussing it in the union. James Matles, addressing a UE class for shop stewards and local officers in Latrobe, Pennsylvania, in November 1968, specifically raised the question of young workers. He observed that, although they had not joined the students' "revolt [against the] status quo and the Establishment... the young people in the shops are involved in a revolt of their own.... It is not political in character. It expresses itself today solely in economic terms, but as it develops, it is bound to have far-reaching political consequences." Matles continued:

> It is only the democratic rank-and-file nature of our union and the day-to-day work of our shop stewards and local officers that have so far prevented these young people

12. UE 1965 Convention Proceedings, pp. 167-168.
13. Business Week, September 24, 1966, p. 49.

> and minority groups from openly breaking with us as is happening in so many other unions.... During the past two years, we have been having widespread discussion in our union on this subject. We are seeking to determine the cause of this revolt and trying to find some trade union answers to it.[14]

The difference between the UE and the AFL-CIO leaders was that the UE not only discussed the new rank-and-file developments, but also related the workers' frustrations to the policies of the Cold War and, as the decade progressed, to the war in Vietnam. For an example of the union's different response to the developments of the mid-1960s, we can look at the UE's 1965 convention. The *General Officers' Report* to the delegates addressed as its second major point, after the condition of the economy, "The Struggle for Peace." The report recalled that the UE had long warned of the dangers of Cold War policies and, unlike the AFL-CIO, blamed the Johnson Administration, the Pentagon, and the South Vietnamese Generals for refusing to negotiate and claiming that "negotiation meant surrender."[15]

The Resolutions Committee presented a proposed resolution noting the widespread support from various

---

14. UE Pamphlet, The Young Worker Challenges the Union Establishment, personal papers of Edward Boehner, former recording secretary of UE local 107, file "1968." The UE had some success in relating to young workers of the period. The author interviewed Tim McDonnell who went to work at the Westinghouse Lester, Pennsylvania plant in 1966 with the intention of resuming his college education when his finances allowed. However, he soon became a shop steward and union activist and worked at the plant until it closed twenty years later. Likewise, John Hovis, after discharge from the Navy, went to work in the Westinghouse Company's Seattle plant where he became active in the UE. Hovis, who by his own account had been "fairly hawkish," changed his thinking as the Vietnam War dragged on, and as the war continued to be discussed at union meetings. Hovis went on to become organizational director of the union and, in September 1986, was elected national president. McDonnell interview July 27, 1987. Telephone conversation with Hovis, August 14, 1987.

15. UE 1965 General Officers' Report, pp. 18 ff.

sections of the American people for a change in policy and calling on the Administration to:

1. stop relying on more troops and bombs;
2. stop quibbling about negotiations with the representatives of the National Liberation Front in South Vietnam;
3. show by deeds our wish to end this terrible war through negotiations, and thereby to prepare the ground for a ceasefire.

The resolution was not voted on immediately. Three delegates spoke in opposition. Kenneth Duffy of California's local 1012 questioned the propriety of the union's taking a stand on foreign policy, which, he argued, should be left to the elected representatives in Washington. In response to the opposition, Fitzgerald noted from the chair that the resolution did not include a call for withdrawing troops, and that such a resolution, which had been submitted for consideration, had not been adopted by the Committee. Other delegates, including District 11 leader William Burch, spoke in favor of the resolution, but argued that it did not go far enough and should have called for troop withdrawal. Burch defended the union's right to debate foreign policy questions just as it debated domestic issues such as unemployment. The *UE News* reported in an article headlined "Resolution for Peace Draws Spirited Debate" that "the resolution passed by voice vote with a smattering of nays."[16]

The following year the *Officers' Report* more directly linked the economic situation to the costs of the Vietnam War, arguing that the Johnson Administration's Great Society legislation was in danger, and that the President had stated, "Because of Vietnam we cannot do all that we should do or all that we would like to do." This section of the report, titled "War Economy Pressure on Living

16. UE 1965 Convention Proceedings, pp. 243-257; also summary of the discussion in the UE News, October 4, 1965, pp. 4-5.

Standards," discussed the effects of the war in terms of inflation, shelving of tax cuts, and scaled-down wage increases. It argued that, while Great Society programs faced elimination or cuts, profits were "skyrocketing."[17] While the UE was still considered an outcast by the AFL-CIO leadership, its Cold War isolation was clearly weakening. The union's 1966 convention in Pittsburgh heard speeches not only by Professors David Montgomery and Seymour Melman, but also by Dick Gregory and Pennsylvania gubernatorial candidate Milton Shapp as well.[18]

As the decade of the 1960s passed its midpoint, then, the American labor movement presented a mixed and changing picture. The leadership of the AFL-CIO, while feeling pressure from below, adhered to its support for the nation's foreign policy, especially where that policy seemed the most likely to adhere to Cold War assumptions—the Vietnam War. At the same time, the pressures from below had already had considerable influence in the electrical unions. The most strident Cold War leader in electrical unionism had suffered a decisive defeat in the IUE, while the UE continued to call for an end to Cold War policies at home and abroad and had emerged as a force for stability and direction in the industry. The full impact of the changes in electrical unionism was not immediately felt, but by 1966, the status quo was on the defensive.

The new IUE leadership knew that it would have to address the fragmented conditions in the industry. In late 1965, seven national unions with GE and Westinghouse contracts formed a Coordinated Bargaining Committee (CBC) to present a united front to the two largest electrical firms. As important a step as this was, it did not yet go beyond the Carey proposal of 1953, which had called for unity in bargaining among "non-Communist"

17. UE 1966 General Officers' Report, pp. 5-12.

18. UE 1966 Convention Proceedings. Montgomery's appearance had special significance as he had been a shop chairman in UE local 475 until District 4 went into the IUE in the spring of 1956.

unions. The exclusion of the UE meant that the only union besides the IUE to hold national contracts with the largest companies would still bargain on its own. IUE president Jennings not only refused to consider cooperation with the UE, he announced a drive to take over bargaining rights from the UE in major plants.[19]

The newly formed CBC did not find the going easy in negotiations with either company. They resisted the unions' efforts to bargain jointly and GE went to court to appeal the National Labor Relations Board decision requiring the company to recognize the CBC. The IUE-led coalition repeatedly stated its determination to pursue the effort, conflicting decisions were appealed, and the issue remained in doubt as the October 2 strike deadline at GE approached.[20]

Two other issues hung over the negotiations of 1966. Each was related to the larger question of whether the IUE leadership would continue to observe the unspoken boundaries of the Cold War consensus. The first issue was the UE's relationship to the Coordinated Bargaining Committee. UE continued to bargain separately, and the CBC showed no signs of wanting a change. In May, IUE official John Callahan appeared ready to revive the Carey tactics of the early 1950s when he charged GE with seeking to divide unions by signing separate contracts with the "discredited" leaders of the UE. After this, however, the CBC publicly ignored the UE, which continued to state its intention to "bust through" the wage guidelines set by the Johnson Administration.[21]

---

19. IUE News, October 28, 1965, p. 1. The seven-member unions of the CBC were the IUE, IAM, IBEW, UAW, American Federation of Technical Engineers, Sheetmetal Workers, and Allied Industrial Workers. Harry Block alleged in his March 17, 1987, interview that a meeting with UE leaders took place following Carey's defeat, but produced no agreement because "we didn't want any commies."

20. NYT, July 14, 1966, p. 20; August 20, 1966, p. 22; September 9, 1966, p. 1; September 22, 1966, p. 43. The issue was not resolved until October 1968; IUE News, November 14, 1968, p. 1.

21. NYT, May 26, 1966, p. 28; June 7, 1966, p. 55. See also UE Economic Report, number 1, March 28, 1966; and number 2, April 11, 1966; and Matles to UE GE and Westinghouse locals, June 20, 1966, "Rank and File Revolt

The other issue was the influence of the Vietnam War on the negotiations. GE's position as a major military contractor became the basis for the Johnson Administration's urgent calls for a settlement without a strike. On the day before the CBC's strike deadline, the unions agreed to move the negotiations from New York to Washington and to a two-week contract extension. The Washington talks proceeded under pressure from the President and the military and included one session in the office of Secretary of Defense Robert McNamara with the Secretaries of the Army, Navy, and Air Force also present. This "briefing" at the Pentagon followed by two days the President's public statement underlining the importance of the operation of GE's plants for the war effort. After summarizing the "wide range" of military equipment produced in the company's facilities, the President continued, "Our men in Vietnam need these planes, these helicopters, these weapons. They are essential to their very lives, and they need them now, not next week or next month."[22]

While the Administration's actions showed its readiness to use the war to secure a contract settlement, they left unanswered questions about whether military production was the real issue. One report noted that Administration officials failed to explain why they had called on the unions to avoid striking the company's "non-defense operations" since GE had claimed that its defense work was concentrated in less than 12 of its 165 plants and that a "selective strike" against non-defense facilities would not interfere with its military programs. The Administration, it appeared, aimed to derail any contract settlement that would violate its wage guidelines and be labeled as inflationary at a time when living costs were already rising. At the same time, the negotiations indicated the difficulty involved in determining

---

in IUE GE Shops," for background and UE assessment of conditions surrounding 1966 negotiations. Boehner 1966 file.

22. NYT, October 3, 1966, p. 1; p. 33.

what constituted "military" production. The union bargaining committee refused to limit the strike threat to non-defense plants since GE was so "integrated" that it could not separate military from civilian work.[23]

The 1966 negotiations with General Electric demonstrated four significant points relating to the deteriorating Cold War consensus, and the October 14 settlement suggested both the strengths and the weaknesses of the coordinated bargaining effort. In the first place, GE workers felt increasingly confident and reflected the new militancy. Although a nationwide strike was avoided, local work stoppages occurred in both UE and IUE plants as well as in plants represented by other unions in the coalition.[24] Second, the effort of the AFL-CIO unions had, despite determined resistance from the company, succeeded in winning a settlement more favorable than in previous years and underscored the effectiveness of the joint bargaining strategy.[25]

On the other hand, the coalition showed obvious weaknesses. The most serious was the continued absence of the UE from the joint negotiations. In addition to its numbers and its national contract, the UE had leaders

23. Ibid., October 3, 1966, p. 46, for editorial on the Administration wage guidelines; October 5, 1966, p. 94, for the union and company positions.

24. Ibid., September 15, 1966, p. 85; October 4, 1966, p. 28; Business Week, October 22, 1966, pp. 37-38.

25. IUE News, October 20, 1966, pp. 6-7; NYT, October 15, 1966, p. 1. The union leaders believed that GE's improved offer would never have been made without coordinated bargaining. The average wage increase for the two previous contracts, 1960 and 1963, had been 2% per year; the 1966 settlement was over 3%. The UE had a different assessment; in a UE pamphlet, "UE Labor News," Matles reported that "While the UE was engaged in direct collective bargaining and was making progress on the Cost of Living issue, the Administration used its power to force the AFL-CIO unions to accept the GE formula that provides for less than half the wage losses sustained by GE workers due to cost of living increases in the past and affords less than 50% protection against future increases.... General Electric's unyielding collective bargaining practice known as 'Boulwarism' has again escaped unscathed as it has ever since 1949 when GE workers were split.... It will be eliminated only when the Company is confronted with negotiating one contract with one militant union that relies on collective bargaining and its own economic power, rather than on Washington politicians to gain its objectives." Boehner 1966 file.

with years of bargaining experience with the major employers that could have helped the CBC effort. Later reports suggested that the IUE leadership had showed a "defeatist attitude" as the strike deadline approached, and that "President Meany of the AFL-CIO had to rescue Mr. Jennings" by visiting the White House and urging President Johnson to intervene.[26]

The IUE's rigid position encountered opposition in 1966 from at least one of its strongest supporters. Monsignor Charles Owen Rice, the UE's longtime adversary, altered his stance. In an article in the *Pittsburgh Catholic* in June, Rice argued that the UE would bolster the joint bargaining effort and should be included. Contending that the "Communist issue [was] meaningless in today's struggle," he observed that "The UE has been building up to a new strength. I do not know the political or ideological complexion of it now, but it seems to be a good aggressive union—big too, 164,000."[27]

The inclusion of the UE would be up for discussion in the future.

Fourth, the manner in which the settlement was reached, under pressure from Cabinet officers, prominently including the Secretary of Defense, demonstrated the restricting influence that the AFL-CIO leadership's ties to U.S. foreign policy continued to wield over the labor movement. The UE's Matles wrote later that the AFL-CIO leadership's "strong institutional support for the Johnson war policies... was a prime factor... inhibiting collective bargaining co-operation between the UE and the IUE" during 1966.[28] To summarize, the 1966 negotiations in the industry demonstrated both the potential effectiveness of coordinated bargaining on the one hand, and, on the other, the critical weakness

---

26. Philip J. Schwartz, Coalition Bargaining (Ithaca, New York State School of Industrial and Labor Relations), 1970, p. 14; Wall Street Journal, August 6, 1969, p. 19.

27. Charles Owen Rice, "Ecumenism in Labor," Pittsburgh Catholic, June 9, 1966.

28. Matles and Higgins, Them and Us, p. 258.

resulting from the continuing Cold War division in electrical labor.

During the next three years, the situation in the American labor movement underwent drastic change. The unraveling of the Cold War consensus in the AFL-CIO accelerated at a rate beyond the control of the Meany leadership, and events in the electrical unions illustrated this trend. While the IUE had already replaced its most vigorous Cold War spokesman at the national level, the process continued in the union's largest district. The New York-North Jersey district, now IUE District 3, experienced another upheaval during 1967–1968. The district president, Milton Weihrauch, who had welcomed the new members "trapped in the Communist dominated UE" a decade earlier, faced charges from the new national leadership in the summer of 1967. Charged with misappropriation of union funds during the decade of the 1960s, Weihrauch was removed from office by a lopsided recall vote in August.[29]

While the pressures on the IUE leadership to drop its Cold War stance intensified, both inside and outside the union, the UE became more outspoken in its calls for a change in the nation's foreign policy, especially its Indochina policy. Every year after 1966, the reports of the general officers argued that the "war economy" threatened the domestic programs originally proposed by the Johnson Administration as well as the general living standards of the American people. The 1968 foreign policy resolution charged that the war had become an "American war" that benefited no one in Vietnam except "Vietnamese generals, landlords, and merchants."[30]

---

29. NYT, July 20, 1967, p. 23; July 21, 1967, p. 14; August 15, 1967, p. 49; September 26, 1967, p. 56. The next spring, Weihrauch pled guilty to one count of embezzlement of union funds, NYT, April 5, 1968, p. 52.

30. UE 1967 Convention Proceedings, pp. 5-14, "War Economy Undermines Living Standards"; UE 1968 General Officers' Report, p. 48, "The Search for Peace." At the 1968 convention, the officers attempted to prevent the discord they observed in the IUE and other unions by reviewing their own union's past. The remarks of Matles and Fitzgerald were reprinted in a booklet entitled A Little Bit of UE History You Should Know. Fitzgerald related

The UE conventions of the late 1960s generally retained the qualities noted by the CIO's George McCray fifteen years earlier. The "good natured and orderly proceedings" were, nonetheless, frequently punctuated by spirited debate. This included the resolutions on foreign policy. One delegate in 1967 asked why the resolutions committee made the United States "the bad guys" in Vietnam, but then went on to say that his brother might be going to Vietnam and that he was "really in a quandary." Fitzgerald responded that, since the government that the union was in a position to influence was "our own," that was what the UE should attempt to do.[31]

As the decade progressed, the conventions heard more urgent calls for action to end the war. For example, in 1969, Leonard Bruneau of local 279 told the delegates that he had recently visited his brother and other servicemen who had just returned from Vietnam. Related Bruneau, "They told me the only way for the war to get over is for the people in America to revolt," and that, while they agreed with the UE position on the war, they had pressed further, asking, "Do you mean it? If you mean it, prove it."[32]

In the fall of 1969, the UE urged its locals to hold plant gate meetings or otherwise show support for the October 15 anti-war rallies held in many cities. After the event, the *UE News* ran a picture and an article on the members

---

the debate over Vietnam to events of the late 1940s: "We have an executive board and we have fights. I am against the war in Vietnam and I don't care who knows it (applause). I say we should stop the bombing there. We have a member of our executive board, Joe Calabrese, that is sitting over there, who has a difference of opinion with me. I hope to win him over some time, but Joe, in all of our disagreements with me on that has never once questioned my Americanism (applause) and I have never once questioned his integrity.... That is the way things should be in this country.... The little man who stood on the floor of this convention years ago and started this bonfire under the loyalty of the officers and the policies and program...of this union, was just a couple of years ago trying to steal the election for president of the IUE... 'the good honest, American trade union,' [laughter] the most laughable thing I ever heard in my life."

31. UE 1967 Convention Proceedings, pp. 352-354.

32. UE News, October 6, 1969, p. 7.

of local 404 at Lite Industries in New Jersey, which produced "bulletproof vests and formerly body bags." At the noon-hour protest meeting, attended by 60 members of the local, workers had expressed their feelings on the war. One woman had told the paper, "Right now we aren't making the shrouds, but you don't feel happy when you make them." Another local member, Jesus La Luz Marin, said that his brother was in Vietnam and continued, "I don't know about the work. I want the war to end."[33]

When UE locals and districts attempted to find common ground with student activists, they found the goal not always easy to reach. In March of 1969, for instance, a conference of the reconstituted UE District 7 in Toledo, Ohio, invited Larry Rubin, an activist from nearby Antioch College, to address the fifty delegates. Rubin spoke about the causes of campus unrest and compared the problems of students to the early struggles of working people, arguing that students resented being "stamped out" as white-collar workers for industry without an opportunity to develop their own ideas. The UE members were skeptical. When they asked why students did not negotiate their problems with administrators, Rubin responded that their attempts to do so did not always succeed, just as workers could not always avoid strikes. While the student leader did not find total agreement, the delegates applauded his presentation strongly when he finished.[34]

Two months later, UE local 610 business agent Tom Quinn told a student rally at the University of Pittsburgh that workers' living standards had suffered as a result of the war. Quinn called for an end to the war and to the "corporate profiteering" arising from it. Sharing the platform with Joseph Yablonski of the United Mine Workers, Quinn also urged the students to be "militant" in seeking a redress of their own grievances.[35]

33. Ibid., October 20, 1969, p. 9, "Anti-War Rallies Biggest in U.S. History."

34. Ibid., March 10, 1969, p. 2.

35. Ibid., June 16, 1969, p. 8.

Thus, by the late 1960s, although the electrical unions remained apart, the UE was forming relationships outside the labor movement which had been impossible for over a decade. Changes were also unfolding inside the movement that would alter the union's situation there as well.

By 1966, the AFL-CIO leadership's unyielding adherence to Cold War positions and policies caused frustration among the former CIO unions. During that year, two foreign policy issues got major attention from the AFL-CIO executive board. When the International Labor Organization (ILO), meeting in Geneva, narrowly elected a delegate from Poland as its chairman, the head of the AFL-CIO delegation, Rudy Faupl, withdrew the delegation from the meeting, giving as his reason that he "could not, in good conscience, sit in the Conference presided over by a representative of a totalitarian country...." Against the advice of Secretary of State Dean Rusk, the AFL-CIO board supported Faupl's action. Six of the nine presidents of original CIO unions, led by Walter Reuther, voted in opposition.[36]

In addition to the ILO boycott and the Vietnam War, a third foreign policy issue soon confronted labor. Victor Reuther, director of the UAW's International Affairs Department, criticized the American Institute for Free Labor Development (AIFLD) for allowing corporate executives to serve on its board of directors. The AIFLD, chartered by the AFL-CIO in 1961, received major financial support from the United States Government through the Agency for International Development (AID). The AIFLD's existence rested on the assumption that American labor could play a key role in preventing the growth of revolutionary movements in Latin America. Victor Reuther's criticism aggravated the existing tension over foreign policy issues at the top level of the AFL-CIO.[37]

---

36. John P. Windmuller, "The Foreign Policy of American Labor," Political Science Quarterly, LXXXII, no. 2 (June 1967), 213.

37. See Frank Koscielski, Divided Loyalties; American Unions and the Vietnam War (New York: Garland Publishing) 1999, pp. 55-83, for an account

During 1966, two executive board meetings and one meeting of the full AFL-CIO council dealt almost entirely with foreign policy issues. In every case, the Reuther forces, generally drawn from the old CIO unions, found themselves outnumbered by union leaders following the Meany policy. On the ILO boycott, they lost twenty-one to six. Likewise, the criticism of the AIFLD was rejected by a vote of twenty-three to two, as Reuther and Joseph Curran of the National Maritime Union cast the only dissenting votes. Reuther's leadership of the moderate forces came in for criticism when he missed the full council meeting, which had been called at his request to review the AFL-CIO's foreign policy positions. In his absence, the council voted unanimously to reaffirm the positions it had taken since the AFL-CIO's founding eleven years earlier.[38] Nevertheless, the differences of opinion that had surfaced and the extraordinary attention given to foreign policy issues during 1966 suggested that the consensus in the labor movement was increasingly unstable.

Over the next two years, open disagreement with the official line emerged. By mid-1967, four national officers of AFL-CIO unions had joined other unionists in the Trade Union Division of the Committee for a Sane Nuclear Policy (SANE) in calling for a "National Labor Leadership Assembly for Peace." The conveners based their appeal on both the cost of the war to the American people, and the damage it caused in Vietnam. The call to the Assembly argued that the "enormous diversion of human wealth and energies into war has grievously undermined every program to meet the needs of our cities..." and that "the culture of our country is being brutalized by a logic which seeks to justify the use of the

---

of the internal debate in the UAW on the Vietnam War and the differences between Reuther and Meany on the issue.

38. Ronald Radosh, American Labor and United States Foreign Policy, p. 443.

most inhumane weapons of war whose primary victims inevitably are the population of Vietnam."[39]

The response to the call surprised the Assembly's organizers. Over 500 trade unionists from sixty-three unions, including forty-five national officers, came to Chicago on a November weekend. The two-day conference issued a policy statement calling for American labor to "play its part in bringing this savage war to a swift and just conclusion...." While this statement did not go far enough to satisfy all those present, the Assembly marked an important step for labor. The participants came from a wide spectrum of the labor movement. They heard prominent guest speakers including the Reverend Martin Luther King, John Kenneth Galbraith, and journalist David Schoenbrun. Victor Reuther blasted the AFL-CIO leadership for its top-down method of handling foreign policy questions and urged labor to reach foreign policy decisions in the same way it reached decisions on collective bargaining or domestic legislation, "upward from the membership following the widest possible discussion in depth by the rank and file."[40]

A UE delegation of thirty-five local leaders and executive board members attended the Chicago conference. Tom Quinn participated as a speaker in a major panel discussion, and the continuations committee included three UE members.[41] The acceptance of the UE and other previously shunned unions, such as the ILWU, did not escape the notice of observers of labor. In a letter to *The Nation*, Michigan State Economics Professor Charles Larrowe pointed out that "sitting side by side" with AFL-CIO unionists were members of "unions that have been in Coventry for eighteen years... the UE, the

39. Quoted in Foner, Labor and the Indo-China War, p. 49.

40. The Nation, November 27, 1967, p. 563, "Labor Meets for Peace."

41. Matles to UE General Executive Board members and Staff Representatives, November 13, 1967, Boehner 1967 file. Matles wrote that this was "the first national gathering of trade union leaders since the split in the CIO that the UE and the ILWU have officially participated in." Also see UE News, November 27, 1967, pp. 6-7.

West Coast longshoremen, even the old United Public Workers...." The Assembly represented, he wrote, "a long step toward ending two decades of red-baiting in the labor movement."[42]

In one important sense, this estimate was accurate. The Labor Assembly for Peace signaled the resurfacing of forces long submerged. The presence of Victor Reuther and UAW vice president Emil Mazey suggested that the largest AFL-CIO union had begun to find the boundaries of the "in-house" debate overly restricting. In a letter to all UAW locals in January 1967, Walter Reuther had charged the AFL-CIO leadership with a long list of abuses of the 1955 merger agreement: failure to organize, failure to address broad social questions such as education and health care, and specifically with a "narrow and negative attitude... on most foreign policy questions."[43]

That the UAW intended to follow through and pursue this shift was demonstrated in the spring of 1968 when the regional leadership joined with the UE and other unions to organize events such as the Labor for Peace conference in Philadelphia on May 18. Here, 225 delegates, including 30 from UE's District 1, heard Senator Joseph Clark call for "a stop to the killing now" and themselves called for an immediate end to the bombing of North Vietnam, diversion of resources from the Vietnam War to the domestic war on poverty, and the inclusion of the National Liberation Front in peace negotiations.[44] Thus, when Walter Reuther led the UAW out of the AFL-CIO in July 1968, foreign policy and international concerns figured prominently among the areas of disagreement. As Reuther pointed out in his 1967 letter to the locals, the issues extended "far beyond considerations of international affairs and [went] to the heart of the fundamental aims and purposes of the American

42. The Nation, December 25, 1967, p. 674.
43. UE News, January 9, 1967, p. 4.
44. Ibid., June 3, 1968, p. 5.

labor movement."[45] In other words, observing the boundaries of the Cold War consensus would no longer be the sole guiding principle for the union's activity.

In June 1969, 500 delegates from the UAW and the Teamsters under President Frank Fitzsimmons met in Washington, D.C. to form the Alliance for Labor Action (ALA) that aimed to "get the American Labor movement on the march." This meeting heard Senator George McGovern call for United States' withdrawal from Vietnam, and the presidents of both unions attacked the Administration's war policy when they spoke. Fitzimmons told the gathering that "the youth of our country [are] up in arms... over the billions of dollars this country spends annually to carry on this war in the Far East when our own people go begging right here at home." He urged that the war, "the bane and plague of Republican and Democratic administrations, must be stopped and must be stopped soon." The *UE News* gave prominent coverage to the ALA meeting.[46] Although the ALA sputtered following the death of Walter Reuther in 1970, the events of the late 1960s indicated that the manufactured "consensus" was coming unglued. Of the three original core industries of the membership of the CIO, two, auto and electrical manufacturing, were now outside the "house."[47]

The breakdown of the consensus in the AFL-CIO leadership apparently reflected the attitudes of large

45. Ibid., January 9, 1967, p. 4.

46. Ibid., June 2, 1969, p. 8. While the ALA's formation showed the extent of the erosion of the Cold War consensus, it did not fulfill its potential. For an analysis, see Gil Green, What's Happening to Labor (New York: International Publishers), 1976, pp. 124-127.

47. The steelworkers' union also experienced unsettled conditions and opposition to the established leadership during the mid-1960s, but the most serious challenge did not occur until the1970s when Edward Sadlowski of the union's District 31 in the Chicago-Gary area ran against Lloyd McBride, I.W. Abel's designated successor. Although Sadlowski won a majority among basic steel workers, McBride prevailed in a disputed election. Ernest DeMaio, former president of UE District 11, in a telephone conversation with the author on March 6, 1986, named McBride as one of the delegates who had physically assaulted him at the 1947 Illinois CIO convention.

numbers of union members. The results of a Gallup Poll in early 1968 suggested that George Meany's unwavering support for the Administration's Vietnam policy did not enjoy anything like unanimous support from members of the labor movement. The poll showed, for instance, that forty-three percent of "adults in union member families" believed that "the United States made a mistake in sending troops to fight in Vietnam." A later poll in the summer of 1969, although not specifically identifying union members, confirmed the lack of consensus among working people regarding Vietnam.[48] (See tables 3-1, 3-2.)

The changing environment finally brought a partial thaw on the collective bargaining front. Beginning in January, representatives of the UE and the IUE met to plan strategy for bargaining with GE and Westinghouse.[49] While the UE did not formally join the AFL-CIO coalition, it was recognized as a key member of the bargaining team, and, in recognition of the UE's experience, Matles was designated the negotiator in charge of "economic" issues. The IUE's John Shambo, of the Schenectady local, took responsibility for "non-economic" issues. Bargaining was coordinated, although two sets of negotiations were carried on with GE because the company insisted on maintaining its interpretation of

---

48. NYT, January 3, 1968, p. 3, for the first poll; also see Koscielski, Divided Loyalties, for an instructive account of the attitudes of members of UAW Ford Local 600, especially his conclusion, pp. 161-165.

49. NYT, Febtruary 2, 1969; Business Week, February 8, 1969, clippings in Boehner 1969 File. BW viewed this development with apprehension: "The bargaining outlook in electrical manufacturing has new, possibly darker aspects this week as a result of a surprise move by two major unions—bitter rivals since the 1940s—to collaborate in negotiations." This bizarre semi-recognition of UE would continue for years. The "Coordinated Bargaining Committee of AFL-CIO GE-Westinghouse Unions" had its own letterhead listing the presidents of the numerous coalition unions, with George Meany's name at the top, but no mention of the UE. See memo from the IBEW's Richard Mills to UE organizing director Hugh Harley February 15, 1973, UEA RG 1.2 Box 1 "Matles 1937-75" ff "Matles, James-Correspondence General Secretary-Treasurer 1973."

Table 3-1
Public Opinion Poll Results: The Vietnam War

Poll results showed that working people, including union members, were divided in their opinions on the war by the mid-1960s. A Gallup Poll report in the *New York Times* on January 3, 1968 presented a markedly different picture than the "unanimous" support accorded the Administration war policies at the 1965 and 1967 AFL-CIO conventions. The questions were asked of "adults in union member families."

"Do you approve or disapprove of the way President Johnson is handling the situation in Vietnam?"

	Approve	Disapprove	No Opinion
National	39%	49%	12%
Union Families	47%	43%	10%

"In view of the developments since we entered the fighting in Vietnam, do you think the United States made a mistake in sending troops to fight in Vietnam?"

	Yes	No	No Opinion
National	45%	46%	9%
Union Families	43%	51%	6%

According to the poll, union families were, by the beginning of 1968, more likely to approve of the Johnson Vietnam policy than the general population, but only by a narrow margin. Union members apparently found it difficult to put themselves on record against Administration policies because labor considered the Johnson domestic program, except for the wage guidelines, worthy of strong support. See, for example, the *NYT*, February 3, 1968 (p. 6), for an account of George Meany's filmed conversation with Johnson at the White House intended as a campaign piece.

the complex court ruling on the right of unions to bargain jointly with the same employer.[50]

By October, it appeared that General Electric was prepared for a major test of its "take-it-or-leave-it"

50. See IUE News, November 14, 1968, p. 1; June 12, 1969, p. 1; NYT, June 29, 1969, p. 52, for the rulings. Business Week, January 31, 1970, p. 29, reported that the two unions had divided the responsibility for "economic" and "non-economic" issues "in recognition of Matles's quarter century or more of bargaining experience with GE."

Table 3-2
Public Opinion Poll Results: The Vietnam War

By mid-1969, workers in "manual" or "blue collar" occupations favored withdrawing troops more strongly than those in "professional or business" categories. Continuing the pattern shown in polls 16 years earlier regarding Korea (see appendix A), respondents with less formal education were more likely to favor withdrawing troops.

"Would you favor or oppose withdrawing all of our troops from Vietnam immediately as suggested by some of our Senators?"

	Favor	Oppose	No Opinion
Educational Level Attained			
College	21%	72%	5%
High School	30%	63%	7%
Grade School	35%	48%	17%
Occupation			
Professional and Business	23%	70%	7%
White Collar	25%	68%	7%
Farmers	36%	48%	16%
Manual	32%	61%	7%

"Should we begin to reduce, month by month, the number of soldiers in Vietnam?"

	Favor	Oppose	No Opinion
Educational Level Attained			
College	57%	27%	16%
High School	59%	25%	16%
Grade School	61%	21%	18%
Occupation			
Professional and Business	55%	27%	18%
White Collar	59%	25%	13%
Farmers	54%	23%	23%
Manual	61%	25%	14%

Source: Gallup Opinion Index, Princeton, New Jersey, Report no. 49, July 1969, p. 11.

bargaining methods of the last two decades, and that, this time, the Republican Administration in Washington would not intervene. The story of the 1969–1970 strike has been told,[51] but its significance in historical context requires emphasis. The level of acceptance and support accorded the UE signaled a dramatic departure from the Cold War isolation the union had faced as recently as three years earlier. The IUE leadership changed direction and accepted proposals the UE had made since the early 1950s.

The events of October 13 showed the extent of the change. In New York City, with the strike deadline looming, the two presidents publicly exchanged visits. Jennings addressed the UE-GE conference Board, and Fitzgerald spoke before the IUE's GE Conference Board. Several members of the IUE group had been in the UE during the 1946 nationwide GE strike, and they welcomed the UE president's call for "no more war between UE and IUE." We can only wonder what thoughts passed through the mind of Albert Fitzgerald on that fall morning as he heard Jennings tell the UE board that "there will be no more playing one against the other.... We're in a basic fight, and when we win it, we'll build on it."[52]

The strike began on October 27 and lasted three months. It was a turning point. The UE's isolation from AFL-CIO unions ended; the union's crucial role in making possible a united front facing the major electrical firms received wide recognition. Financial support came from wide sections of the labor movement including the UAW, which represented a section of GE workers, and from the AFL-CIO. The settlement reached in late January, in Matles's words, while "not the whole loaf, had quite a bit of bread in it." For the first time in over two decades, GE had significantly altered its initial proposals and had, in short, been forced to negotiate

51. Matles and Higgins, Them and Us, pp. 262-287.
52. UE News, October 20, 1969, p. 3.

a contract.[53] The changed relationship between the two electrical unions also meant less antagonism and at least some level of cooperation in organizing unorganized shops. Inter-union correspondence even indicates that the cooperation went beyond the UE and the IUE and included other unions such as the IBEW.[54]

The GE strike proved what close observers of labor already knew. Major sections of the movement no longer felt obliged to conform to the boundaries of the Cold War consensus. Even the most unbending Cold War supporters acknowledged the new situation. Support for the GE strikers, including all unions on strike regardless of their affiliation, had been urged by Walter Reuther and had come from the AFL-CIO and the UAW. Support also came from students on a number of campuses, notably Michigan State and Holy Cross where students protested the presence of GE recruiters during the strike.[55]

Evidence of the change came quickly from electrical workers. In February, the *IUE News*, which had virtually never mentioned the Vietnam War previously, printed an editorial urging the Nixon Administration to "heed the warnings of organized labor" and to plan ahead for a peacetime economy. The editorial observed, citing an article in the *Monthly Labor Review*, that unemployment was apparently rising "even without the end of the Vietnam War," but that this was "a small foretaste of what would come."[56] (See table 4-1.)

The IUE, after the GE strike, joined a growing number of AFL-CIO unions on record against the war. By the end of February 1970, the leaders of twenty-two national

---

53. Matles and Higgins, Them and Us, p. 281; Business Week, January 31, 1970, pp. 28-29.

54. UE Archives, RG 1.2 FF "Matles, James Correspondence 1973" IBEW's Richard Mills to UE Organization Director Hugh Harley, February 15, 1973; Matles to IUE Secretary-Treasurer David Fitzmaurice, September 24, 1973.

55. Matles and Higgins, Them and Us, p. 285; NYT, November 9, 1969, p. 62, for the labor support. See NYT November 11, 1969, p. 6; December 13, 1969, p. 21, for the campus activity.

56. IUE News, February 19, 1970, p. 4; Monthly Labor Review, February 1970, pp. 3-10, "Increase in Defense Related Employment."

Table 4-1
Private Defense Generated Employment 1965-1969

	1965	1967	1968	1969
Total number of jobs	2,102,000	3,082,000	3,574,000	3,400,000

Source: Bureau of Labor Statistics, Monthly Labor Review, February, 1970, pp. 3, 4.

unions had publicly joined a call for the immediate withdrawal of troops from Vietnam and for the redirection of resources to domestic uses.[57] After the strike, it was clear that the AFL-CIO leadership could no longer claim to speak for a clear majority of organized workers, especially on international matters. Public opinion polls, the statements of top and middle level trade union leaders, and the increasing reluctance or refusal of union members to allow Cold War ideas or arguments to determine their actions all indicated that monolithic labor support for Cold War policies did not exist.

The breakdown of the consensus by no means ended the reign of the Cold War labor leadership. On the contrary, the early 1970s saw increasing activity by both sides. The extension of the Indochina War into Cambodia at the end of April 1970 brought sharply divergent responses from different sections of labor. These underlined the nature of the disagreement and the high priority that the Nixon Administration still attached to gaining active and public support from labor. While the leaders of the UAW, the American Federation of State, County, and Municipal Employees, the Teamsters, the UE, and various local and regional labor bodies issued statements calling for an end to the war, and rank-and-file workers joined anti-war activities in greater numbers than previously, the Cold War forces also ratcheted up their activity.[58]

57. Foner, Labor and the Indo-China War, pp. 76-77.
58. Ibid., pp. 85-88.

Table 4-2
Private Employment Attributable to Department of Defense (D.O.D)
Expenditures Selected industries 1965, 1968

	1965 Private Employment			1968 Private Employment		
Industry	*Total*	*D.O.D.*	*Per cent*	*Total*	*D.O.D.*	*Per cent*
Construction	3,120,000	67,000	2.2 %	3,225,000	75,000	2.3 %
Manufacturing						
Total	17,611,000	1,391,000	7.9 %	19,527,000	2,353,000	12.1 %
Aircraft	602,000	331,000	55.0 %	851,000	616,000	72.4 %
Communications Equipment	533,000	195,000	36.7 %	666,000	257,000	38.6 %
Machine Shop Products	180,000	29,000	16.3 %	227,000	63,000	27.8 %
Engines & Turbines	88,000	7,000	7.6 %	107,000	12,000	11.0 %
Electrical Industrial Equipment	349,000	34,000	9.7 %	417,000	57,000	13.6 %
General Industrial Machinery & Equipment	251,000	15,000	5.9 %	290,000	27,000	9.1%
Metalworking Machinery & Equipment	293,000	21,000	7.0 %	345,000	37,000	10.6 %

Source: Bureau of Labor Statistics, Monthly Labor Review, February, 1970, pp. 3, 4.

The labor support for the Nixon policies came primarily from the New York building trades whose members staged several "demonstrations" during May. These widely publicized actions had much to do with perpetuating the image created by George Meany's leadership of the AFL-CIO during its fifteen-year existence. But these "hard hat" demonstrations, it turned out, required a second look and deeper analysis than they at first received. Evidence soon surfaced that many of the construction workers who had participated in the largest (and peaceful) march on May 20 had been told by contractors and union officials that they would be paid for the time spent at the demonstration and that failure to attend would mean loss of a day's pay. After the largest march on May 20, President Nixon personally thanked Peter Brennan, president of the New York Building Trades Council for his support and invited Brennan to the White House. Brennan accepted.[59]

Other developments showed, however, that the consensus was beyond repair. The relationship between the two electrical unions continued to develop and contacts between the UE and other unions opposed to the war continued. The 1971 UE convention in Los Angeles heard speeches not only by Harry Bridges of the West Coast Longshoremen, but also by new UAW president Leonard Woodcock and the IUE's Jennings. Jennings told the UE delegates that the recent GE strike had done "more to bring the labor movement together than any other thing in twentysome odd years; because for the first time in years, people were fighting together to take the bosses on."[60]

The 1971 UE convention also heard an address by John Kerry, president of the Vietnam Veterans Against the War (VVAW) and passed two resolutions on foreign policy. One specifically addressed the Vietnam War; the

---

59. For accounts of the May events in New York see Time, May 25, 1970, p. 21; Foner, Labor and the Indochina War, pp. 88-91; Koscielski, Divided Loyalties, pp. 19, 20.

60. UE News, September 13, 1971, p. 7.

other called on the government to direct the nation's resources away from "outlays for military goods" and institute a "Foreign Policy for Peace." The floor discussion again included calls for the union and its locals to increase their efforts to mobilize active opposition to the war. District 7 president Richard Neibur emphasized the importance of getting more "working people to speak out," and local 107's James Hart called for legislation to prevent any future American president sending "our boys to fight and die in immoral, unconstitutional and unlawful wars again."[61]

By the summer of 1972, the growing assertiveness of the anti-war forces in the labor movement led to the organization of a broader Labor for Peace conference than the Labor Assembly of 1967. This gathering at the Teamsters' Joint Council in St. Louis in June had the support and participation of five independent unions, including the UE and fourteen affiliates of the AFL-CIO. The *UE News* gave extensive coverage to the conference and the 985 delegates including 50 from the UE.[62]

The year 1972 provided even more dramatic proof of the end of the consensus. Developments in the labor movement during the presidential campaign could hardly have been imagined four years earlier. These resulted from factors related to, but not limited to, the Vietnam War. By 1972, no one called for continuing direct United States military involvement in Vietnam. Whether Washington would continue to play a role in any other form, such as aerial bombing, was unclear, but few politicians or labor leaders doubted the unpopularity of the war.

Yet, the changes in the labor movement did not find ready acceptance in all quarters. Old, more basic differences from two decades earlier re-emerged, but in

---

61. UE 1971 Convention Proceedings, pp. 105-107, 324. UE conventions were, by this time, larger than they had been a decade earlier. This reflected the union's growth during the decade. The Credentials Committee reports at the 1962 convention listed 150 delegates; at the 1969 convention, the report listed 230 delegates.

62. UE News, July 26, 1972, pp. 1, 6, 7.

new conditions. For the first time in the organization's history, the AFL-CIO leadership refused to support the Democratic presidential candidate; the executive council voted twenty-seven to three in July to make no endorsement. George Meany issued a statement charging that "a showdown" with the "new politics [became] necessary when a small elite of suburban types and students took over the apparatus of the Democratic Party."[63] While it at first appeared that the "showdown" might become a bitter reminder of the battles of two decades earlier, this did not happen, in part because of the number of major unions ready to support the McGovern candidacy, and the speed with which they acted.

By mid-August, a committee of the leaders of sixteen AFL-CIO unions had formed for that purpose. The committee included not only Paul Jennings of the IUE, but also the leaders of the International Association of Machinists (IAM) and the International Brotherhood of Electrical Workers (IBEW) as well. In fact, IBEW president Joseph Keenan chaired the group, which from the outset stated its intention to work with sympathetic unions. Since both the UAW and the UE endorsed the Democratic ticket and actively supported the campaign, all five of the unions that had competed in the electrical and machine industries during the 1950s and 1960s were in the same camp in 1972.[64] The size and determination of the independent labor forces caused President Meany to moderate his election rhetoric. When the AFL-CIO council met in September, he reiterated his position that member unions were free to make their own decisions and urged labor to work for the election of a friendly Congress.[65] Times had changed since 1948.

Two final points deserve emphasis regarding labor's participation in the 1972 election. First, the McGovern

63. NYT, July 20, 1972, p. 1.

64. For the committee's formation, see NYT, August 15, 1972, p. 24. For UE activity in the campaign along with other unions, see UE News, September 21, 1972, p. 3; October 30, 1972, pp. 1, 6, 7.

65. Business Week, September 2, 1972, p. 17.

labor committee, although it included the labor anti-war forces, included other unions as well. Joseph Beirne of the Communications Workers joined on the basis of McGovern's pro-labor voting record and in spite of disagreement on the war. On the other hand, the Teamsters broke with their UAW allies and endorsed Nixon.[66]

Second, while the 1972 election may have been a debacle for the Democratic Party, this is a superficial judgment when considering labor's role. Broad forces in labor displayed remarkable independence from the Meany leadership of the AFL-CIO. This was not always easy, despite Meany's decision to allow member unions to make their own choices. The AFL-CIO president suspended the charter of the Colorado Labor Council for endorsing McGovern. He personally addressed the steelworkers' convention in a successful bid to prevent that union from taking similar action. When the machinists' convention endorsed the Democratic ticket, Meany cancelled a planned appearance there, a decision the delegates applauded.[67]

While post-election reports emphasized labor's unprecedented desertion of the Democratic Party, the widespread resistance to Meany's efforts to keep Labor out of the McGovern camp was an equally remarkable feature of the election. In a campaign remembered for the illegal activities of the victors, for the large spending advantage enjoyed by the Republicans and for the subsequent disgrace of the winning candidate, thirty-two international unions, including all the major unions in the electrical industry, played a role independent of the AFL-CIO leadership.[68]

The prospects for the resurgence of labor's left-center coalition were thus still decidedly murky by

---

66. NYT, August 15, 1972, p. 24; August 18, 1972, p. 36.

67. Ibid., September 13, 1972, p. 32.

68. This figure is from Carl Gershman, The Foreign Policy of American Labor, p. 76, note 8. The NYT noted on August 29, 1972, that, in the New York area, the unions supporting McGovern were generally the old CIO unions (p. 37).

1973. A form of it emerged in support of the McGovern candidacy. The determination shown by a broad section of labor by refusing to accept George Meany's position suggested the potential for independent political activity, despite the sobering election-day results. The fact that neither major party fielded a candidate who made continuation of the Cold War an issue—the incumbent visited both Moscow and Peking before the election—indicated the extent of the erosion of support for it. The election-day results might delay the realignment taking place in the labor movement, but the Cold War consensus had disintegrated. The increasing unity of action in the electrical industry held the possibility of further developing an independent course. The UE and its supporters and allies could take encouragement from these developments, having seen the end of its isolation. While they could claim that events had justified their stand on the Cold War, whether labor's independent potential would soon be fulfilled remained unclear.

Conclusion

In these pages, we have dealt with a part of the American labor movement that was not part of the movement's public face for much of the period covered and that survived defeats and disappointments during the decade and a half after World War II. The left-center coalition that pioneered industrial unionism in the electrical manufacturing industry certainly suffered major setbacks during the first post-war decade. This does not mean, however, that it had no influence or significance, or that historians can afford to ignore it.

Our story suggests, rather, that the left—originally in the CIO—and in the UE in particular, along with center forces that worked with the left, continued to play a role as an integral, if not always recognized, section of the movement, even in the most adverse circumstances. The persistent question in the electrical industry for two decades was: Who would or could step forward to replace the ostracized leaders and their supporters who had ceased to exist in the eyes of AFL-CIO officials? By the late 1960s, it was clear that the industry would not be unified without the left-center coalition that these leaders represented. The Cold War barriers then began to melt.

Workers in other industries, of course, also felt the effects of the Cold War. The CIO unions that joined with the AFL in 1955 experienced increasing stress during the 1960s. This resulted, at least in part, from the refusal of their leaders to challenge the restricting Cold War policies of the AFL leadership. The withdrawal of the auto workers from the AFL-CIO in 1968 resulted in large part from differences over political Cold War-related issues.

The UE, on the other hand, won renewed recognition and acceptance while it adhered to its positions and, in fact, intensified its opposition to the Vietnam War. By the end of the decade, not only the UE, but also many

AFL-CIO unions and the two largest independents, the auto workers and the Teamsters, opposed the war. At the same time, the breakthrough in the 1969 negotiations with General Electric indicated the respect accorded the UE and the viewpoint that it represented. James Matles, long the head of the union's GE negotiating team, was put in charge of "economic" issues for the union coalition.

The UE undertook one other action that demonstrated its leaders' determination to break through Cold War barriers. In the fall of 1972, the union responded to an invitation from the Power and Electrical Workers Union of the USSR. A nine-member UE delegation spent two weeks in the Soviet Union in an effort to expand trade possibilities and personal contacts. UE president Fitzgerald, who led the delegation, thus made his second visit after a gap of twenty-seven years. A delegation from the UE's New England district (District 2) had earlier traveled to Washington to urge that restrictions on trade with the USSR be relaxed. The District 2 delegation was the union's response to high unemployment in the machine tool industry in the region. The UE members argued that a large potential market for American machine tools existed in the USSR. They met with high officials of the State, Commerce, and Defense Departments as well as with Congressmen and Senators, "and met with a sympathetic response everywhere but at the Pentagon." The *UE News* gave prominent coverage to the Soviet tour and the delegates' report of their journey.[1] Times had clearly changed since the 1950s.

They had not changed everywhere, however. The "free trade union" leadership associated with George Meany remained firmly in place. Although the U.S. Supreme Court declared the anti-Communist affidavit clause of the Taft-Hartley Act an unconstitutional bill of attainder in 1965, the AFL-CIO formally barred Communists

1. UE News, November 13, 1972, p. 9; November 27, 1972, pp. 1, 3; December 11, 1972, pp. 1, 5-7; December 25, 1972, pp. 6-7.

from holding union office until the late 1990s. The American labor movement has yet to fulfill the potential that it seemed to hold in 1973, as the Cold War consensus weakened. The accelerated decline of the nation's basic manufacturing sector robbed labor of its territory of greatest strength. While aggressive organizing in the public sector, and recently in service industries, has gone forward, organized labor's share of the work force has, until recently, steadily declined. That might be considered the "bad" news.

The good news is that this situation is, at the time of this writing, sparking renewed and strenuous debate in the movement. This represents a giant positive step. Labor's need to try new strategies and approaches is bringing forth a tide of proposals and ideas from workers and from labor's allies. When we look back half a century, we can recall a time when such open discussion was stifled and unwelcome, but the pressure for change—and especially for a break with Cold War ideas and foreign policy—has deep historical roots in American labor, as we have argued here. During the three decades since the Cold War consensus collapsed in the labor movement, the ground has been prepared by countless rank-and-file unionists, as well as some of their leaders. The work of the Labor Leadership Assembly for Peace, the National Coordinating Committee for Trade Union Action and Democracy (TUAD), Jobs with Justice, and others have brought labor to the point where input and discussion are becoming a part of life in the movement. In addition, labor's role in recent election campaigns has expanded its influence far beyond its formal membership.

Here, we should turn again to considering the international context. The end of the Cold War was, to be sure, a momentous series of events that changed the environment in which American workers and their organizations struggle. The collapse of the Soviet Union and the socialist governments in Eastern Europe, of course, had global ramifications. It was at once an enormous disappointment to liberation movements around the world and an enormous perceived "success"—some would say an intoxicant—for major sections of the U.S. ruling class and foreign policy establishment. For American labor and its leaders, it presents a new set of problems and challenges, but perhaps it also presents opportunities. U.S. workers are, of necessity, coming to realize that the decisions, aims, and policies of corporate America profoundly impact millions of people—including workers—around the planet as well as workers in our own country. The challenge for us is, therefore, to find the ways to forge new relations and unity with workers and their organizations abroad.

The question mark is, in this writer's opinion, whether the current debate in our own labor movement will include a hard and critical look at American labor's international record and future outlook. This has proven a tough issue to confront, but there are hopeful signs. As we noted at the outset, the summer of 2004 saw several major unions take the step of directly challenging the U.S. Administration's Iraq War policy. In June of 2005, a delegation of Iraqi trade unionists toured U.S. cities at the invitation of U.S. Labor Against the War; they found willing and ready dialogue partners in the U.S. labor movement. A month later, the AFL-CIO took a step that could signal a change of direction after 60 years of actively supporting aggressive U.S. foreign policy. An increasing number of local, state, and regional bodies have gone on record against the Iraq War and called for the rapid withdrawal of the troops. Labor's participation has expanded and deepened the base of the peace movement.

The broader international picture also shows positive signs. The International Confederation of Free Trade Unions has merged with other organizations to form the International Trade Union Confederation (ITUC—Some might notice the dropping of the provocative term "free" from the name). The World Federation of Trade Unions (WFTU) is still alive and well as an independent entity. The two organizations now attend the same meetings and confront common issues. For example, as of this writing, the ITUC is planning to open contacts with the All China Federation of Trade Unions (ACFTU), a step that had previously been considered off-limits by trade unions in capitalist countries. All this activity gives hope for labor's future. If American labor will work to find its place as a leader among the working people of the planet, then it will be ready to fulfill its potential in its own country as well.

Appendix A
U.S. Labor and the Korean War

The Korean War 1950–53 solidified U.S. Cold War policy. The North Korean "aggression" proved the necessity of the fourfold increase in the military budget from 1950 to 1951. The original version is still largely accepted without question by historians in this country, despite a serious challenge that appeared in 1952 (before the war ended) in journalist I.F. Stone's book *The Hidden History of the Korean War.* Stone suggested that the war was actually provoked by an insecure, unpopular, and reactionary South Korean government in a bid for U.S. support, and that this support had probably been promised in advance since John Foster Dulles and other high-ranking American officials had visited South Korea, and the border with the north, a few days before the war's outbreak.

In any case, the leaders of the CIO, now functioning without their organization's "left-progressive wing," immediately and energetically supported the Truman Administration's decision to intervene on the Korean peninsula.

By early 1951, however, it was already clear that the CIO position would prove difficult to sustain. With the war barely six months old, signs of "war weariness" were already evident in the United States. Widespread concern that the war would escalate and spread surfaced around the globe. Let us compare the positions and statements of the leaders of the CIO on the one hand, and the UE on the other, regarding the world situation and the war at about this time. We can then suggest some tentative conclusions regarding who was more accurately representing American workers.

The CIO:

Secretary-treasurer James Carey, in a speech to the Ohio CIO council, called the "growing tide of isolationism... Communism's fifth column" in the United States. "Carey branded isolationists virtual traitors... and called on organized labor to educate all Americans on the real way to fight Communism, with arms, with ideas, with economic aid." (CIO News, 1/29/51 p. 6)

CIO representatives, along with those of the AFL on the United Labor Policy Committee, "renewed organized labor's support of our country's struggle against Soviet imperialism... at a meeting with Secretary of Defense George Marshall." (CIO News, 1/22/51, p. 6)

The UE:

The *UE News* criticized the Truman Administration for U.S. opposition to the cease-fire proposal made by the Arab nations at the UN and which had the tacit support of "practically every important nation in the world including France, Britain, and India." The editorial suggested that the Administration wanted a wage freeze and a tax increase and that its leaders believed that they needed the war emergency to secure support for these policies. (UE News, 2/26/51, p. 2) The UE gave prominent coverage to the cease-fire proposal of Senator Edwin C. Johnson (D-Colo.) and sent a delegation to see Johnson to express this support. (UE News, 5/28/51, p. 2; 6/25/51, p. 1)

Also, the *UE News* reprinted an editorial from a small Pennsylvania newspaper, the *York Gazette and Daily*, which had sharply criticized "high labor union officials" for their support for the foreign policy of the Truman Administration. The editorial read in part:

> The American labor movement has... sacrificed almost all its objectives because its leaders refused to see that these could be obtained only if a larger objective, peace, were attained... their greatest failure has been their utter

> lack of responsibility in the cause of world peace... No group is better situated to lead a constructive struggle for peace than the working people....
>
> Developments show that many Americans are fearful of global war...not the representatives of labor, but those of conservative interests are now speaking out.... Many Americans are looking for leadership which can provide a rational, genuine program for peace.... How much brighter the future of the world would seem if officials of labor unions in this country had so conducted themselves these past few years that they were ready to accept this leadership. (UE News, 2/26/51, p. 2; see chapter IV, n. 53.)

Most of the literature continues to assume that the leadership of the AFL and the CIO were in the "mainstream" of American public opinion, and that the "left led" unions, such as the UE, represented the "fringe." However, the results of Gallup polls taken during early 1951 suggest that the truth may well have been the opposite.

Survey 469-K January 22, 1951 Question 3:

"In view of developments since we entered the fighting in Korea, do you think the United States made a mistake in deciding to defend South Korea or not?"

Yes....................49%
No......................38%
No Opinion...........13%

Question 6:

"Now that Communist China has entered the fighting in Korea with forces far outnumbering the United Nations troops there, which one of these courses would you yourself prefer that we follow: Pull troops out of Korea as fast as possible, or keep our troops there [against] these larger forces?

Pull out.................66%
Stay there...............25%
No opinion...............9%

Survey 487-K April 2, 1951 Question 4a:

"Do you think the United States made a mistake in going into the war in Korea, or not?"

Yes....................51%
No......................35%
No opinion............14%

Perhaps the most revealing results were those in answer to the above question when they were grouped according to the educational level reached by the respondents.

Survey 471-K March 28, 1951 Question 4:

"Do you think the United States made a mistake in going into the war in Korea, or not?"

College
Mistake..............43%
Not a mistake.........50%
No opinion

High School
Mistake..............50%
Not a mistake.........41%
No opinion............9%

Grade School
Mistake................52%
Not a mistake.........35%
No opinion...........13%

What is most striking about these results, besides the general level of dissatisfaction with the war, is that the dissatisfaction increases among respondents with less formal education. While not conclusive, they suggest that those with grade school and high school educations realized that their sons were the ones paying the price of the U.S. war policy in a far-off country on the other side of the planet. While some of their leaders had, through their own effort and sacrifice, managed to earn college degrees, most electrical workers, in common with most CIO members and most Americans at the time, had not had the opportunity. Therefore, these figures compel us to wonder how accurately James Carey and the other CIO leaders were representing their constituents when they labeled "isolationists" as "virtual traitors." Were they speaking for their members, or were they attacking them?

Appendix B
Selected Biographies of "Generation" Members

Pat Barile: President of UE local 428 at the Sonotone Corporation in White Plains, New York, during the 1940s and early '50s. He ran for Congress as the candidate of the American Labor Party in West Chester County in 1948. When his political/union activity cost him his job at Sonotone, the local continued to elect him president. After District 4 joined the IUE in 1956, Barile worked as an organizer for that union for the rest of the decade of the 1950s. By his own account, he was dismissed from the IUE in 1960 after refusing to get involved in the UE-IUE labor board election at the Lynn General Electric plant. In August 2001, he did an extensive interview with the author covering his career as electrical worker, union officer, and as an organizer on the staff of the UE and later the IUE. As of this writing, he continues his political activity and writing of his own.

Barile grew up in Jersey City and learned about politics from his father, who was a leader in the Italian immigrant community during the Depression years. The transcript of his interview with the author is in the Communist Party collection at the Tamiment Library of NYU.

David Davis: Business Agent of Local 155, Philadelphia. One of the early organizers in the machine tool industry in what became UE District 1, Davis served as business agent and organizer for most of the life of the union from the early '30s until the early '50s. He did not hide his membership in the Communist Party USA. In his district position, he helped to organize demonstrations and rallies in support of the GE strike in the winter of 1946, activity which brought him recognition and less than favorable mention in the national print media at the time.

In the summer of 1953, Davis was one of nine Philadelphia CP leaders arrested on Smith Act charges. Their Philadelphia trial was in some ways unique. For instance, several prominent establishment law firms agreed to defend the accused and provided (generally young and inexperienced) attorneys to do so; the decision was made to fight the case as a Civil Rights issue rather than a political trial. Davis was the one defendant represented by his union lawyer. The nine were convicted and served months in prison before their convictions were reversed on appeal, and Davis gave up his union position, but he continued to be supportive of the cause. The three-page statement he issued upon leaving his position in November 1953 stands as an eloquent expression of the beliefs of a "left wing" trade union leader from that time. He wrote, in part:

> 1) I believe that every American is entitled to a decent job, at decent wages, and in decent working conditions, and to bring up his children without fear; 2) I believe that this land properly belongs to the working people and farmers who built it; 3) I believe that the working people and farmers, who are the majority in this country, should have the major governing power. This is democracy; 4) I believe that we can live in peace with the rest of the world. I believe that these things that I stand for are what many workers and farmers stand for; but even though you may not agree with all of my ideas, most people will agree that I have the right to express them, in accordance with our American traditions; that I should not go to jail for my ideas; and that I should be able to remain with my family, and with you, to fight for a better life for all of us.

The last message we have from him is his hand-written note to Julius Emspak that Davis penned in April 1959 upon hearing that the Subversive Activities Control Board had dropped its proceedings against the UE. Davis wrote, "This victory is particularly significant since it was the government that moved to drop the charges, thus actually admitting that when its stable of stool pigeons has to submit to real cross examination they haven't a leg to stand on."

While the facts of his early life are sketchy, Davis was apparently born a Russian Jew in the first decade of the 20th century. His name at the trial was given as "Davis (aka Dubensky)." He was remembered as a highly effective and principled trade union leader during his nearly quarter century of activity in Philadelphia metal working unionism.

Sources: Davis to Emspak, April 5, 1959, UE Archives, Record Group 1.2, ff "Emspak, Julius Correspondence 1936-1962"; Statement by David Davis to "Dear Fellow Members of Local 155 UE," November 10, 1953, in UE Archives RG D1 ff 796; Interviews with David Cohen, former counsel for UE Local 155, December 2, 2004, and January 13, 2005, and former members of UE local 155; Harris, Howell John, *Bloodless Victories: The Rise and Fall of the Open Shop in the Philadelphia Metal Trades,* Cambridge: Cambridge University Press, 2000; Labovitz, Sherman, *Being Red In Philadelphia: A Memoir of the McCarthy Era,* Philadelphia: Camino Books, 1998; *Time*, March 11, 1946, "The Riot Act."

Ernest Demaio: President of UE District 11 in Illinois and Wisconsin during the 1950s and '60s. Demaio held key posts in the union during much of the period covered in this book. For example, at national conventions, he served as chair of the resolutions committee for several years and, as such, dealt with the issues that the members deemed important enough to want discussed by their leaders. Demaio was one of the "left-wingers" who did not leave the union during the mid-'50s at the time of the AFL-CIO merger. After his retirement from the UE in 1974, he served several years as the United Nations representative of the World Federation of Trade Unions.

Born in New Haven, Demaio, by his own account was the son of an IWW activist and from a large family. As a young worker, he was fired from his job after a violent encounter with his supervisor who had belittled his participation in the campaign to free Sacco and Vanzetti. He then became one of the first organizers hired by the new electrical and radio union in the mid-1930s. In retirement, Demaio returned to Connecticut where he was interviewed by the author in October 1986.

Carl Gray: President and Business Agent of the 7,000-member UE Local 107 at the Westinghouse steam turbine plant (known among workers as the "steam division") in Lester, Pennsylvania, during the 1950s. He first joined the labor movement as a seaman during the Depression and came to work at Westinghouse during the 1940s. He led the local through the 10-month strike of 1955–56 and was one of the 26-member negotiating committee that spent 19 days at the Delaware County prison farm at Broad Meadows for violating an injunction in March of 1956. He was also one of the leaders in the successful effort to keep the local in the UE during the decade of raiding and intra-union warfare. After his career in the UE, Gray worked as an organizer for AFSCME. In his 1986 interview with the author, he defended the UE's opposition to the Vietnam War and argued that "the UE represented the majority; the AFL-CIO represented the bosses."

James B. (Jack) Hart: A chief steward in UE local 107 during the late 1940s and '50s, and field organizer for the union during the '60s and '70s. Born in Americus, Georgia, Hart came north and went to work in the maintenance department at the Westinghouse turbine plant in Lester (Essington), Pennsylvania, near Philadelphia in July 1941. During the late 1940s, he was elected steward and later chief steward of several departments, where he broke new ground as an African-American in an elected position representing racially integrated departments.

In 1963, Hart was hired as a field organizer for the UE and worked for the union until he retired in 1981. In his July 1986 interview with the author, he vigorously defended the UE position on the Vietnam War and told how he had become interested in anti-war activities. He took a leave from his union job to travel with a delegation to the Soviet Union in 1975. Hart also spoke with pride the union's involvement and of his own work in the Civil Rights movement during the 1960s. During that period, Hart was instrumental in founding a rank-and-file group of African-American electrical workers in UE District 1, calling themselves "the Carthaginians" who, early on, publicized and supported the anti-apartheid struggle in South Africa.

Russ Nixon: Served as the UE's Washington representative from 1941 until the early 1960s with a break for military service during WWII. In Washington, Nixon oversaw the union's exhaustive research on economic and labor issues and testified before Congress on numerous occasions. One of Nixon's early experiences with a Congressional committee was in March 1947 when the House Labor Committee called him to testify about Communist influence in the UE. This appearance was newsworthy because of what the press called a "dramatic reversal of roles" as Massachusetts Congressman John F. Kennedy questioned the witness. Kennedy had been a student in Nixon's class at Harvard and was now questioning his former teacher. The reported exchange went as follows:

> Mr. Kennedy: Do you think that Communism is a threat to the economic and political system of the United States?
>
> Mr. Nixon: I do not think it is a threat. What I do think is a threat is our failure to meet the economic needs of our people.

Nixon was born in Minnesota in 1913. He graduated from UCLA, 1934; received his MA from Harvard, 1938; his PhD from Harvard, 1940. He was an Economics instructor at Harvard during 1938–1939; went to work for WPA in January 1941; for UE in December 1941. Nixon enlisted in the Army in April 1944; worked for the U.S. Treasury Department tracking Nazi assets in Europe 1945; resigned in protest early in 1946, saying the

U.S. government was not serious about de-Nazification in Europe and that the three Western powers (U.S., England, and France) were forming a bloc to isolate the Soviet Union.

Nixon's correspondence is in the UE Archives RG 1, "Washington Representative Russ Nixon 1946–1955"; his biographical information is also in the Archives in the UE FBI files Box 28 File# 100-66573 and in UE photos Box 25.

Helen Quirini: A leading activist at the GE Schenectady works first hired in 1941. She worked in different departments, became a shop steward, an officer of local 301, the UE's largest, and later an organizer for the union during the early 1950s. She was a leader in the struggle for women's equality on the job and in the union. Called to testify before Congressional committees more than once, her strongly worded testimony (see chapter V) helps to recreate for readers the atmosphere of the early Cold War years. She grew up in Schenectady, attended public school, played on high school sports teams, gave up going to college in order to help support her family, and, as of this writing, still lives in Schenectady where she is active on retiree and pension issues.

Quirini has written and published two books: *A Personal Memoir of World War II* (1997), which contains much information about her work experiences and her union career; and *The Story of Local 301 IUE AFL-CIO* (1987), which she co-authored with Henry Antonelli. She has also done extensive interviews for the "Schenectady General Electric in the Twentieth Century Project."

Ernest Thompson: Business manager for UE locals 427 and 446 in the Jersey City area during the late 1940s and executive officer of the Hudson County CIO Council from 1942–50. In 1943, he became the first African-American field organizer for the UE. From 1951 to '56, Thompson served both as director of the UE's National Fair Practices Committee and as a leading organizer of the National Negro Labor Council, which, at its peak, claimed over 50,000 members in 53 cities. The Council led the nation's first mass job campaigns by African-Americans and targeted several companies including General Electric in Louisville, Kentucky. Under pressure from the Subversive Activities Control Board, the Council disbanded in 1956, and that same year Thompson's work with the UE ended when District 4 went into the IUE. Thompson then became a leader in community and political organizing in the area around Newark and Orange, New Jersey, where he lived until his death in January 1971.

Thompson spent his early years with his family on a farm in Maryland and came to live with his aunt in Jersey City when he was 13. His papers comprise Manuscript Collection 1180 at the Rutgers University Libraries Special Collections and University Archives.

Appendix C

Letter from John Williamson, National Labor Secretary, Communist Party USA

To Philip Murray, President, Congress of Industrial Organizations

September 15, 1949

Explaining how he sees Murray's position as having changed over the previous three years and offering to work with Murray "on the basis of a minimum program representing the interests of labor."

Source: Rutgers University, IUE Papers, Box 28, copies in File Folders 5 and 13.

COMMUNIST PARTY, U. S. A.
National Office
35 East 12th Street - New York 3, New York

September 15, 1949

Mr. Philip Murray, President,
Congress of Industrial Organizations,
718 Jackson Place, N. W.,
Washington 6, D. C.

Dear Sir and Brother:

Innumerable news items have appeared during the past year in which you or your fellow officers are quoted attacking the Communist Party and sometimes the so-called "Communist-dominated" affiliates of the CIO. We have until now ignored your alleged charges and distortions of Communist policy. Since there are no "Communist-dominated" affiliates of the CIO, we cannot speak for them. If, as we have reason to suspect, by "Communist-dominated" affiliates, you mean those Internationals whose membership have adopted a union policy on political questions at variance with the majority of CIO opinion, I assume they are well able to take care of themselves.

However, this letter is written because the *CIO News* of August 15th devotes an entire page to comment on an article written by me in the magazine *Political Affairs* for January 1949 on the 1948 CIO Convention. Disregarding such questions as the belated discovery of this article and the fact that *CIO News* ignored significant sections of it, I welcome this opportunity to compare what we Communists said nine months ago with the claims of the dominant CIO leaders. I furthermore believe that it will benefit the whole labor movement to examine what has since happened to our respective analyses and perspectives.

In the Portland Convention, the majority associated with you and Walter Reuther rode the Truman bandwagon. You declared:

> "We put all our might and effort ... toward the election of President Truman and a liberal Congress; and we won. The people won. Thank God for that ..."

Walter Reuther and Jacob Potofsky used their own adjectives to describe Truman's victory. Carey, in fact, on another occasion elevated Truman to a pedestal higher than Franklin D. Roosevelt. No speech of a majority supporter at that Convention was complete, without singing hozannahs to Truman and promising a new "New Deal" legislative program. You promised the repeal of the Taft-Hartley Act by Truman almost with the finality of God himself.

Ten months of the new Truman Administration have gone by. And in spite of the siren songs of all the trade union leaders associated with you, as to the benefits labor would gain, the failure and betrayal of Truman and the Democratic Congress majority have been so clear that a process of disillusionment has set in among the workers. Contrast your estimate and that of your associates with that made by the Communist Party's General Secretary, Eugene Dennis, a few days after the 1948 election. He said in part:—

> "Many people believe they are going to get what they want from the Truman Administration and the Democratic majority in the bi-partisan Congress. But these illusions will be — or, at least,

can be — relatively short-lived. We are not entering another New Deal 'era." The Administration and the bipartisan Congress are committed to an anti-Communist drive at home and abroad, and to an aggressive imperialist war policy and a war economy. This cannot but determine the character of, and set definite limits upon, the scope of Truman's promised social and labor reforms."

The roll call of Truman promises that have never been delivered on is a long one. Suffice it here to single out two:

1. Truman promised unequivocal repeal of the infamous Taft-Hartley Act. On this basis he gained substantial trade union support, making inroads even among Wallace supporters. In exchange for this promise the entire Right-wing trade union leadership of both CIO and A.F. of L. supported the bipartisan imperialist foreign policy. During the election campaign they fought against the Progressive Party and its candidate, Wallace, the organized expression of the independent political action of labor and its allies.

What actually happened regarding repeal of the Taft-Hartley Act? The CIO asked for the "two-package" procedure to guarantee repeal of Taft-Hartley. But Truman (with a clear-cut Democratic majority, despite Brother Riordan's article) presented a "one-package" proposal which included some "little" (Thomas Lesinski) amendments, as crooked as they were tricky. Truman recommended "repeal" but with a catch to it. The catch consisted of some "little" amendments deliberately opening the door to some "bigger" amendments (Sims) and finally to the Taft proposals, which actually meant keeping the original Taft-Hartley Act on the statute books. This is how today, ten months after the election, the Truman promise to repeal the Taft-Hartley Act remains an empty promise.

Incidentally, it is a known fact that CIO Legislative Directors of unions under Right-wing leadership supported both the Lesinski and the Sims amendments. And yet the article in CIO News has the audacity to state, "The work of your /meaning in reality the Left-Progressive unions which according to you, Mr. Murray are "Communist-controlled"/ lobbyists hurt the cause of liberation to a great degree.."

2. Truman promised civil rights legislation, particularly to the Negro people. But here again he shamefully betrayed that promise. Truman has not only refused to deliver on his civil rights promises in terms of legislation against lynching, poll tax, for an F.E.P.C., etc. He is directly responsible for the present wave of repression, such as: the trial of thought and books in Foley Square, the Loyalty Oaths, the proposed Mundt-Ferguson and Hobbs Bills, etc. It is the Truman assault on civilization which set the stage for the fascist attacks on the great American Paul Robeson and the people who attended his concert at Peekskill. This attack has aroused great concern amongst many liberty-loving Americans, who recognize that the bestial and hateful anti-Negro, anti-Communist, anti-Jewish atmosphere in Peekskill is a warning that the rights of all trade unionists, all minorities, all true democrats are in danger. Unfortunately, you, Brother Murray, remained silent on the storm trooper attack at Peekskill. When this silence on the threat of fascism is accompanied by your vilent anti-Communist attacks, it would seem that the lesson of Hitler fascism has been forgotten by you.

There is really no need for long argumentation to show that our analysis of Truman and the Democratic Party has proven correct. All one needs is to ask the workers in any shop in the country, "Are you better off today than you were last November?" And the answer will invariably be, "We are worse off."

Let us for a moment examine the question of foreign policy. It is particularly bad-timing for your spokesman, Mr. Riordan, to refer to the Marshall Plan, because the presence here of the British Bevin-Cripps Delegation crying for dollar-aid at this very moment, dramatizes the complete failure of the Marshall Plan to do what you claimed it would at Boston and Portland. Furthermore, would you say that the North Atlantic Pact and the Arms Bill are proof of your position that the Truman foreign policy is designed to help the peoples of Europe recover from the ravages of war? Obviously, military alliances and arms will do precisely the opposite. Your spokesmen claim that the Marshall Plan is popular amongst the American workers. Of course, the majority of those who originally swallowed your false analysis of the Marshall Plan supported it because they honestly believed it would feed the hungry, clothe the naked and house the homeless people of our wartime allies. Besides, you created the illusion that the Marshall Plan would provide jobs and prosperity at home. But now it is abundantly clear that the Marshall Plan, North Atlantic Pact and Arms Bill are all part of the scheme for war preparations and war. Now more and more trade unionists see that the Marshall Plan has in fact worsened conditions in most industries right here at home. That is why millions of American workers are beginning to realize that the Communist position on the Marshall Plan has been correct and that your position has been wrong and in effect gave aid to the warmongers, the monopoly enemies of labor.

Editor Riordan loses all control of himself and writes, "Williamson, like all other Communist leaders, hates the very thought of CIO President Philip Murray." This is childish nonsense. Communist leaders don't hate you. We have been sharply critical of your policies during the last few years because we believe that they are detrimental to the interests of labor and the nation. Communists have worked in alliance with you in the past, and would do so now, on the basis of a minimum program representing the economic and political interests of labor and that would allow democracy and autonomy in the affairs of the C.I.O. When Communists and Leftwingers were in alliance with you from 1935 to 1946; when you welcomed the cooperation of Communists in organizing the unorganized; when you hired scores of SWOC organizers and directors whom you knew to be Communists; we were no different then than we are now. Then, as now, we believed in Socialism and you believed in Capitalism. Nevertheless, we were able to work together on the basis of a fighting militant trade union program.

The interests of the workers and trade unions demand united action today of all forces, irrespective of their ideological differences. The burning issues confronting all workers and all trade unions are clear. The need for united action against the attacks of the employers, government boards and anti-labor courts is equally clear.

Just as ideological differences between Communists and non-Communists did not prevent joint action and a united CIO from 1935 to 1946, it is equally possible today.

Consequently, if we Communists take sharp issue with you today, Editor Riordan should ask you and not me, "How's your party line change these days..."

Many examples could be given of who did the changing, but let me cite only four.

I am sure you remember when you supported and voted in 1946 for an official CIO foreign policy resolution that stated in part:

"We know that an enduring peace requires an early agreement ... for world disarmament. Grandiose demonstrations of military power ... do not lend themselves to ... trust. As a result our nation now has an annual military budget of billions of dollars ...

"Above all the common people of this country demand that there be a fulfillment of the basic policy of our late President Roosevelt for friendship and unity among the three great wartime allies...

"The President recognized that friendship and unity could flow, only from understanding, negotiation and agreement and not from maneuver, pressure and denunciation...

"We reject all proposals for American participation in any bloc or alliance which would destroy the unity of the Big Three..."

How does that square with what you said on foreign policy in Portland and throughout last year, Brother Murray? Clearly, it is you who has changed.

I am sure you have not forgotten that forthright speech in Pittsburgh on December 4, 1945, where you characterized the Truman Administration in the following words:

"A very serious crisis faces our nation today. It would be unwise and hypocritical not to face this fact"...

"What is the answer of the federal administration to this diabolical plot of American industry?"...

"The sole answer of the federal administration is to seek legislation directed against labor"...

"To all this arrogance /of the trusts/ the federal administration yields in abject cowardice. Its rancor is confined to labor."...

"To date the federal administration has completely ignored the grave human problems which stand unsolved."

"The federal administration instead is embarked upon a policy of continued appeasement of American industry in the face of its contemptuous attitude toward the American people..."

"It is within this framework that the proposed legislation of President Truman must be viewed and its real intent understood."

"The design... is to weaken and ultimately destroy labor union organizations..."

How does that square with what you said in praising Truman in Portland or throughout the year since then, Brother Murray? Clearly it is you who has changed.

You cannot have forgotten that decisive speech you made in 1947 at the UAW Convention on the issue of autonomy, where you stated:

> "We never determine the course of action of our affiliates... They were sovereign, autonomous unions, and in matters of great moment we got together and we considered and advised with each other, but in the end we left the ultimate decision to each of the International unions for important policy decisions. There is a reason for that. I hope the day never comes in the history of the CIO when it shall take upon itself the power to dictate or to rule or to provide by policy methods of dictation and ruling that run counter to the very principles of true democracy."

This is only one of many similar speeches by you which were basic CIO policy and in fact constituted the very cornerstone of the founding policies of CIO at its Constitutional Convention.

Yet today, what Reuther said in Portland about "Get clear ... or clear out of CIO" was proposed by you at the last CIO Executive Board meeting. It was you who proposed motions adopted by majority vote, declaring that all CIO Board members must "conform" to majority political policies, or "resign" or be kicked out. This was accompanied by decisions to lift charters. At the N. Y. State CIO Convention last week, Vice-President Haywood is quoted as saying that the Left-wing unions "may as well get out now" or they will be kicked out.

In nearly every issue of CIO News, Editor Swim has a special assignment to explain away this change in fundamental policy regarding autonomy. Despite Swim's twisting of the truth, the issue of autonomy is as simple as you stated it in 1947. It is not a question, as Swim distorts it, of having a situation in the national CIO where "All affiliates should be permitted to vote on policy matters. But none should be required to adhere to policies thus determined." This is not the position of the left, progressive internationals. The issue is the majority effort to force autonomous international unions to conform on broad political issues, such as; whom to support in election campaigns, what foreign policy is in the interests of our nation, etc.

How do these actions and all the threats to expel the Left Progressive Internationals at the coming Cleveland Convention square with what you yourself so truthfully said in 1947 on autonomy, Brother Murray? Clearly it is you who have changed.

As late as 1946 you made a statesmanlike presentation of your attitude towards Communists in your own Steel Workers Union, which you must remember. You stated;

> "We ask no man his national origin, his color, his religion or his beliefs. It is enough for us that he is a steel worker and that he believes in trade unionism... Our union has not been and will not be an instrument of repression. It is a vehicle for economic and social progress... As a democratic institution, we engage in no purges, no witch-hunts. We do not dictate a man's thoughts or beliefs. Most important of all we do not permit ourselves to be stampeded into course of action which create division among our members and sow the disunity which is sought by those false prophets and hypocritical advisers from without who mean us no good."

True, you violated this solemn commitment at the subsequent Steel Union Convention, insofar as Nick Migas was concerned.

For the past 12 months you and your associates who have been slandering the Communist Party, have forgotten the role the Communists played in helping to build the C.I.O. But, clearly it is you and not we who have changed.

We Communists, as a working-class political party, speak out plainly on issues confronting labor and the trade unions. We do this, not to interfere in the affairs of the trade unions, but because we know that without strong trade unions receiving the active support of their membership, the vital needs of the entire nation for peace, security and democracy can never be realized.

Brother Murray: The main concern of the Communists today as ever is to promote the united action of labor in defense of its economic and political needs. We are sharply aware of the dangers facing the labor movement. We see clearly the arrogance of the employers, their refusal to grant the just wage and contract demands of the unions, and their preparations to weaken or smash the unions wherever they feel the unions are weak. And the employers don't make any distinction between the workers of Right or Left-led unions, when their profits are involved.

We have forewarned the workers of the developing economic crisis which already has created 6 million unemployed and 9 million part-time workers and has struck the Negro workers with special savagery.

We emphasize the encroachment of reaction upon the rights of the people and especially the trade unions as exemplified not only by the Taft-Hartley Act but also by the attacks on picket lines, by injunctions, etc.

The policy you are following today, egged on by Walter Reuther who thinks of himself as the top man in CIO majority circles, threatens much more than the Left-Progressive Internationals and their membership — serious as that is. A thousand times more important is the fact that the very existence of all trade unions will be jeopardized, that the gains realized by the workers over the years through militant struggles will be threatened.

What is being prepared as your "anti-Communist policies for the Cleveland Convention" in effect threaten to nullify the great historical step of American labor, symbolized by the organization of the CIO in 1936. They threaten to undermine the great tradition of progressive trade unionism that was represented by the CIO in its first decade of existence, and to destroy the growing coalition of labor and the Negro liberation movement that was evidenced in the CIO in its early years. Your red-baiting pro-imperialist policies are throwing back the American labor movement which stood forth in the first decade of the CIO as the champion of the nation in opposition to Wall Street trusts and their representatives in government, even though it earned you the attacks of all reactionary forces.

We stand as uncompromising today as always for the unity of the labor movement. We are particularly firm in our stand for a united CIO, for a united wage fight, for a united fight to repeal Taft-Hartley. We are against splits, against secessions and against expulsions. We believe that there is room in a trade union for differences especially on political issues. And those issues can and should be openly debated. We believe your policies are harmful to the CIO members. We will try to influence workers to return the CIO to its founding policies of militant trade unionism, inner democracy and autonomy, and away from class collaboration, expulsions and blind conformity. But all this can and should be realized within the framework of the C.I.O. [illegible] political party where people voluntarily obligate themselves to the common political line of that party. Trade unions are elementary economic organizations, uniting workers of different political beliefs. They can grow and prosper if they adopt a fighting policy in the interests of their members and never forget that their enemies are the employers, especially the big trusts, and all the political instruments of the trusts. Progressive trade union leaders try to influence their affiliates and members to adopt political policies and candidates that correspond to their interest as workers - but they cannot impose such policies upon them, either as individuals or as affiliates.

Editor Swim in the Sept. 5 issue of CIO News says that if the forces standing for autonomy in the CIO (whom he deceitfully limits to Communists) were successful they would be able to say, "The patient died but the operation was a great success." Brother Murray, you and not Allan Swim know that the CIO policies from 1935 to 1946 proved successful. The patient did not die. These founding policies organized and built the CIO. They inspired workers and all the oppressed people of our nation.

The immortal Scottish poet Robbie Burns, whose writings you are no doubt well acquainted with, in a different setting, well said:

"Oh, wad some power the
giftie gi'e us
To see oursel's as others see us!

It wad frae monie a
blunder free us
And foolish notion:

What airs in dress an' gait
wad lea'e us,
and e'en devotion!"

I hope, since it was found possible to devote an entire page in CIO News to attacking my article and viewpoint, that you will see that this answer is given equal space.

Sincerely yours,

/s/ JOHN WILLIAMSON

John Williamson,
National Labor Secretary,
Communist Party, U.S.A.

uopwa-16

A Note on Sources
The Historiography of Labor and the Cold War

The evolving historical treatment of the electrical unions is a story in itself. Here, the author should mention a few of the milestones he encountered in his research.

Historians have given attention to the electrical workers; in fact, the UE and the IUE are probably among the most written about unions in the recent American past. Over the years, the value and quality of the work have dramatically improved, but it has not been an easy process. An early effort to make sense of their experience with industrial unionism and its political implications was Max Kampleman's *The Communist Party vs. the CIO* in 1957, which unabashedly shows its Cold War origins. Kampleman was Senator Humphrey's aide at the time of the 1952 hearings on Communist influence in the labor movement conducted by the Humphrey subcommittee, and the book is an expanded version of his doctoral thesis. I mention this work primarily to show how far historians had to come back in restoring the electrical unions to a better place in the annals of labor history.

The next published work of alleged scholarship appeared two decades later and did give some space to the UE as part of the rise and fortunes of industrial unionism. This was Bert Cochran's *Labor and Communism; the Conflict that Shaped American Unions* in 1977. While Cochran presents a more layered view of the CIO's early years, and of the auto workers especially, his treatment of the electrical unions leaves the reader with many questions and, I would argue, wrong impressions. His title suggests his Cold War bias.

Meanwhile, researchers were digging in and producing more useful work on electrical and other workers as well, although much of it remained unpublished. A sort of trio of the most important seminal dissertations would have to include 1) James Prickett, "Communists and the Communist Issue in the American Labor Movement 1920–1950" (UCLA 1975) that argues that the left-led unions were more democratic than those under right domination; 2) Leroy Lenburg, "The CIO and American Foreign Policy 1935–1955" (Penn State, 1973) on the unequal contest between the left and the right, which had official support, in the CIO after World War II; and 3) Ronald Filippelli, "The United Electrical, Radio and Machine Workers of America 1933–1949; the Struggle for Control" (Penn State, 1970). Of these, the only one ever published was the last mentioned (see below).

In 1974, James Matles, along with James Higgins, did what more labor leaders should do when he put his memories about his union activity on paper. Everyone interested in the problems and challenges facing the labor movement today could benefit from reading *Them and Us*. Appearing as it did, immediately after the U.S. withdrawal from Vietnam (and a year before Matles's sudden fatal heart attack), this work, in a way, perhaps had the long-term effect of encouraging a new generation of labor historians to look critically at American labor's lot during the Cold War years.

By the 1980s, researchers who dared to deal with the politics of the labor movement were publishing. Most useful is Roger Keeran's *The Communist Party and the Auto Workers' Unions* in 1980. On the electrical industry specifically, the appearance of Ronald Schatz's pioneering study, *The Electrical Workers: A History of Labor at GE and Westinghouse 1923–1960*, in 1983, indicated that enough time had passed for scholars to look objectively at electrical workers and their efforts to organize. This book broke new ground. It takes us into the world of the factories in the two big electrical chains, and sheds light on their employees' work lives, their relationships on the job, and their reasons for wanting a union. Any future research on electrical workers must take Schatz's research into account. However, his discussion of the effects of the Cold War on electrical workers and his brief treatment of the 1950s leave many questions unanswered. That the UE's size and influence declined is hardly debatable, but how much is not clear. What happened in electrical unionism during and after the mid-1950s? Is the label "left wing" adequate to describe the UE? While Schatz appears to accept the democratic rank-and-file nature of the union for the earlier period, he gives little credibility to its positions during the 1950s.

Still another decade passed before we got a level-headed assessment of the politics of electrical unionism. Filippelli and Mark McColloch, formerly the archivist at the UE's Pittsburgh archives, published what some now consider a companion volume to Schatz's social history. Their *Cold War in the Working Class; the Rise and Decline of the United Electrical Workers* (1995) deals fairly with the role of Communists and others on the left in building the electrical workers' union and documents the widespread attacks that the union faced during the decade and a half after World War II.

The most recent decade has seen the appearance of decidedly worthwhile and relevant contributions. Michael J. Bonislawski's 2002 dissertation, "Field Organizers and the United Electrical Workers: A Labor of Love, Struggle and Commitment," includes a wealth of information on the union's organizers and argues for the political diversity of the UE. Jane LaTour's series of interviews with former UE research director, Nathan Spero, provide a look at the union through the eyes of one of the people primarily responsible for its consistent ability to generate reports and statistics of value to the entire labor movement. Frank Koscielski's book *Divided Loyalties: American Unions and the Vietnam War* (New York: Garland Publishing, 1999) focused on the attitudes of members of UAW Local 600 who had been at work during the Vietnam years. He found many workers reluctant to talk about their thinking during the period of the war, but many of those that did expressed disagreement with the Meany/AFL-CIO position. Most recently, Rosemary Feurer's *Radical Unionism in the*

Midwest, 1900–1950 (2006) persuasively begins to make the link between militant trade unionism at the community level and a class outlook on the larger world.

On the broader topic of the origins of the Cold War, we do not find the same process of generally improving research and analysis. The Cold War's apparent end and the perceived "victory" of the United States have generated more celebration and justification than questioning, but there are exceptions. Benjamin O. Fordham's *Building the Cold War Consensus: The Political Economy of U.S. National Security Policy 1949–1951* (Ann Arbor: U. of Michigan Press) 1998, persuasively argues that domestic concerns of various business groups and their political allies, rather than "response to external threats to core values," drove the development of U.S. global policy at that time. But much of the most helpful work remains the earlier efforts of authors such as Dana Fleming, Joyce and Gabriel Kolko, Lloyd Gardner, Daniel Yergin, and, yes, David Horowitz. I would make two special recommendations: 1) Godfrey Hodgson's *America in Our Time* (New York: Doubleday) 1986, includes his analysis of "the establishment" and its role in the nation's affairs after World War II, which I found extremely helpful, and 2) *Cold War Critics*, a volume edited by Thomas Patterson, which appeared in 1971. This collection should be on the reading list of anyone seeking to understand our nation's foreign policy stance during the post-World War II decades. One can find here essays about journalists (such as I.F. Stone and Walter Lippman), politicians (such as Henry Wallace and Glenn Taylor), leaders of the African-American community (such as W.E.B. DuBois), and others who questioned or opposed the foreign policy of the Truman Administration during the late 1940s. However, the reader will look in vain here for an essay, speech, or article by or about a member or leader of the American labor movement. One aim of *Generation of Resistance* is to argue that the most informed, thoughtful, and persistent critics of U.S. Cold War policies prominently included trade unionists.

Another aim is to encourage researchers to continue the effort to address labor's political and international fortunes during the Cold War and since. The opportunities for research in American labor history are, happily, becoming almost too numerous to track. I must mention the following repositories, which were among the first and the most helpful for me. The UE Archives at the University of Pittsburgh's Archives and Records Center; the IUE Papers, sometimes referred to as the James Carey Papers at Rutgers University; the James Carey Papers at the Archives of Labor and Urban Affairs, Wayne State University (here is Carey's correspondence in his capacity as an officer of the CIO); the John Foster Dulles Papers, Seeley G. Mudd Manuscript Library, Princeton University; and the Oral History of the American Left at New York University's Tamiment Library.

Finally, allow me a couple of random thoughts on the importance of original sources. There is now so much material available that the possibilities for re-interpretation and new thinking about "old" questions are mind-boggling. Recently, for instance, the UE Archives have gained possession of FBI files on many of the union's leaders and activists during the period covered in this book. My own reaction upon sifting through some of these records surprised me. It soon became obvious that many FBI reports submitted during the decade of the 1950s simply summarized easily available public information. One wonders what the Bureau meant by "investigation." Agents seem to have made a practice of sending in reports drawn from press descriptions of public meetings and quoting the speakers mentioned in the articles.

In fact, one report contains this startling admission, "... since passage of the Labor Management Relations Act of 1947 [Taft-Hartley], union leaders have ceased to participate in open Communist activities and, therefore, it has not been possible for us to develop sufficient evidence to form the basis for a petition before the Subversive Activities Control Board." In other words, this report suggests the Federal Bureau of Investigation often depended not on going under cover and ferreting out hard-to-get sensitive information about suspected "subversives," but on observing "open activities" and collecting data available to any member of the general public. These FBI files do contain valuable factual biographical information, but, I would argue, they often reveal as much about the Bureau, its tactics, and its underlying assumptions as they do about the "subjects" who were being investigated.

One other thought: for anyone accustomed to thinking of "Communists" or "Marxists" as overly dogmatic or mechanical, reading the Communist press from the post-World War II period might bring some surprises. For instance, I found the regular "World of Labor" columns by George Morris in the *Daily Worker* to provide nuanced and reflective analysis of then-current developments in labor that still give helpful insight decades later.

The hope here is that *Generation of Resistance* will move this continuing process forward by 1) refocusing attention on how the leadership of the electrical unions dealt with the overwhelmingly adverse circumstances that confronted them during the depths of the Cold War and how they related to their members in that context, and 2) to what extent leaders in the electrical industry succeeded in presenting a program and a vision of trade unionism that can be considered a viable alternative to the Cold War brand of unionism pursued by the leaders that dominated the AFL-CIO during the period covered.

Bibliography

Archives and Manuscript Collections

Personal Papers of Edward Boehner, former recording secretary, United Electrical, Radio and Machine Workers local 107, Lester, Pennsylvania.

Congress of Industrial Organizations, Office of the Secretary-Treasurer, James B. Carey Papers, Archives of Labor and Urban Affairs, Walter P. Reuther Library, Wayne State University.

Collection of the International Union of Electronic, Electrical, Salaried, Machine and Furniture Workers, AFL-CIO; Special Collections and University Archives; Rutgers University Libraries, New Brunswick.

John Foster Dulles Papers, Seeley G. Mudd Manuscript Library, Princeton University.

Historical Collections and Labor Archives, Penn State University.

Schenectady General Electric in the 20th Century; Department of History; University at Albany (www.Albany.edu/history).

Tamiment Library and Robert F. Wagner Labor Archives, New York University.

UE Archives; United Electrical Workers/Labor Collections; Archives Service Center; University of Pittsburgh.

Urban Archives, Temple University, Philadelphia.

Public Documents

U.S. House of Representatives, Subcommittee of the Committee on Education and Labor, Investigation of Communist Infiltration of the United Electrical, Radio and Machine Workers of America, 80th Congress, 2nd Session, 1948.

———, Committee on Un-American Activities, Hearings Regarding Communism in the Labor Movement in the United States, 80th Congress 1st Session, 1947.

———, Committee on Un-American Activities, Investigation of Communist Activities in the Newark, N.J. Area, 84th Congress, 1st Session, 1955.

U.S. Senate, Permanent Subcommittee on Investigations of the Committee on Government Operations, Subversion and Espionage in Defense Establishments and Industry, 83rd Congress, 2nd Session, 1954.

———, Subcommittee of the Committee on Labor and Public Welfare, Communist Domination of Unions and National Security, 82nd Congress, 2nd Session, 1952.

Union Publications

American Federation of Labor-Congress of Industrial Organizations, Convention Proceedings, 1959, 1965, 1967, 1969.

Congress of Industrial Organizations, Convention Proceedings, 1947-1954.

United Electrical, Radio and Machine Workers of America, Convention Proceedings, 1946-1955, 1957-1973.

Interviews

Unless otherwise noted, taped interviews are by the author; conversations were with notes by the author.

Pat Barile, former president of UE Local 428, field organizer for UE District 4 and organizer for IUE District 4; taped interview, August 14, 2001.

Harry Block, former president of UE District 1 and IUE District 1; taped interview, March 17, 1987.

Francis Bradley, former business agent of UE Local 107; taped interview, October 9, 1986.

David Cohen, former counsel for UE Local 155 and other District 1 locals; December 2, 2004 and January 13, 2005, conversation with notes.

Archer Cole, former international representative of UE District 4; at the time of the interview IUE director of organization; telephone conversation, February 27, 1987.

Ernest DeMaio, former president of UE District 11, former representative of the World Federation of Trade Unions to the United Nations; conversation November 22, 1985; taped interview, October 2, 1986.

Albert Fitzgerald, president of UE, transcript of interview by Ronald Filippelli, October 10, 1968; Pennsylvania State University, Historical Collections and Labor Archives.

James Hart, former chief steward UE Local 107; former field organizer, UE District 1; taped interview, July 28, 1986.

John Hovis, UE director of organization at the time of the interview, elected national president of UE in September 1987; telephone conversation, August 14, 1987.

Carl Gray, former president and business agent of UE local 107, former international representative of UE District 10; taped interview, December 12, 1986.

Louise Koszalka, former shop steward UE local 155 and later a member of IUE local 123; taped interview, February 21, 1987.
Max Helfand, former business agent UE local 155; taped interview, March 23, 1987.
James Matles, secretary-treasurer of UE at the time; transcript of interview by Ronald Filippelli, October 5, 1968; Pennsylvania State University, Historical Collections and Labor Archives.
Tim McDonnell, former shop steward UE local 107; taped interview, July 27, 1987.
James Mitchell, former Secretary of Labor, transcript of interview by Philip A. Crowe, July 22, 1967; Dulles Oral History Project, John Foster Dulles Papers, Seeley G. Mudd Manuscript Library, Princeton University.
David Montgomery, former shop chairman UE local 475; conversation with notes, July 29, 1987.
Helen Quirini, former recording secretary UE local 301 and legislative representative UE District 3; conversation with notes, September 8, 2005.
Ben Riskin, former editor Federated Press, former UE international representative; taped interview, October 10, 1986; conversation with notes, May 20, 1987.
Russell Senkow, business agent UE local 107; conversation with notes, June 4, 1986; taped interview, November 21, 1986.
Donald Tormey, formerly of UE local 201, two typed letters to the author in answer to questions, December 11, 1986; April 11, 1987.
Philip Van Gelder, former field organizer UE District 1, October 7, 1986.

Books

Acheson, Dean. Present at the Creation: My Years in the State Department. New York: W.W. Norton, 1969.
Allen, Bruce and Arie Melnik. The Market for Electrical Generating Equipment. East Lansing: Michigan State University.
Aronowitz, Stanley. False Promises: The Shaping of American Working Class Consciousness. New York: McGraw-Hill, 1974.
Aronson, James. The Press and the Cold War. New York: Bobbs-Merrill, 1970.
Backman, Jules. The Economics of the Electrical Manufacturing Industry. New York: New York University Press, 1962.
Bell, Daniel. The Coming of Post Industrial Society: A Venture in Social Forecasting. New York: Basic Books, 1973.
Boyer, Richard O. and Herbert M. Morais. Labor's Untold Story. New York: United Electrical, Radio and Machine Workers of America, 1955, 1965, 1971.

Brody, David. Workers in Industrial America: Essays on the Twentieth Century Struggle. New York: Oxford University Press, 1980.

Caute, David. The Great Fear. New York: Simon and Schuster, 1978.

Cochran, Bert. Labor and Communism: The Conflict that Shaped American Unions. Princeton: Princeton University Press, 1977.

Cook, Blanche Wiesen. The Declassified Eisenhower: A Divided Legacy. Garden City, New York: Doubleday, 1981.

DeCaux, Len. Labor Radical: From the Wobblies to CIO. Boston: Beacon Press, 1970.

DeSantis, Hugh. The Diplomacy of Silence: The American Foreign Service, The Soviet Union and the Cold War 1933-1947. Chicago: University of Chicago Press, 1980.

Donovan, John C. The Cold Warriors: A Policy Making Elite. Lexington, Massachusetts: D.C. Heath, 1974.

Donovan, Robert J. Tumultuous Years: The Presidency of Harris S. Truman 1949-1953. New York: W.W. Norton, 1967,1982.

Feurer, Rosemary. Radical Unionism in the Midwest 1900-1950. Urbana: University of Illinois Press, 2006.

Fleming, Denna F. The Cold War and Its Origins 1917-1960. Garden City, New York: Doubleday, 1961.

Filipelli, Ronald. American Labor and Postwar Italy 1943-1953. Stanford: Stanford University Press, 1989.

——— and Mark McCulloch, Cold War in the Working Class: The Rise and Decline of the United Electrical Workers. Albany: State University of New York Press, 1995.

Fink, Gary M. ed. in chief. Biographical Dictionary of American Labor. Westport, CT: Greenwood Press, 1984.

Foner, Philip. American Labor and the Indo-China War. New York: International Publishers, 1971.

Fordham, Benjamin O. Building the Cold War Consensus: The Political Economy of U.S. National Security Policy 1949-1951. Ann Arbor: University of Michigan Press, 1998.

Foster, William Z. Outline History of the World Trade Union Movement. New York: International Publishers, 1956.

Freeland, Richard M. The Truman Doctrine and the Origins of McCarthyism: Foreign Policy, Domestic Politics and Internal Security 1946-1948. New York: Alfred A. Knopf, 1972.

Gaddis, John Lewis. The United States and the Origins of the Cold War 1941-1947. New York: Columbia University Press, 1972.

Gallup, George. The Gallup Poll: Public Opinion 1937-1971. New York: Random House, 1975.

Garber, Marjorie and Rebecca Walkowitz. Secret Agents: The Rosenberg Case, McCarthyism and Fifties America. New York: Routledge Press, 1995.

Gardner, Lloyd C. Architects of Illusion: Men and Ideas in American Foreign Policy 1941-1949. Chicago: Quadrangle Books, 1970.

Gershman, Carl. The Foreign Policy of American Labor. Beverly Hills: Sage Publications, 1975.

Gilbert, James. Another Chance: Postwar America 1945-1985. Chicago: The Dorsey Press, 1986.

Ginger, Anne Fagan and David Christiano. The Cold War Against Labor. Colorado University Press, 1993.

Godson, Roy. American Labor and European Politics. New York: Crane Russak, 1976.

Goldberg, Arthur. Labor United. New York: McGraw-Hill, 1956.

Green, Gil. What's Happening to Labor? New York: International Publishers, 1976.

Harris, Howell John. Bloodless Victories: The Rise and Fall of the Open Shop in the Philadelphia Metal Trades 1890-1940. Cambridge: Cambridge University Press, 2000.

Herod, Andrew. Labor Geographies. New York: Guilford Press, 2001.

Hoerr, John. Harry, Tom, and Father Rice: Accusation and Betrayal in America's Cold War. Pittsburgh: Pittsburgh University Press, 2005.

Hogan, Michael J. The Cross of Iron: Harry S. Truman and the Origins of the National Security State. Cambridge: Cambridge University Press, 1978.

Hunter, Allen, ed. Rethinking the Cold War. Philadelphia: Temple University Press, 1998.

Johnston, Eric. American Unlimited. Garden City, New York: Doubleday Doran, 1944.

Kepley, David R. The Collapse of the Middle Way: Senate Republicans and the Bipartisan Foreign Policy. New York: Greenwood Press, 1988.

Kessler-Harris, Alice. Out to Work: A History of Wage Earning Women in the United States. New York: Oxford University Press, 1982.

Kimeldorf, Howard. Battling for American Labor: Wobblies, Craft Workers, and the Making of the American Labor Movement. Los Angeles: University California Press, 1999.

Kolko, Gabriel and Joyce Kolko. The Limits of Power: The World and United States Foreign Policy 1945-1954. New York: Harper and Row, 1972.

———, Gabriel. The Politics of War: The World and United States Foreign Policy 1943-1945. New York: Random House, 1966.

Koszielski, Frank. Divided Loyalties: American Unions and the Vietnam War. New York: Garland Publishing, 1999.

Labovitz, Sherman. Being Red in Philadelphia: A Memoir of the McCarthy Era. Philadelphia: Camino Books, 1998.

Larson, Simeon. Labor and Foreign Policy: Gompers, the AFL and the First World War. Rutherford, New Jersey: Farleigh Dickinson University Press, 1975.

Leab, Daniel J., Ed. The Labor History Reader. Urbana: University of Illinois Press, 1985.

Leffler, Melvin P. A Preponderance of Power: National Security, the Truman Administration and the Cold War. Stanford: Stanford University Press, 1992.

Levinson, Andrew. The Working Class Majority. New York: Coward McCann, 1974.

MacShane, Denis. International Labour and the Origins of the Cold War. Oxford: Clarendon Press, 1992.

Matles, James and James Higgins. Them and Us: Struggles of a Rank and File Union. Englewood Cliffs, New Jersey: Prentiss-Hall, 1974.

McColloch, Mark. White Collar Workers in Transition: The Boom Years 1940-1970. Westport, Conn.: Greenwood Press, 1983.

McGeever, Patrick J. Charles Owen Rice: Apostle of Contradiction. Pittsburgh: Duquesne University Press, 1988.

Melman, Seymour. The Defense Economy: Conversion of Industries and Occupations to Civilian Needs. New York: Praeger, 1970.

———, The Permanent War Economy: American Capitalism in Decline. New York: Simon and Schuster, 1985.

Messer, Robert L. The End of an Alliance: James F. Brynes, Roosevelt, Truman, and the Origins of the Cold War. Chapel Hill: University of North Carolina Press, 1982.

Milkman, Ruth. Gender at Work: The Dynamics of Job Segregation by Sex During World War II. Urbana: University of Illinois Press, 1987.

Montgomery, David. Workers Control in America. New York: Cambridge University Press, 1979.

Navasky, Victor S. Naming Names. New York: Viking Press, 1980.

Noble, David. Forces of Production: A Social History of Industrial Automation. New York: Alfred A. Knopf, 1984.

Oshinsky, David. Senator Joseph McCarthy and the American Labor Movement. Columbia: University of Missouri Press, 1976.

Paterson, Thomas. Cold War Critics: Alternatives to American Foreign Policy in the Truman Years. Chicago: Quadrangle Books, 1971.

Pelling, Henry. American Labor. Chicago: University of Chicago Press, 1960.

Preis, Art. Labor's Giant Step: Twenty Years of the CIO New York: Pioneer Publishers, 1964.

Purcell, Theodore V. and Daniel P. Mulvey. The Negro in the Electrical Manufacturing Industry. Philadelphia: University of Pennsylvania, Wharton School, Industrial Research Unit, 1971.

Quirini, Helen. Helen Quirini and General Electric: A Personal Memoir of World War II. Schenectady: Helen Quirini, 1997.

——— and Henry Antonelli. The Story of Local 301 IUE-AFL-CIO: Reflections. Schenectady: Helen Quirini and Henry Antonelli, 1987.

Radosh, Ronald. American Labor and United States Foreign Policy. New York: Random House, 1969.

Raines, John, Lenora Berson and David Gracie, eds. Community and Capital in Conflict: Plant Closings and Job Loss. Philadelphia: Temple University Press, 1982.

Rodden, Robert. The Fighting Machinists: A Century of Struggle. Washington, D.C.: Kelly Press, Copyright Pending.

Rose, Lisle A. The Cold War Comes to Main Street: America in 1950. Lawrence: University Press of Kansas, 1999.

Rosswurm, Steve, ed. The CIO's Left Led Unions. New Brunswick: Rutgers University Press, 1992.

Sampson, Anthony. The Arms Bazaar: From Lebanon to Lockheed. New York: Viking Press, 1977.

Schatz, Ronald. The Electrical Workers: A History of Labor at General Electric and Westinghouse 1923-1960. Chicago: University of Illinois Press, 1983.

Schwartz, Philip J. Coalition Bargaining. Ithaca: New York State School of Industrial and Labor Relations, 1970.

Scott, Jack. Yankee Unions Go Home! How the AFL Helped the U.S. Build an Empire in Latin America. Vancouver: New Star Books, 1976.

Silverman, Victor. Imagining Internationalism in American and British Labor 1939-1949. Chicago: University of Illinois Press, 2000.

Sims, Beth. Workers of the World Undermined: American Labor's Role in U.S. Foreign Policy. Boston: South End Press, 1992.

Somerville, John. The Communist Trials and the American Tradition. New York: Cameron Associates, 1956.

Stone, Isidor F. The Hidden History of the Korean War. New York: Monthly Review Press, 1952.

Theoharis, Athan. Seeds of Repression: Harry S. Truman and the Origins of McCarthyism. Chicago: Quadrangle Books, 1971.

Thomas, Kenneth W. Cold War Theories. Baton Rouge: Louisiana State University Press, 1981.

Troy, Leo and Neil Sheflin. The Union Source Book. West Orange, New Jersey: Industrial Relations Data and Information Services, 1985.

Tucker, Robert. The Radical Left and American Foreign Policy. Baltimore: Johns Hopkins University Press, 1971.

Tugwell, Rexford. A Chronicle of Jeopardy. Chicago: University of Chicago Press, 1955.

Walton, Richard J. Cold War and Counter Revolution: The Foreign Policy of John F. Kennedy. New York: The Viking Press, 1972.

Wehrle, Edmund F. Between a River and a Mountain: The AFL-CIO and the Vietnam War. Ann Arbor: University of Michigan Press, 2005.
Weiler, Peter. British Labour and the Cold War. Stanford: Stanford University Press, 1988.
Williamson, John. Dangerous Scot: The Life of an American "Undesirable." New York: International Publishers, 1969.
Windmuller, John P. American Labor and the International Labor Movement 1940-1953. Ithaca: The Institute of Industrial and Labor Relations, 1954.
Yergin, Daniel. Shattered Peace: The Origins of the Cold War and the National Security State. New York: Houghton Mifflin, 1977.
Zeiger, Robert H. American Workers, American Unions 1920-1985. Baltimore: Johns Hopkins University Press, 1986.

Articles

Atwell, Mary Welek. "Eleanor Roosevelt and the Cold War Consensus." Diplomatic History, III (winter, 1979), 99-113.
Blum, Albert. "Why Unions Grow." Labor History, 9 (winter, 1968), 39-42.
Braden, Thomas. "I'm Glad the CIA is Immoral." Saturday Evening Post, 240 (May 20, 1967), 10-12.
Brooks, Thomas R. "Black Upsurge in the Unions." Dissent, 17 (March-April 1970), 127-134.
Brown, Irving. "Absolute Dictatorship vs. Relative Freedom." American Federationist, (June, 1952), 7.
Carey, James B. "Trade Unionist in Moscow." New Republic, CXV (August 5, 1946), 136-137.
"Coalition Bargaining: The Acid Test." Business Week, 1928 (August 6, 1966), 61.
"Defense Orders Head for Plateau." Business Week, 1934 (September 24, 1966), 50-52.
"Defense Production Buoys Up Steel." Business Week, 1923 (July 9, 1966), 43.
"The Demand Is More–Much More." Business Week, 1927 (August 6, 1966), 118-122.
Dennison, Bill and George Meyers. "Trade Unionists Fight for a Peace Policy." Political Affairs, LXVI (June, 1987), 3-11.
Eisenberg, Carolyn. "Working Class Politics and the Cold War: American Intervention in the German Labor Movement 1945-1949." Diplomatic History, VII (Fall, 1983), 283-306.
"Electrical Unions Square Off." Business Week, 1254 (September 12, 1953), 173-174.
"Federation Steps Up Its Attack on GE." Business Week, 2099 (November 22, 1969), 38-39.

"The First Automation Strike." Fortune, LII (December 1955), 57-62.

"GE Settles Down to a Long Ordeal." Business Week, 2096 (November 1, 1969), 36.

"The GE Strike: It's Starting to Hurt." Business Week, 2097 (November 8, 1969), 13-15.

"GE Strikers Back Their Leaders." Business Week, 2097 (November 8, 1969), 102,107.

"George Meany Finds Europe Soft on Communism." American Federationist, (January, 1952), 4.

Hahn, Harlan. "Dove Sentiments Among Blue Collar Workers." Dissent, 17 (May-June, 1970), 202-205.

Harriman, Averell. "Our Foreign Policy in Perspective." American Federationist, (January, 1953), 11.

Henle, Peter. "Some Reflections on Organized Labor and the New Militants." Monthly Labor Review, 92 (July, 1969), 20-25.

"Hint of a Break in GE Deadlock." Business Week, 2098 (November 15, 1969), 44, 46.

"Impact of the GE Strike on Production of Defense Itmes." Business Week, 2107 (January 17, 1970), 44.

"Is Big Labor Playing Global Vigilante." Business Week, 2919 (November 4, 1985), 92-94.

"Johnson Draws Bead on GE." Business Week, 1936 (October 8, 1966), 145-147.

Kannenberg, Lisa. "The Impact of the Cold War on Women's Trade Union Activism: The UE Experience." Labor History, 34 (Spring-Summer 1993), 309-323.

Kaufman, Burton. "The United States Response to the Soviet Economic Offensive of the 1950s." Diplomatic History, II (Spring, 1978), 153-165.

Kersten, Charles. "We Are Protecting Spies in Defense Plants." Reader's Digest, 62 (January, 1953), 27-31.

McAuliffe, Mary S. "Liberals and the Communist Control Act of 1954." Journal of American History, LXIII (September, 1976), 351-367.

Marshall, Scott. "The Trade Unions and Peace." Political Affairs, LXV (January, 1986), 13-17.

Meany, George. "Labor Looks at Capitalism." American Federationist, (December, 1966), 1.

———. "No Return to Isolationism." American Federationist, (October, 1972), 13-14.

Meyers, George. "Labor's Shift to the Left." Political Affairs, LXVII (January, 1988), 29-34.

———. "The 16th Convention of the AFL-CIO." Political Affairs, LXV (January, 1986), 5-12.

Miller, James E. "Taking Off the Gloves: The United States and the Italian Election of 1948." Diplomatic History, VII (Winter, 1983), 35-55.

"The Mood Is Militant." Business Week, 1934 (September 14, 1966), 47-49.

Morris, George. "The AFL-CIO Merger." Political Affairs, XXXIV (March, 1955), 30-40.

"New Number to Live By." Business Week, 1938 (October 22, 1966), 37-38.

O'Brien, FlS. "The 'Communist Dominated' Unions in the United States since 1950." Labor History, 9 (Spring 1968), 184-210.

"On the Trail of Runaway Plants." Business Week, 1927 (August 6, 1966), 114-116.

"The Overhaul of General Electric" Fortune, LII (December, 1955), 110 ff.

Rice, Charles Owen. "Confessions of an Anti-Communist." Labor History, 30 (Summer 1989), 449-462.

"The Rough Road to GE's Settlement." Business Week, 2108 (January 24, 1970), 28-29.

Schatz, Ronald. "American Labor and the Catholic Church." International Labor and Working Class History, 20 (Fall 1981), 46-53.

Sears, Ben (John B.). "Divided We Fall: A Lesson From Labor History." Political Affairs, 84 (July, 2005) 62-66.

Simon, Hal. "The Labor Merger." Political Affairs, XXXV (January, 1956), 51-65.

———. "Some Concepts of Our Trade Union Work." Political Affairs, XXXVI (February, 1957), 49-57.

Soapes, Thomas F. "A Cold Warrior Seeks Peace: Eisenhower's Strategy for Nuclear Disarmament." Diplomatic History, IV (Winter, 1980), 55-71.

Swift, John. "The Left Led Unions and Labor Unity I." Political Affairs, XXXII (July, 1953), 33-42.

———. "The Left Led Unions and Labor Unity II." Political Affairs, XXXII (August, 1953), 37-50.

"UE Admits Dark Days." Business Week, 1310 (October 9, 1954), 171-172.

"Union Labor: Less Militant, More Affluent." Time, 86 (September 17, 1965), 42-43.

Velie, Lester. "Red Pipeline Into Our Defense Plants." Saturday Evening Post, 225 (October 18, 1952), 19-21, 106-110.

Walker, J. Samuel. "No More Cold War: American Foreign Policy and the 1948 Soviet Peace Offensive." Diplomatic History, V (Winter, 1981), 75-91.

Weiler, Peter. "The United States, International Labor and the Cold War: The Breakup of the World Federation of Trade Unions" Diplomatic History, V (Winter, 1981), 1-22.

Widick, B.J. "Labor Meets for Peace." The Nation, 205 (November 27, 1967), 561-563.

———. "Strong Arm of the Status Quo." The Nation, 201 (December 27, 1965), 516-518.

Weisbrot, Mark. Online commentary. Business Week, (July 29, 2004).

Windmuller, John P. "The Foreign Policy Conflict in American Labor." Political Science Quarterly, LXXXII (June, 1967), 205-234.

———. "The ICFTU after Ten Years: Problems and Prospects." Industrial and Labor Relations Review, 14 (issue 2, 1961), 257-272.

"Winds of Change Ruffle Unions' Top Executives." Business Week, 1933 (September 17, 1966), 71-73.

Winpisinger, William. "A Labor View of Concersion." Economic Notes, 54 (February, 1986), 405.

Wittner, Lawrence S. "The Truman Doctrine and the Defense of Freedom." Diplomatic History, IV (Spring, 1980), 161-187.

Zahavi, Gerald. "Passionate Commitments: Race, Sex, and Communism at Schenectady General Electric 1932-1954." Journal of American History, 83 (September, 1996), 514-548.

Newspapers

CIO News. 1947-1955 [weekly].

Daily Worker. 1949-1952.

IUE-CIO News. 1949-1955 [bi-weekly].

IUE-AFL-CIO News. 1956-1973 [bi –weekly].

New York Times. 1945-1973.

New York Herald Tribune. January 29, January 30, 1950.

People's Daily World. February 26, 1987; March 11, 1987; December 29, 1987.

Evening Bulletin (Philadelphia). 1952-1954.

Philadelphia Inquirer. 1952-1954; May 28, 1987; June 5, 1987.

UE News. 1945-1949 [weekly]; 1950-1973 [bi-weekly].

Wall Street Journal. August 21, 1953.

Unpublished Materials

Emspak, Frank. "The Breakup of the Congress of Industrial Organizations (CIO) 1945-1950." Ph.D. Dissertation, University of Wisconsin, 1972.

Filipelli, Ronald L. "The United Electrical, Radio and Machine Workers of America 1933-1949: The Struggle for Control." Ph.D. Dissertation, Pennsylvania State University, 1970.

Lenburg, Leroy J. "The CIO and American Foreign Policy 1935-1955." Ph.D. Dissertation, Pennsylvania State University, 1973.

Prickett, James R. "Communists and the Communist Issue in the American Labor Movement 1920-1950." Ph.D. Dissertation, University of California, Los Angeles, 1975.

Weed, Roy. "The Westinghouse-UE Strike at Lester 1955-1956: A Case Study in Industrial Conflict." Master's Thesis, Temple University, 1961.

Index